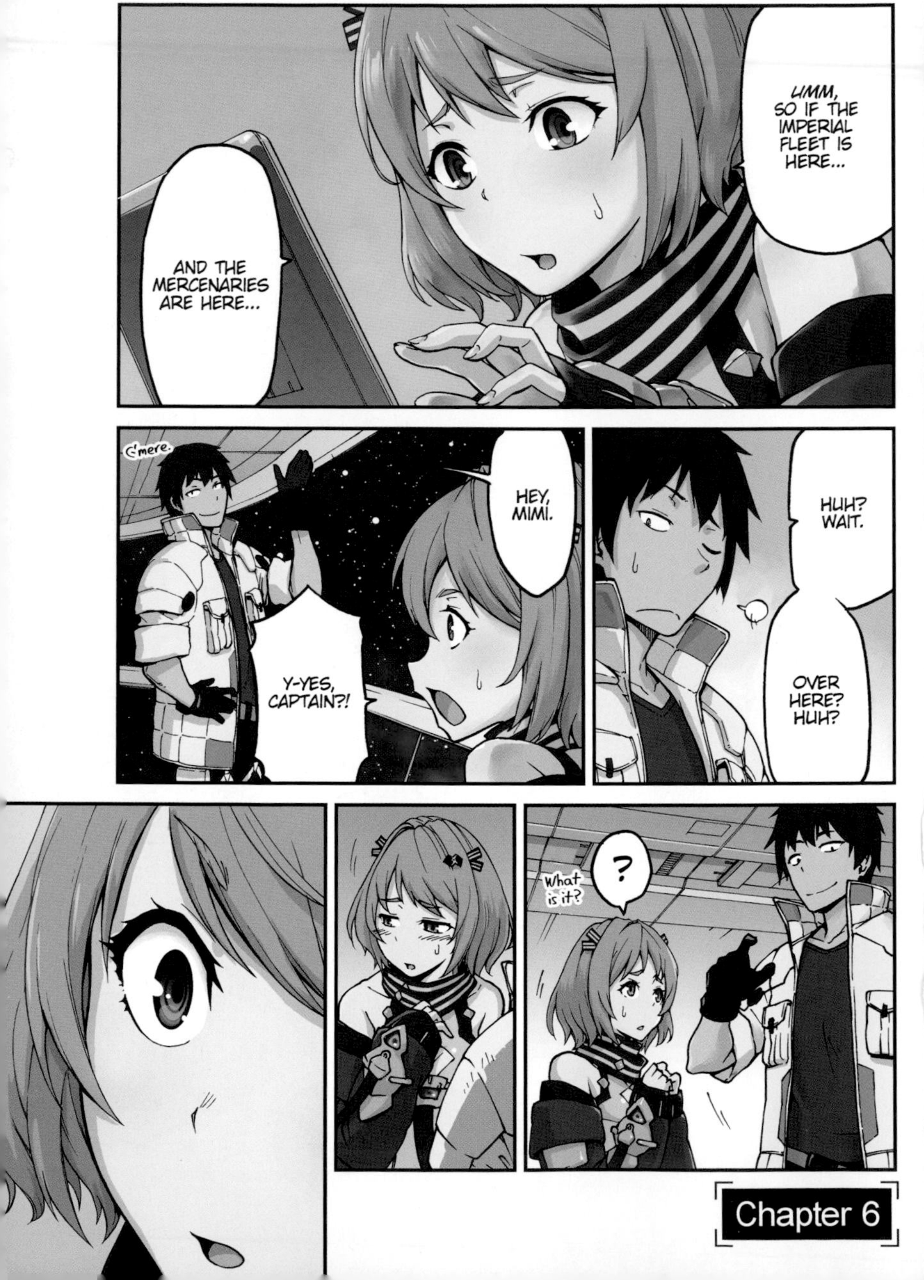
UMM, SO IF THE IMPERIAL FLEET IS HERE...
AND THE MERCENARIES ARE HERE...
HUH? WAIT.
OVER HERE? HUH?
HEY, MIMI.
C'mere.
Y-YES, CAPTAIN?!
?
What is it?
Chapter 6

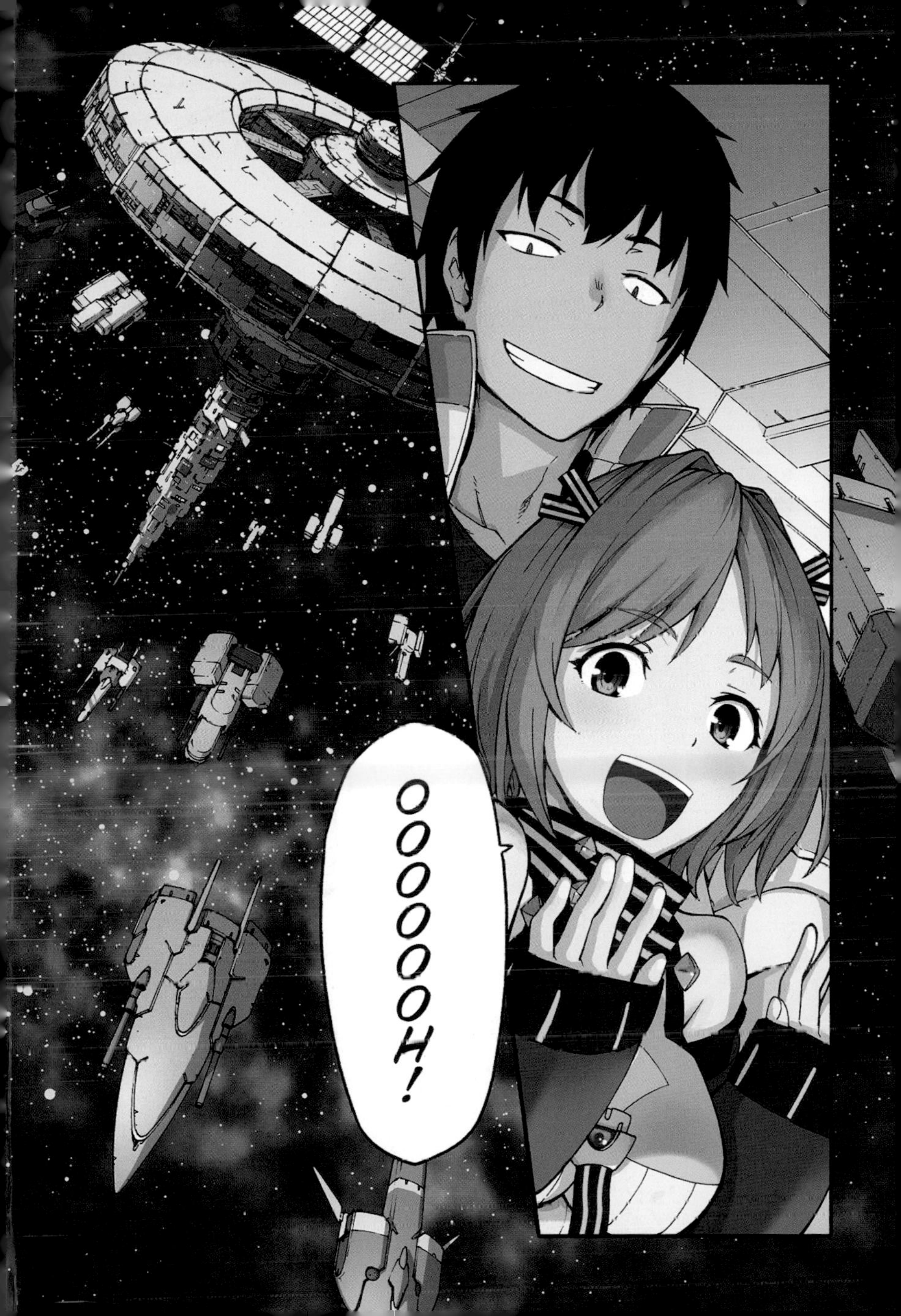
OOOOOOOH!

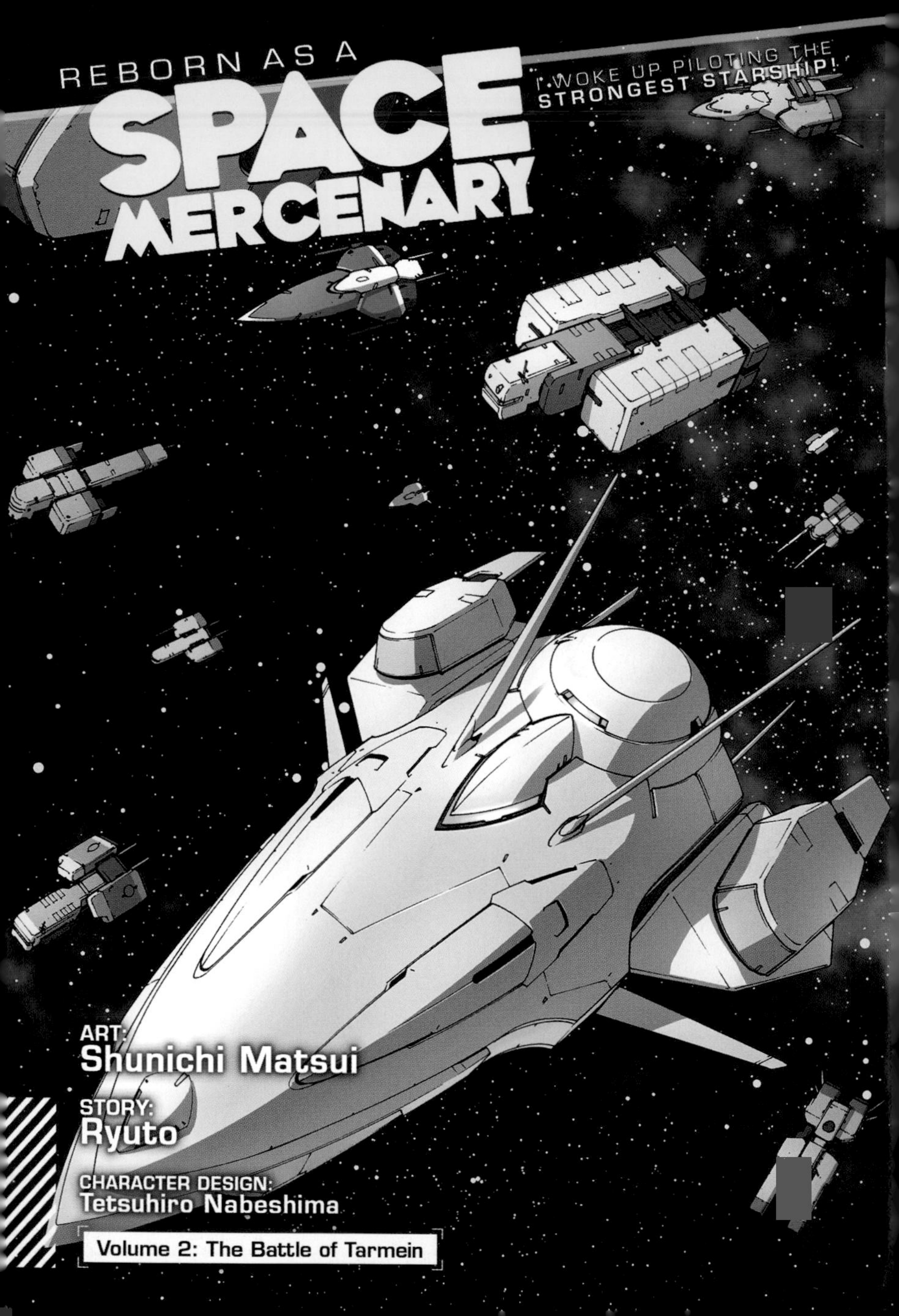
REBORN AS A
SPACE
MERCENARY
I WOKE UP PILOTING THE
STRONGEST STARSHIP!
ART:
Shunichi Matsui
STORY:
Ryuto
CHARACTER DESIGN:
Tetsuhiro Nabeshima
Volume 2: The Battle of Tarmein

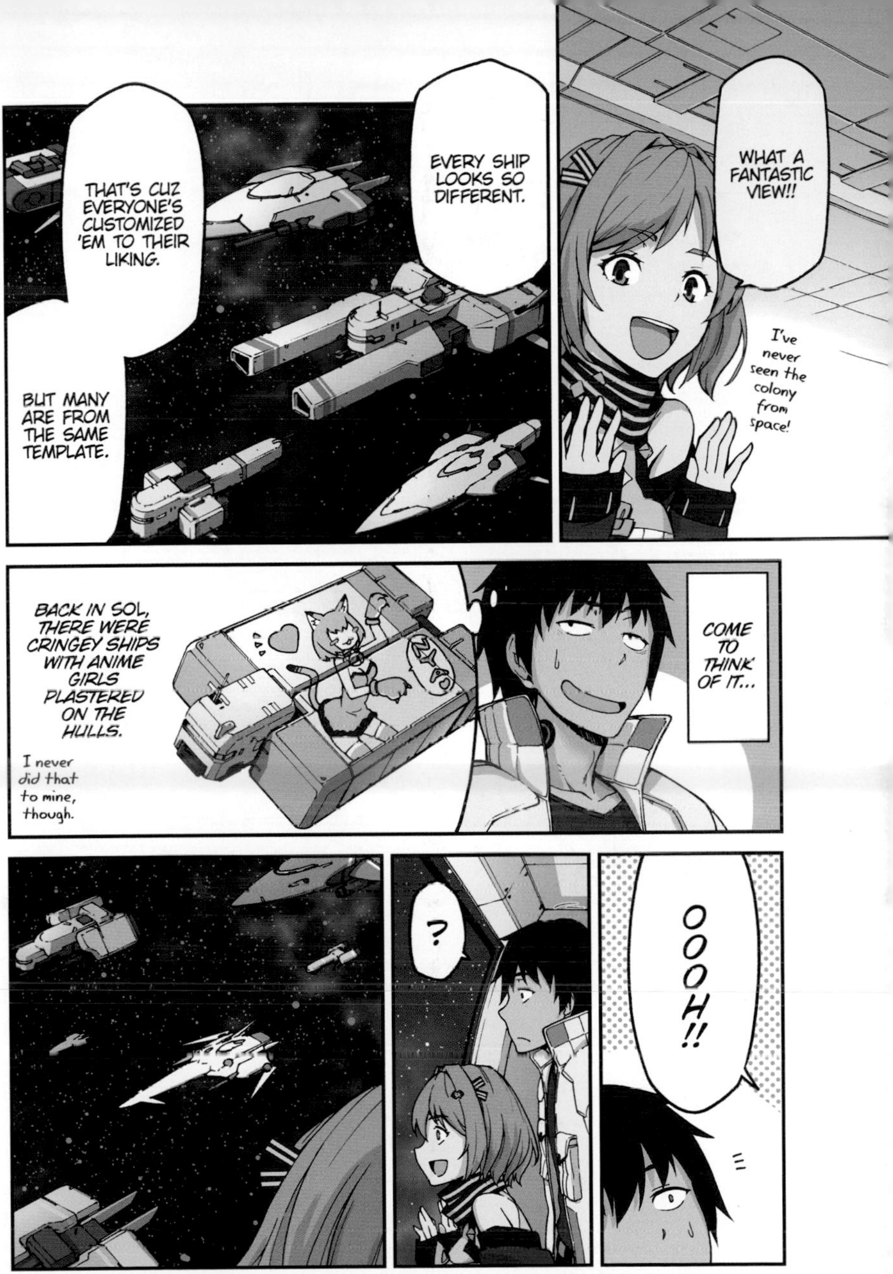
WHAT A FANTASTIC VIEW!!
I've never seen the colony from space!
EVERY SHIP LOOKS SO DIFFERENT.
THAT'S CUZ EVERYONE'S CUSTOMIZED 'EM TO THEIR LIKING.
BUT MANY ARE FROM THE SAME TEMPLATE.
COME TO THINK OF IT...
BACK IN SOL, THERE WERE CRINGEY SHIPS WITH ANIME GIRLS PLASTERED ON THE HULLS.
I never did that to mine, though.
OOOOH!!
?

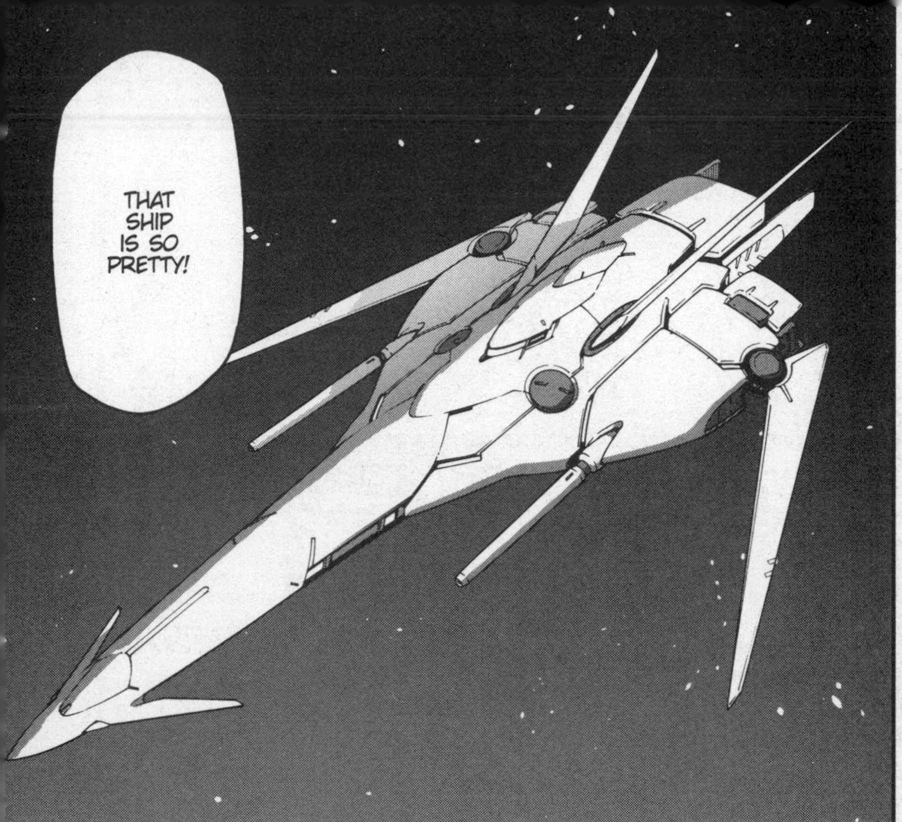
THAT SHIP IS SO PRETTY!

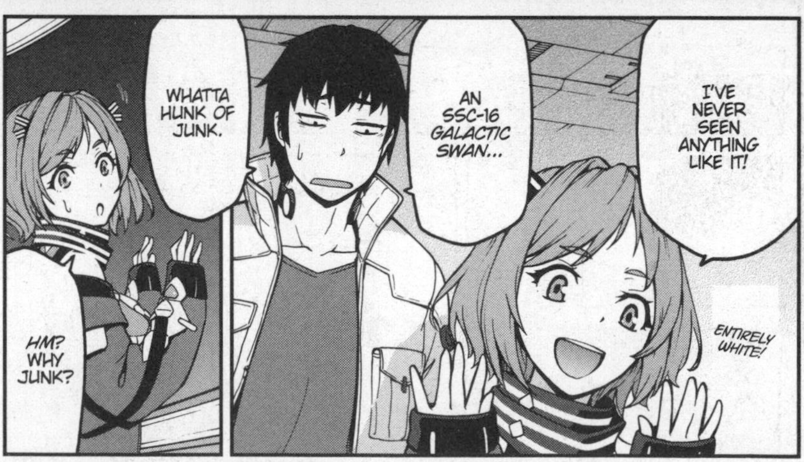
I'VE NEVER SEEN ANYTHING LIKE IT!
ENTIRELY WHITE!
AN SSC-16 GALACTIC SWAN...
WHATTA HUNK OF JUNK.
HM? WHY JUNK?

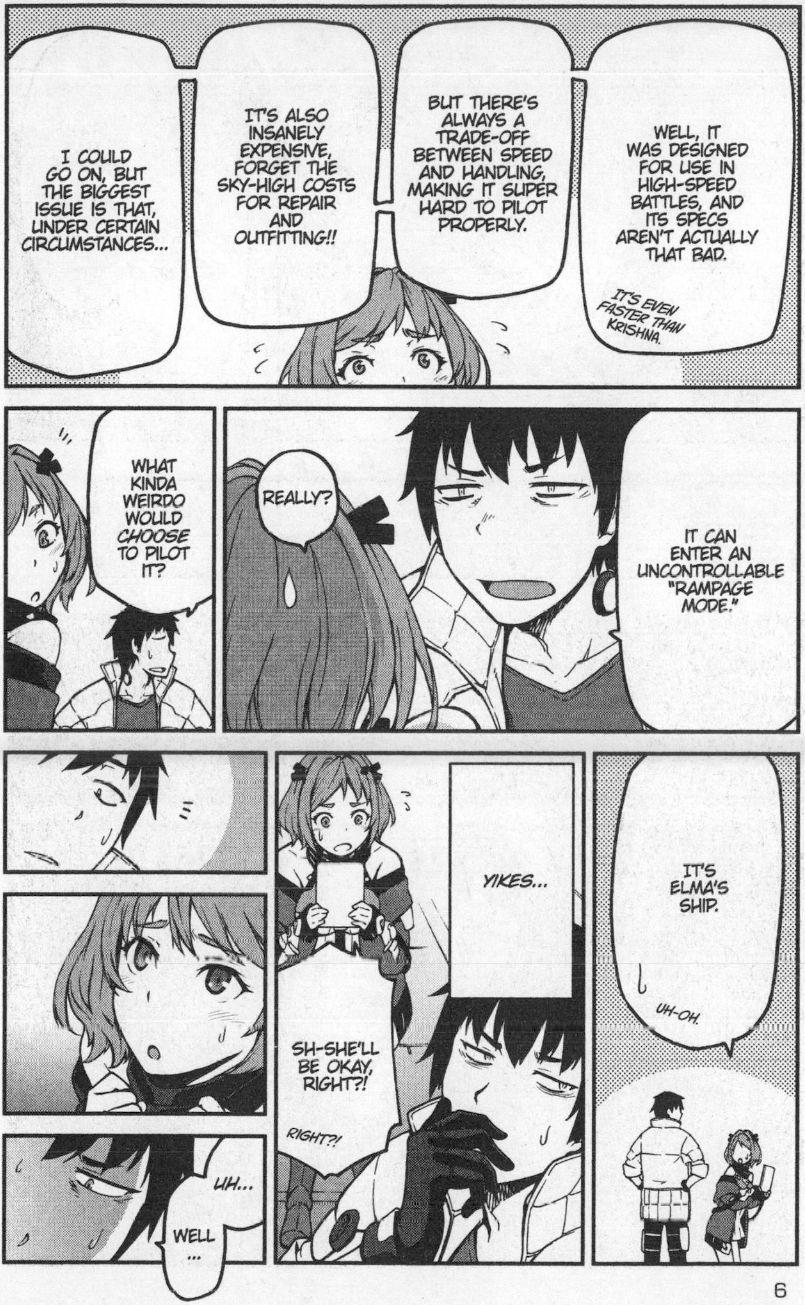
WELL, IT WAS DESIGNED FOR USE IN HIGH-SPEED BATTLES, AND ITS SPECS AREN'T ACTUALLY THAT BAD.
IT'S EVEN FASTER THAN KRISHNA.
BUT THERE'S ALWAYS A TRADE-OFF BETWEEN SPEED AND HANDLING, MAKING IT SUPER HARD TO PILOT PROPERLY.
IT'S ALSO INSANELY EXPENSIVE, FORGET THE SKY-HIGH COSTS FOR REPAIR AND OUTFITTING!!
I COULD GO ON, BUT THE BIGGEST ISSUE IS THAT, UNDER CERTAIN CIRCUMSTANCES...
IT CAN ENTER AN UNCONTROLLABLE "RAMPAGE MODE."
REALLY?
WHAT KINDA WEIRDO WOULD CHOOSE TO PILOT IT?
IT'S ELMA'S SHIP.
UH-OH.
YIKES...
SH-SHE'LL BE OKAY, RIGHT?!
RIGHT?!
UH...
WELL ...

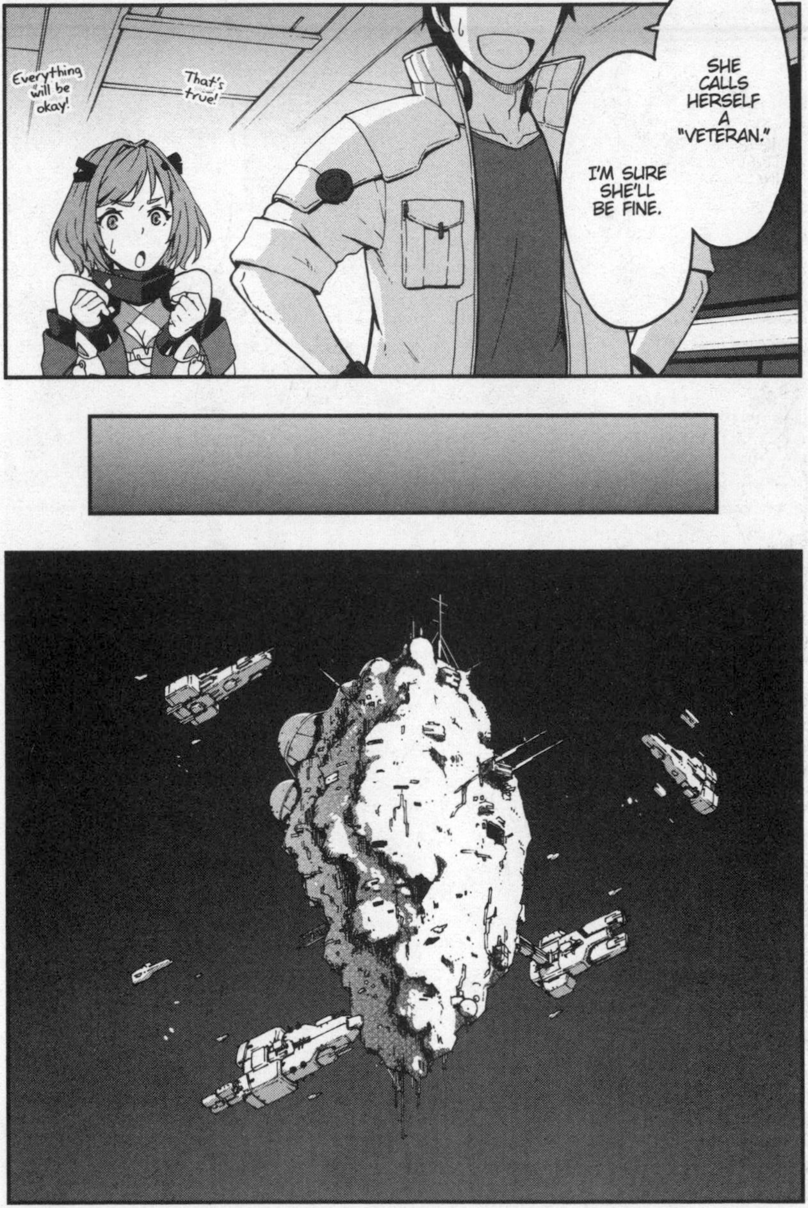
SHE CALLS HERSELF A "VETERAN."
I'M SURE SHE'LL BE FINE.
That's true!
Everything will be okay!

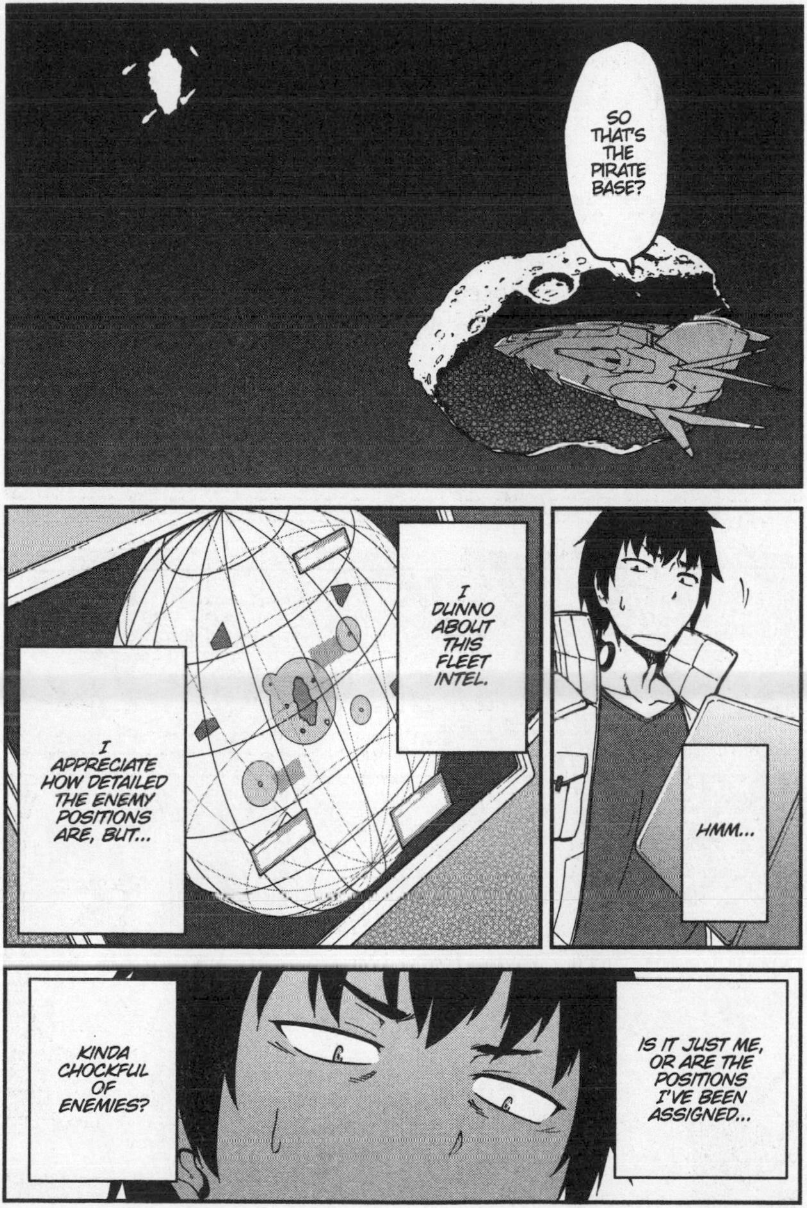
SO THAT'S THE PIRATE BASE?
HMM...
I DUNNO ABOUT THIS FLEET INTEL.
I APPRECIATE HOW DETAILED THE ENEMY POSITIONS ARE, BUT...
IS IT JUST ME, OR ARE THE POSITIONS I'VE BEEN ASSIGNED...
KINDA CHOCKFUL OF ENEMIES?

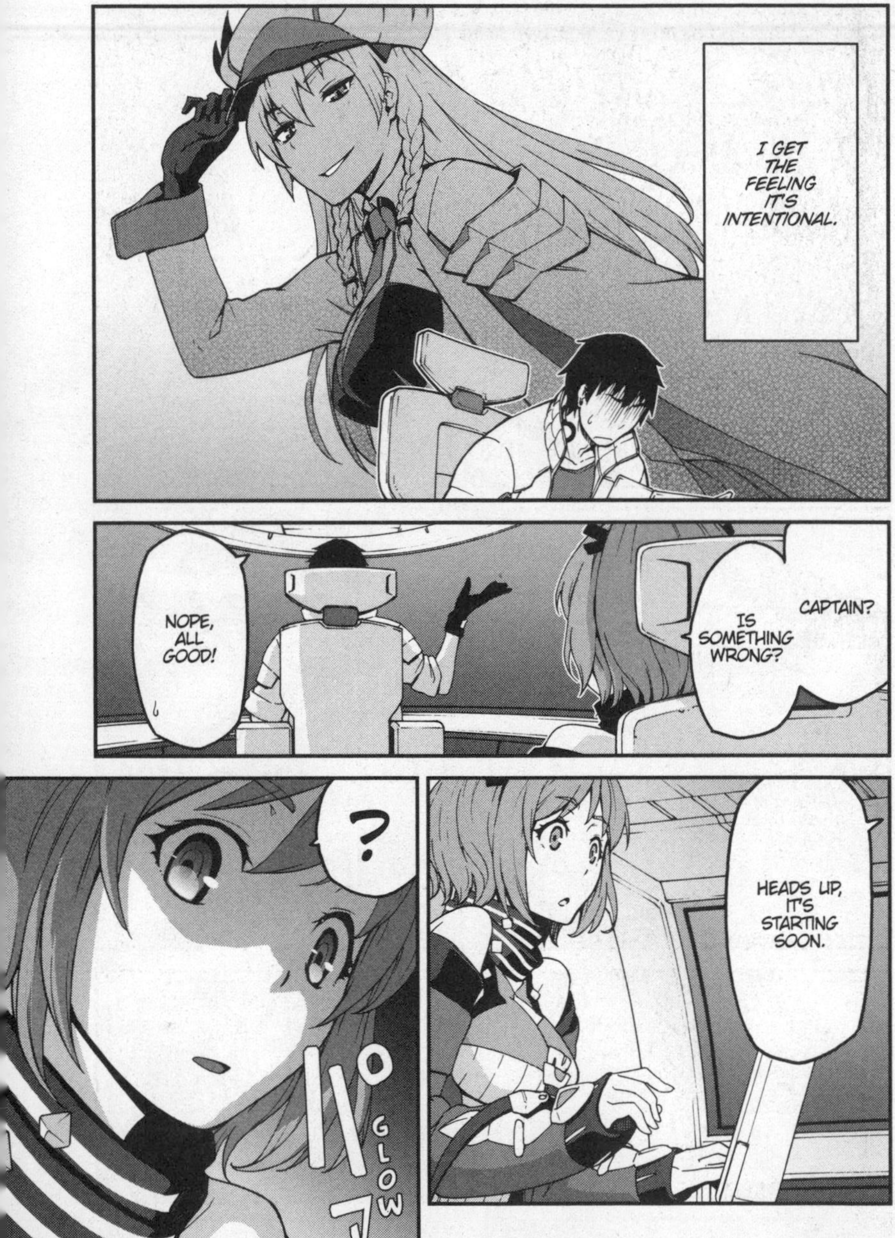
I GET THE FEELING IT'S INTENTIONAL.
CAPTAIN? IS SOMETHING WRONG?
NOPE, ALL GOOD!
HEADS UP, IT'S STARTING SOON.
?
GLOW

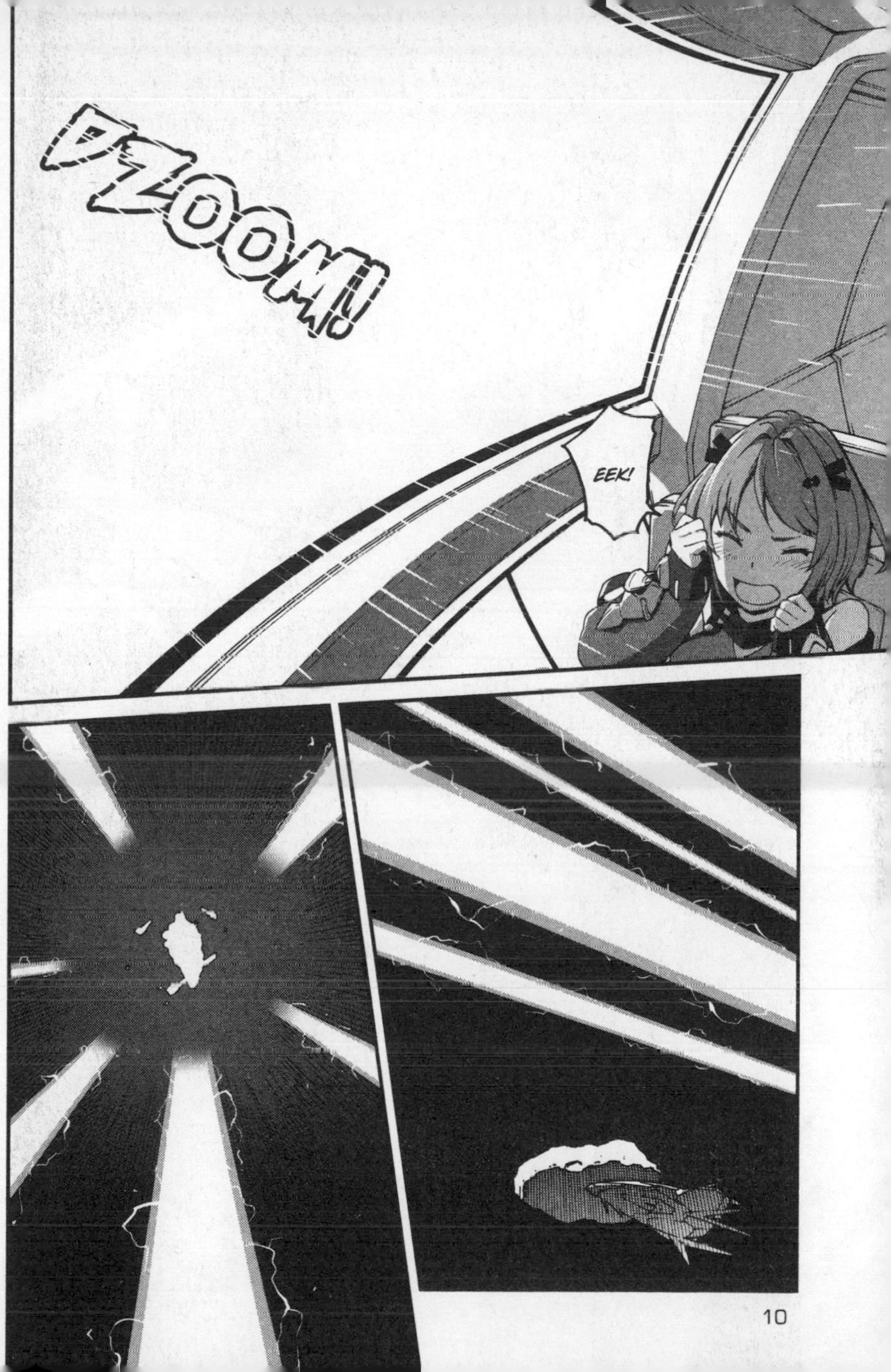
DZOOM!
EEK!

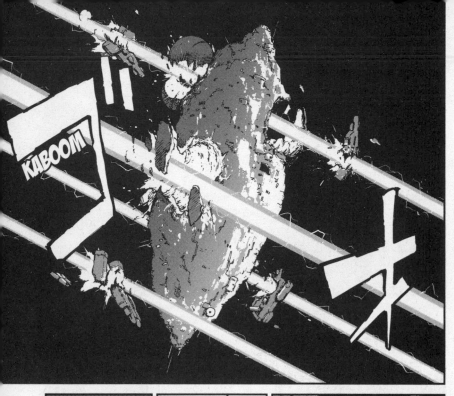

KABOOM

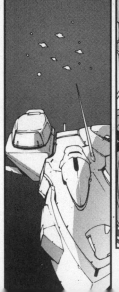

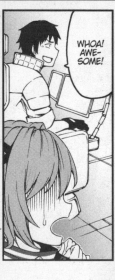

WHOA! AWE-SOME!

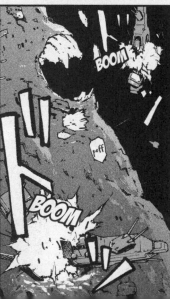

BOOM

poff

BOOM

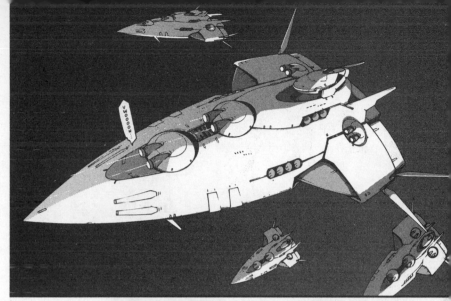

WOW...

WITH THAT RANGE AND POWER, NOT EVEN *KRISHNA* WOULD STAND A CHANCE.

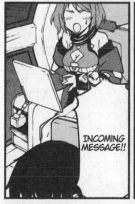

INCOMING MESSAGE!!

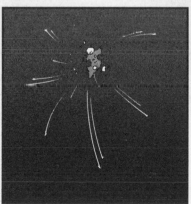

HM?

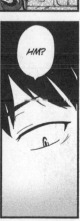

12

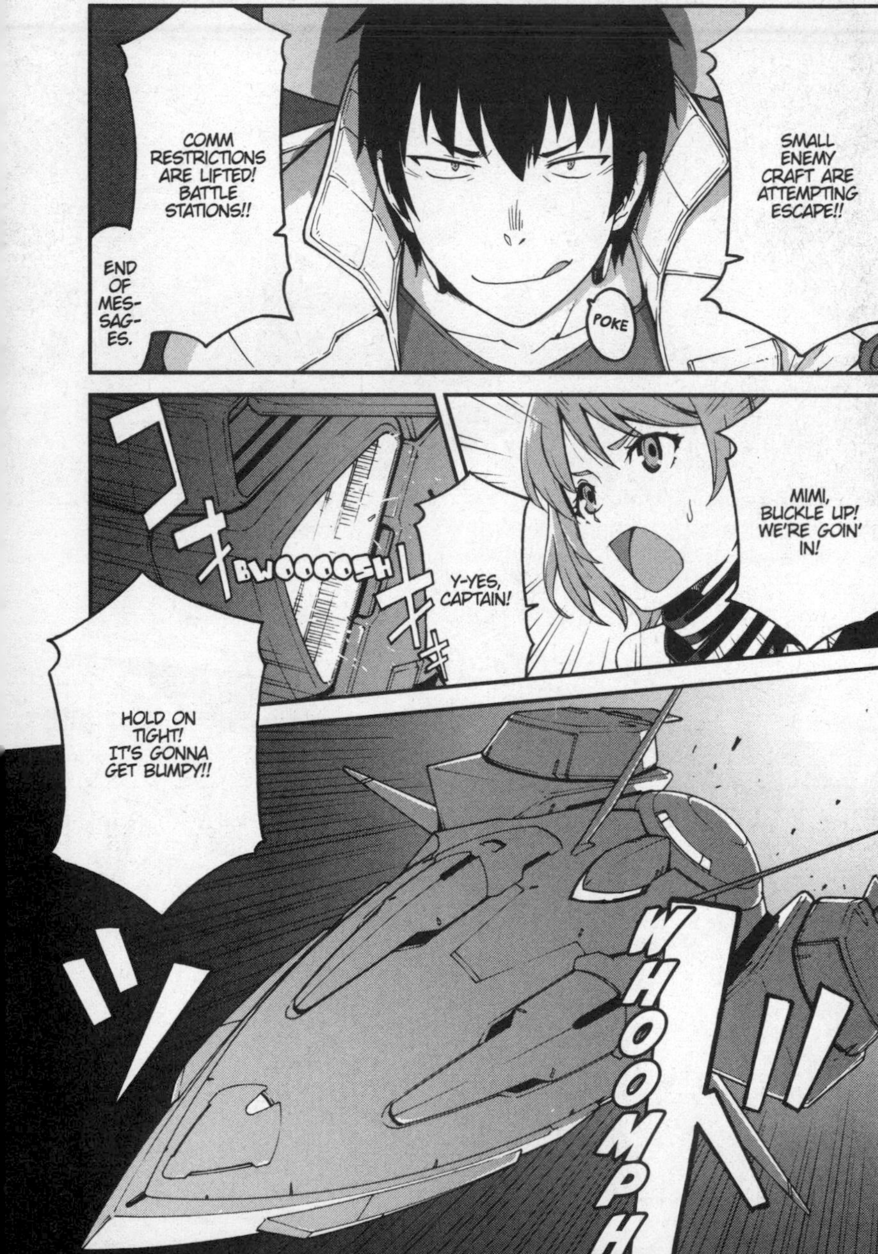
SMALL ENEMY CRAFT ARE ATTEMPTING ESCAPE!!
COMM RESTRICTIONS ARE LIFTED! BATTLE STATIONS!!
POKE
END OF MES-SAG-ES.
MIMI, BUCKLE UP! WE'RE GOIN' IN!
Y-YES, CAPTAIN!
BWOOOOOSH
HOLD ON TIGHT! IT'S GONNA GET BUMPY!!
WHOOMPH

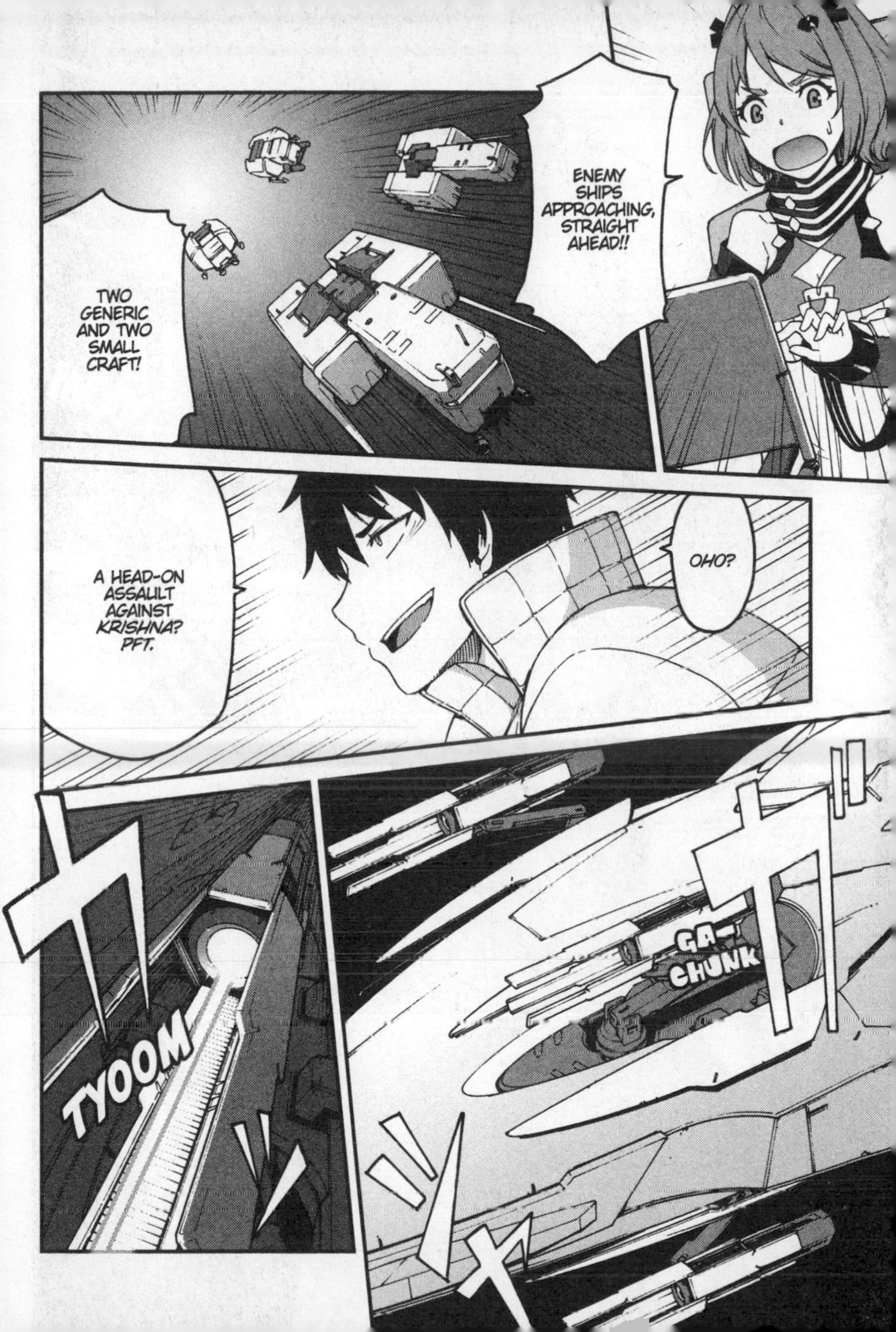
ENEMY SHIPS APPROACHING, STRAIGHT AHEAD!!
TWO GENERIC AND TWO SMALL CRAFT!
OHO?
A HEAD-ON ASSAULT AGAINST KRISHNA? PFT.
GA-CHUNK
TYOOM

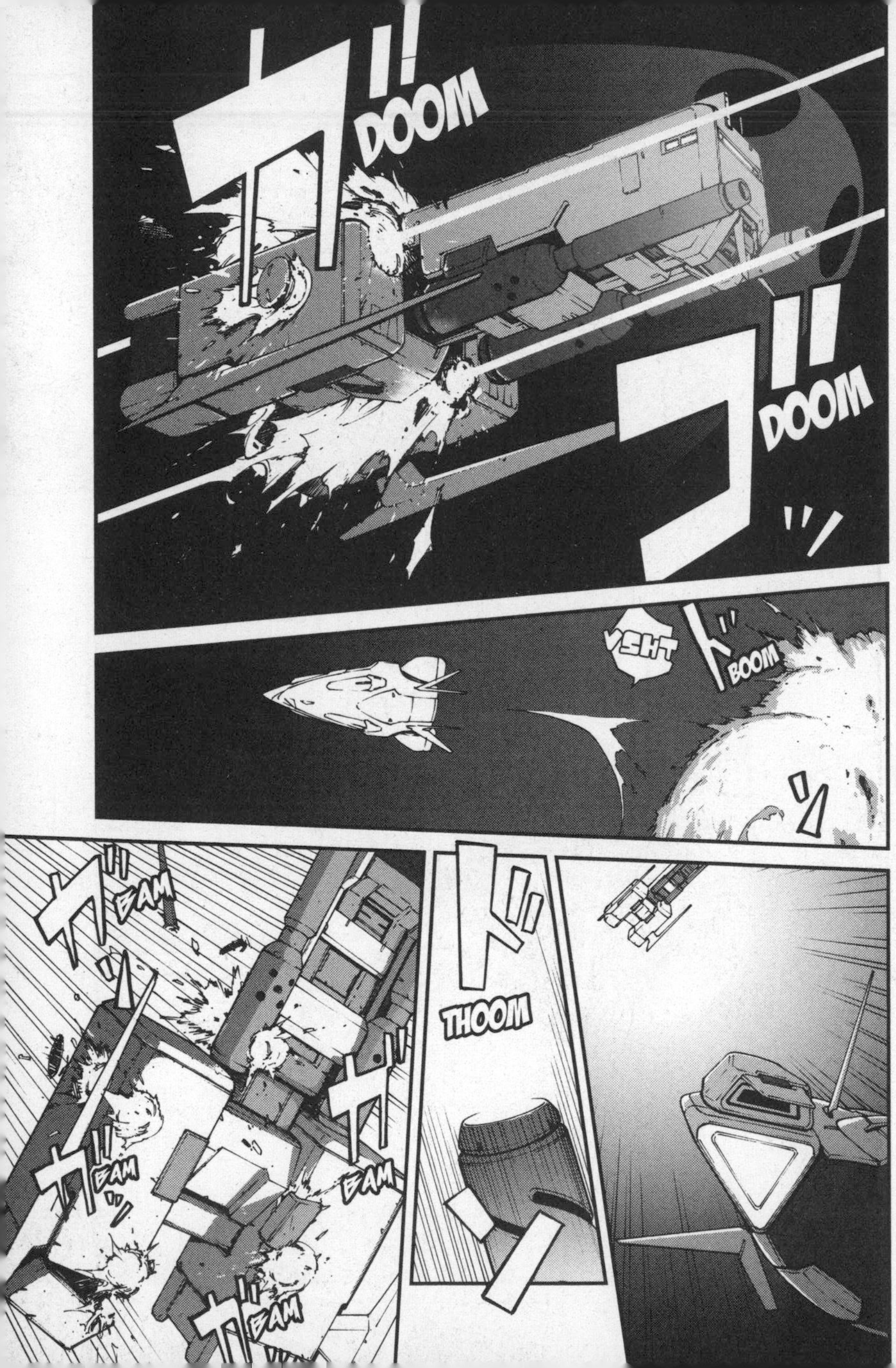
DOOM
DOOM
VSHT
BOOM
THOOM
BAM
BAM
BAM
BAM

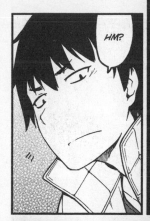

BWOOM
HM?
WE GOT SOME RUN-NERS!
PFFFT!
YOU REALLY EXPECT TO OUTRUN ME...
Ka-chunk
IN SOME MODDED GENERICS?!!
Ka-thunk

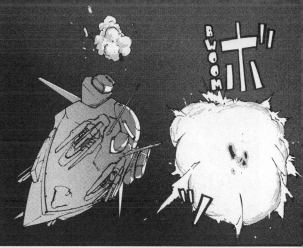

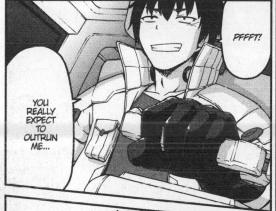

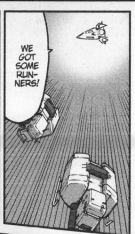

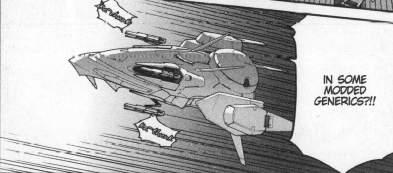

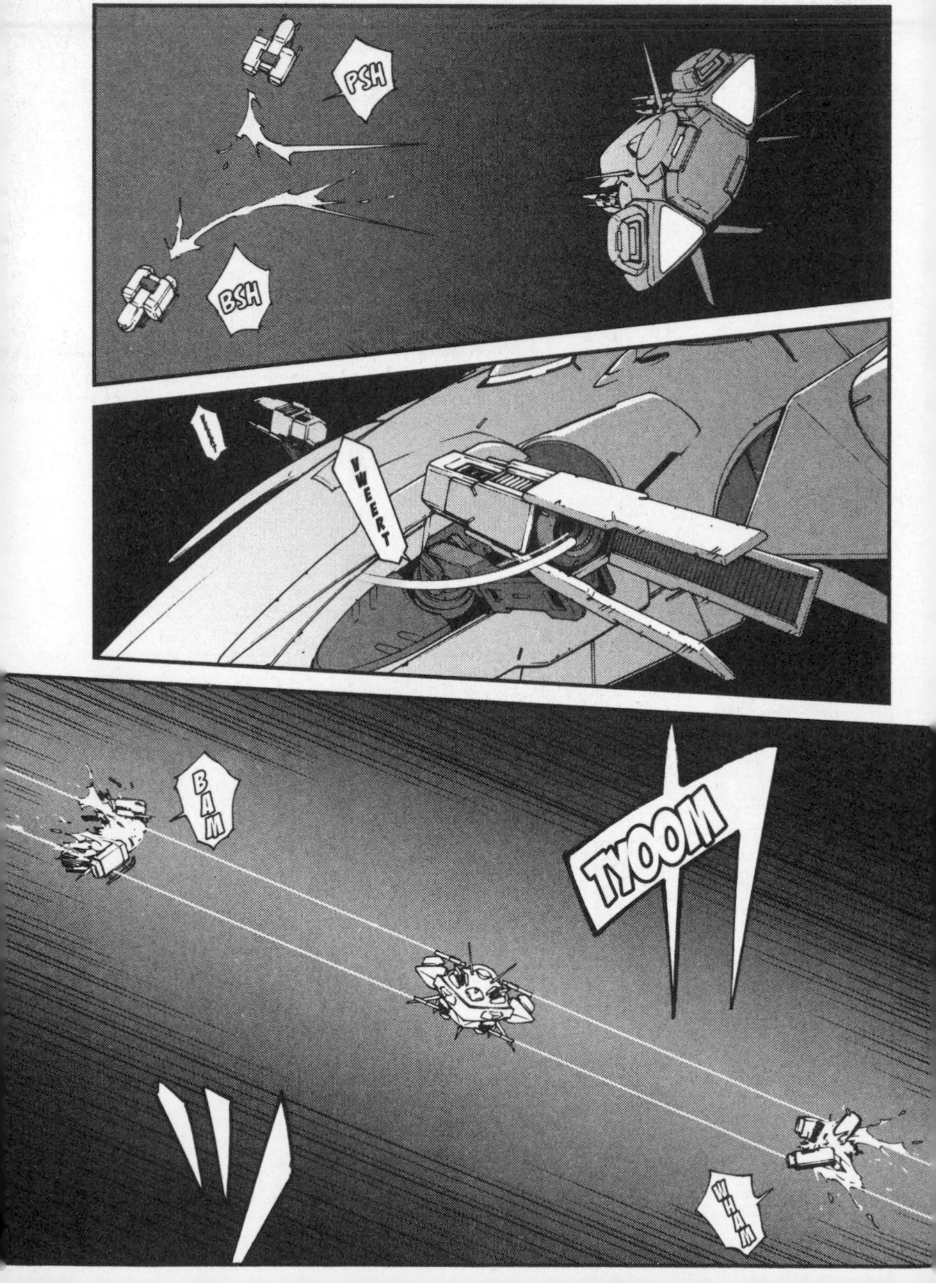
PSH
BSH
VWEERT
TYOOM
BAM
WHAM

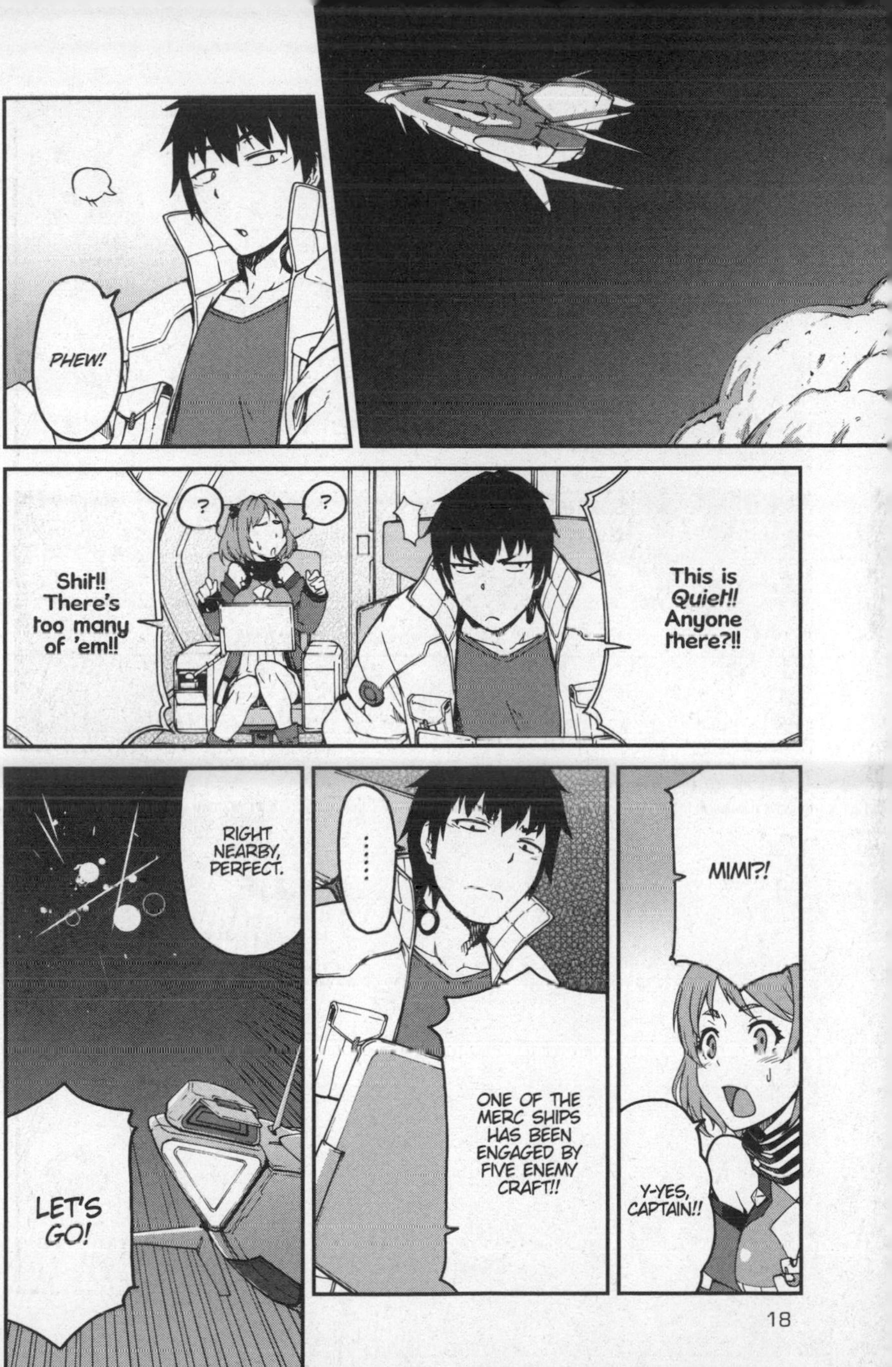

PHEW!
?
?
This is Quiet!! Anyone there?!!
Shit!! There's too many of 'em!!
MIMI?!
Y-YES, CAPTAIN!!
......
ONE OF THE MERC SHIPS HAS BEEN ENGAGED BY FIVE ENEMY CRAFT!!
RIGHT NEARBY, PERFECT.
LET'S GO!

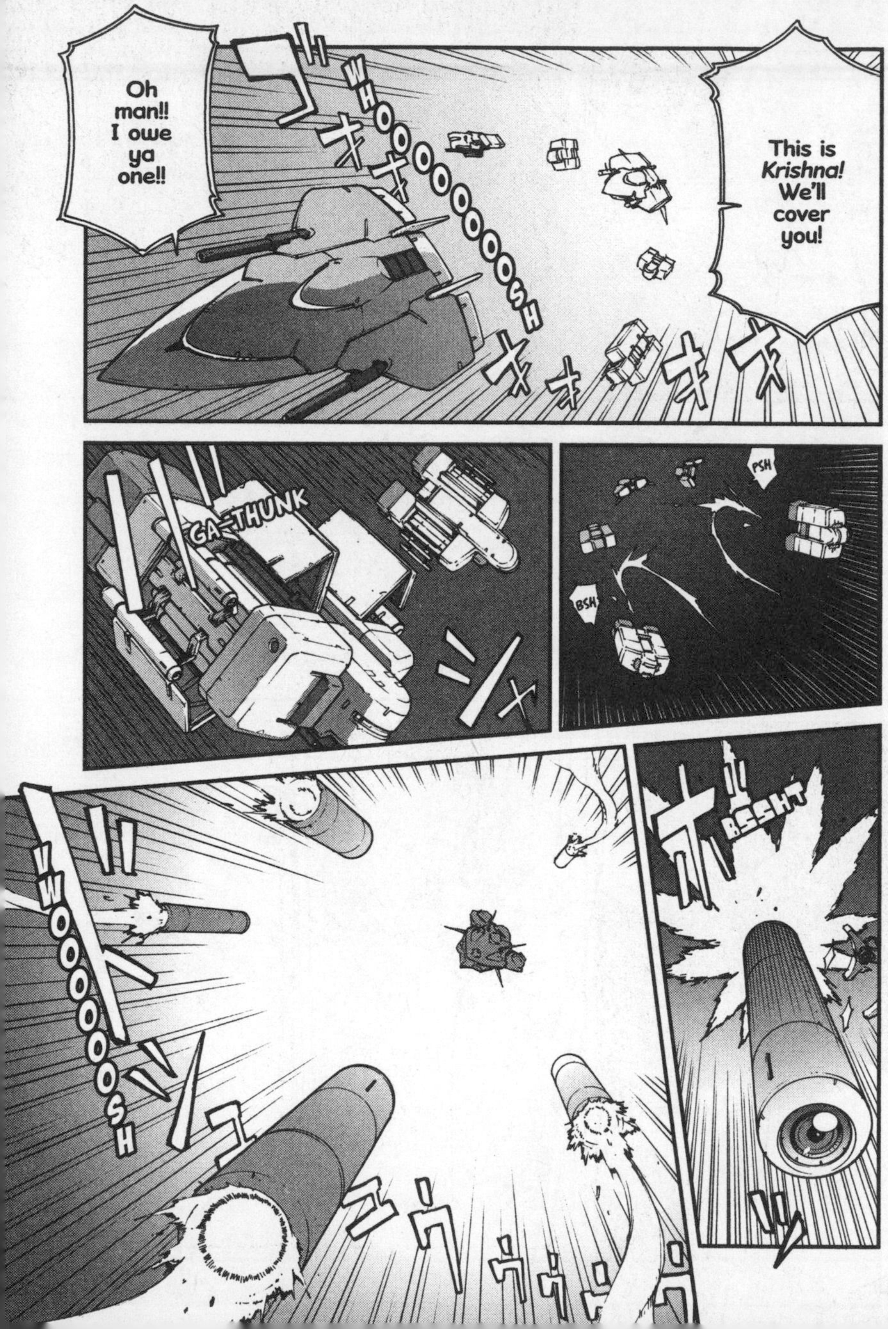
This is Krishna! We'll cover you!
Oh man!! I owe ya one!!
WHOOOOOOOOSH
PSH
BSH
GA-THUNK
BSSHT
VWOOOOOOSH

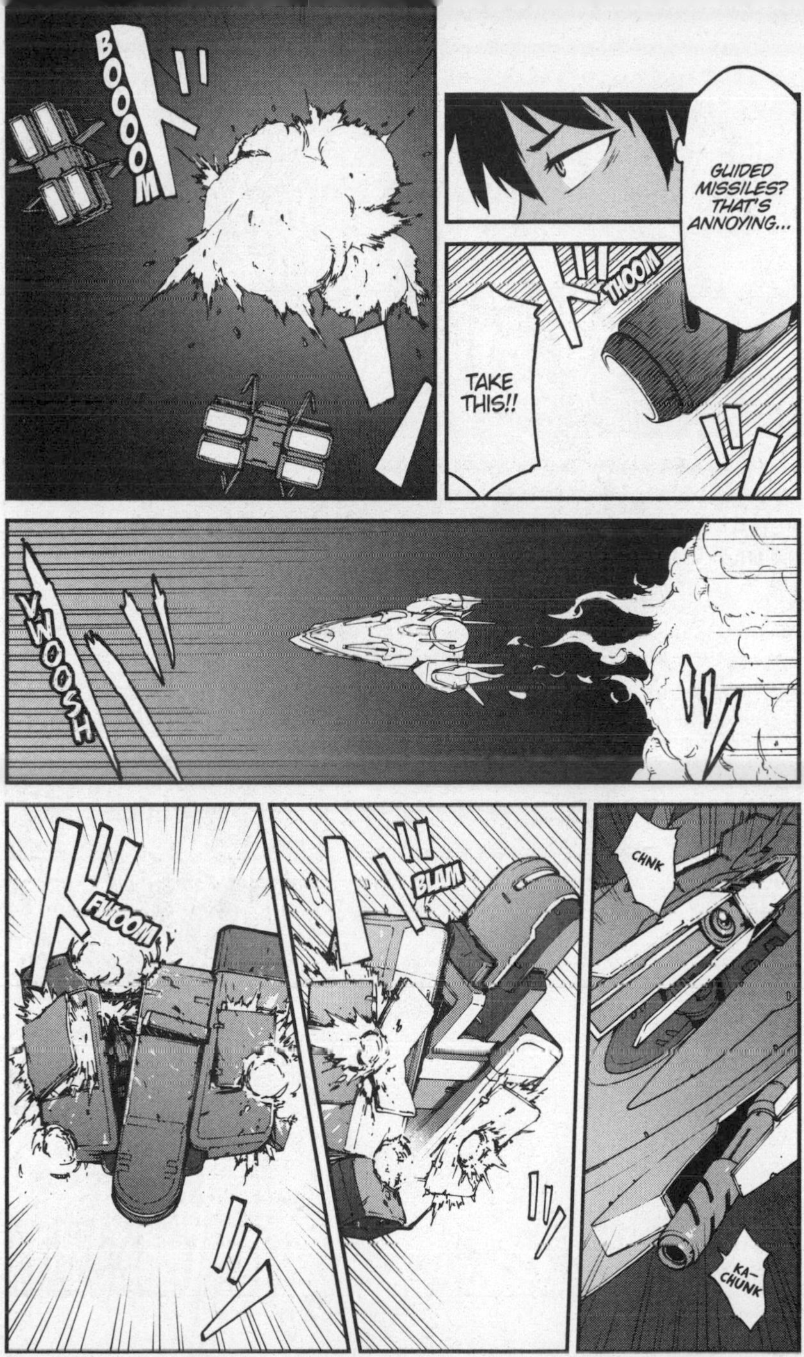
GUIDED MISSILES? THAT'S ANNOYING...
THOOM
TAKE THIS!!
BOOOOM
VWOOSH
CHNK
KA-CHUNK
BLAM
FWOOM

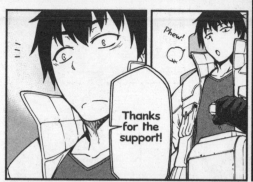

KABOOM
BOOSH
Phew!
Thanks for the support!
You got the rest of 'em? Nice work!
Five at once woulda been the end of me.
I gotta resupply.
Stay safe out there.
Right, see ya later.
Same to you.
MIMI, HOW'RE THINGS LOOKING?
UMM, OVERALL, THE FLEET IS WINNING.
BUT...
THERE ARE THREE MIDSIZE CRAFT NEAR THE FLEET CAUSING A LOT OF TROUBLE.

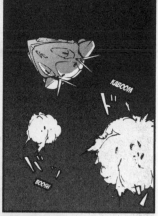

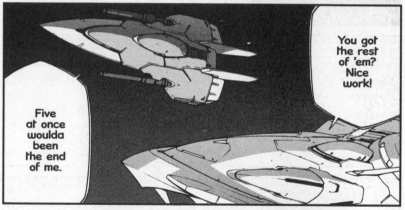

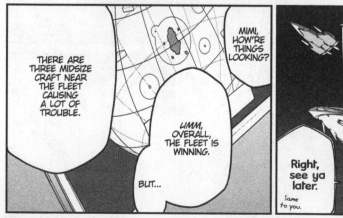

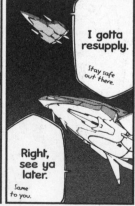

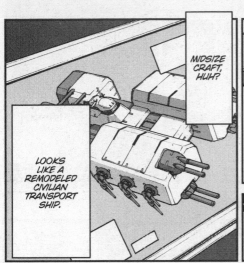

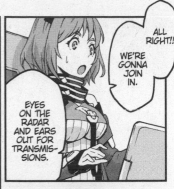

ALL RIGHT!!
WE'RE GONNA JOIN IN.
EYES ON THE RADAR AND EARS OUT FOR TRANSMIS-SIONS.
YES, CAPTAIN!
GLANCE
MIDSIZE CRAFT, HUH?
LOOKS LIKE A REMODELED CIVILIAN TRANSPORT SHIP.
KRISHNA'S SHIELDS SHOULD WITHSTAND THEM, BUT...
BUT I CAN'T OVERLOOK THE MIDSIZE PULSE LASERS OR THE ANTI-PROXIMITY TURRETS.
I'M NOT GONNA FIGHT 'EM HEAD-ON IF I CAN HELP IT.
MIMI.
IT'S GONNA GET A BIT COLD, BUT HANG IN THERE.
O-OKAY... WHAT'S THE PLAN?

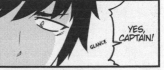

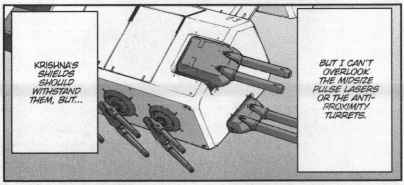

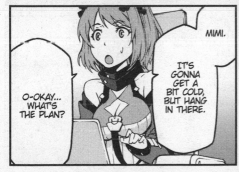

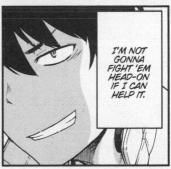

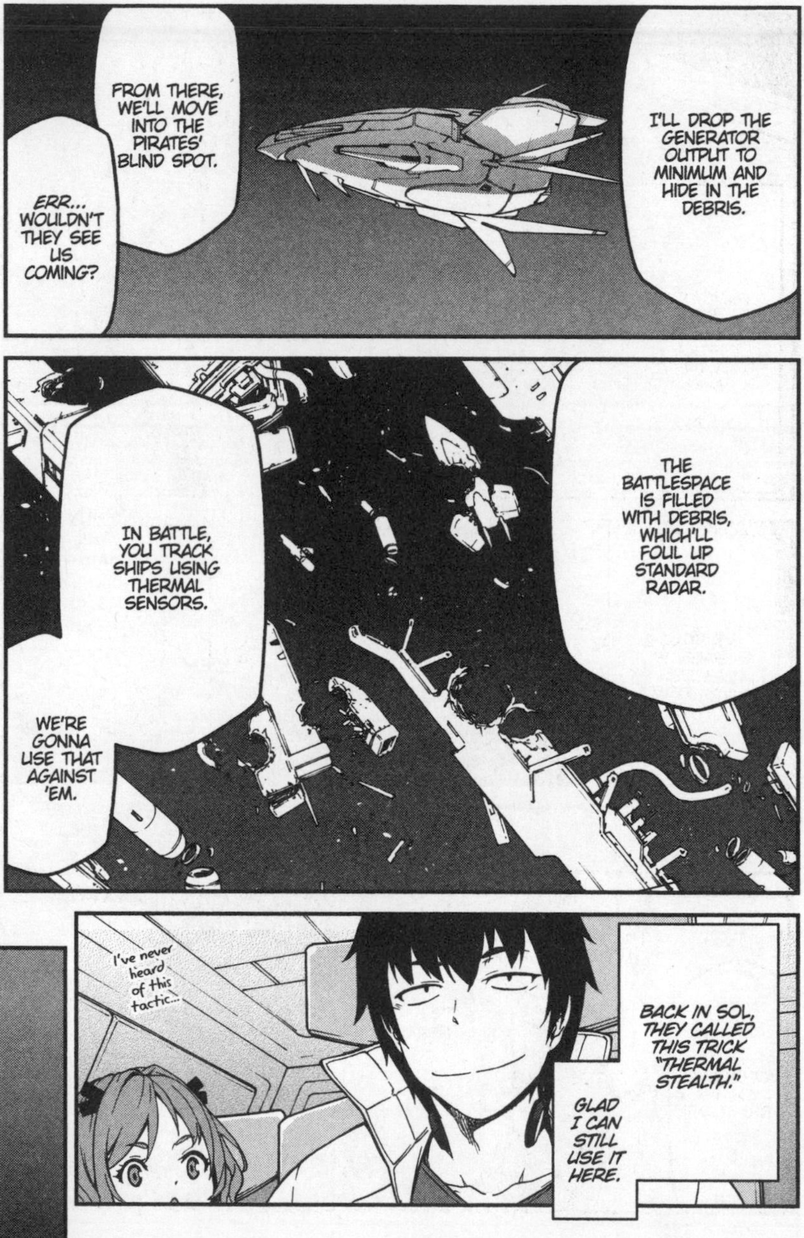
I'LL DROP THE GENERATOR OUTPUT TO MINIMUM AND HIDE IN THE DEBRIS.
FROM THERE, WE'LL MOVE INTO THE PIRATES' BLIND SPOT.
ERR... WOULDN'T THEY SEE US COMING?
THE BATTLESPACE IS FILLED WITH DEBRIS, WHICH'LL FOUL UP STANDARD RADAR.
IN BATTLE, YOU TRACK SHIPS USING THERMAL SENSORS.
WE'RE GONNA USE THAT AGAINST 'EM.
BACK IN SOL, THEY CALLED THIS TRICK "THERMAL STEALTH."
GLAD I CAN STILL USE IT HERE.
I've never heard of this tactic...

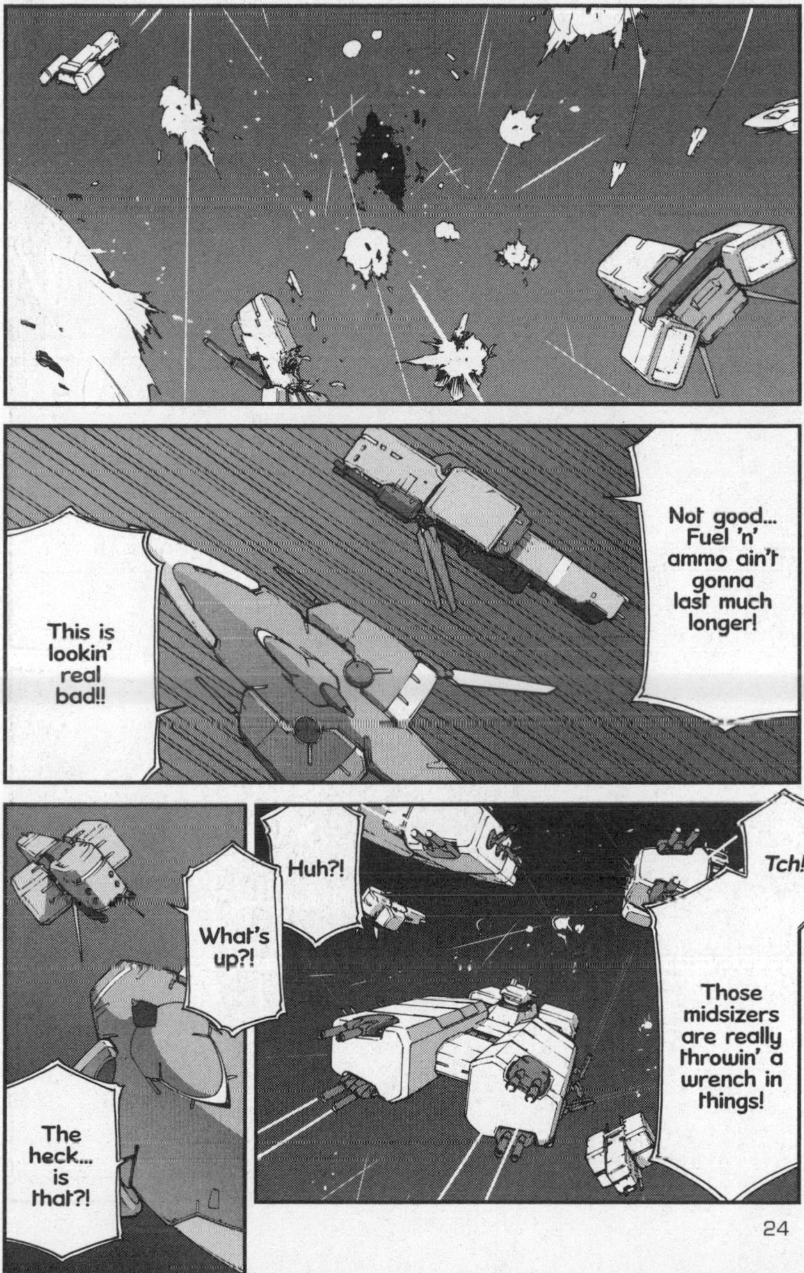
Not good... Fuel 'n' ammo ain't gonna last much longer!
This is lookin' real bad!!
Tch!
Those midsizers are really throwin' a wrench in things!
Huh?!
What's up?!
The heck... is that?!

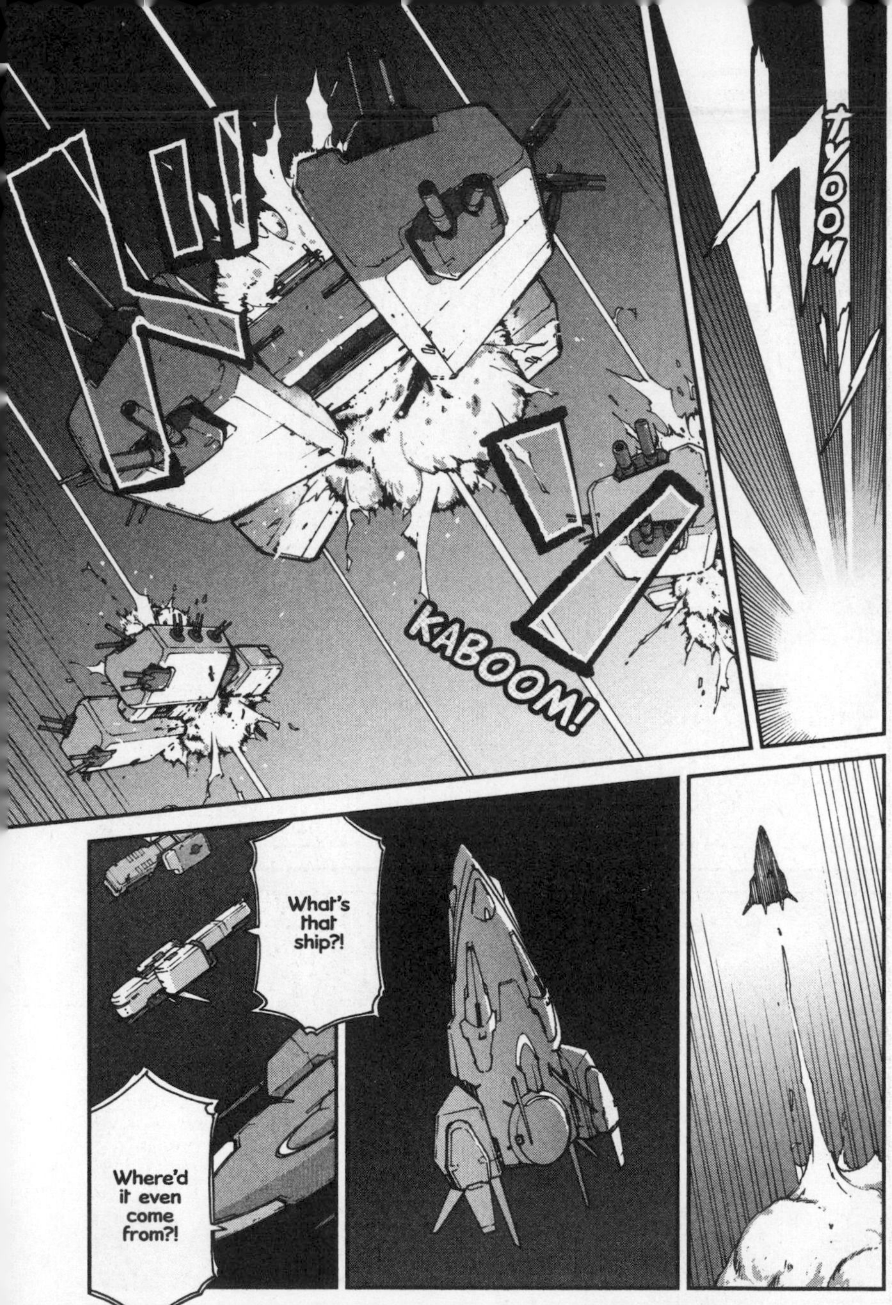
TYOOM
KABOOM!
What's that ship?!
Where'd it even come from?!

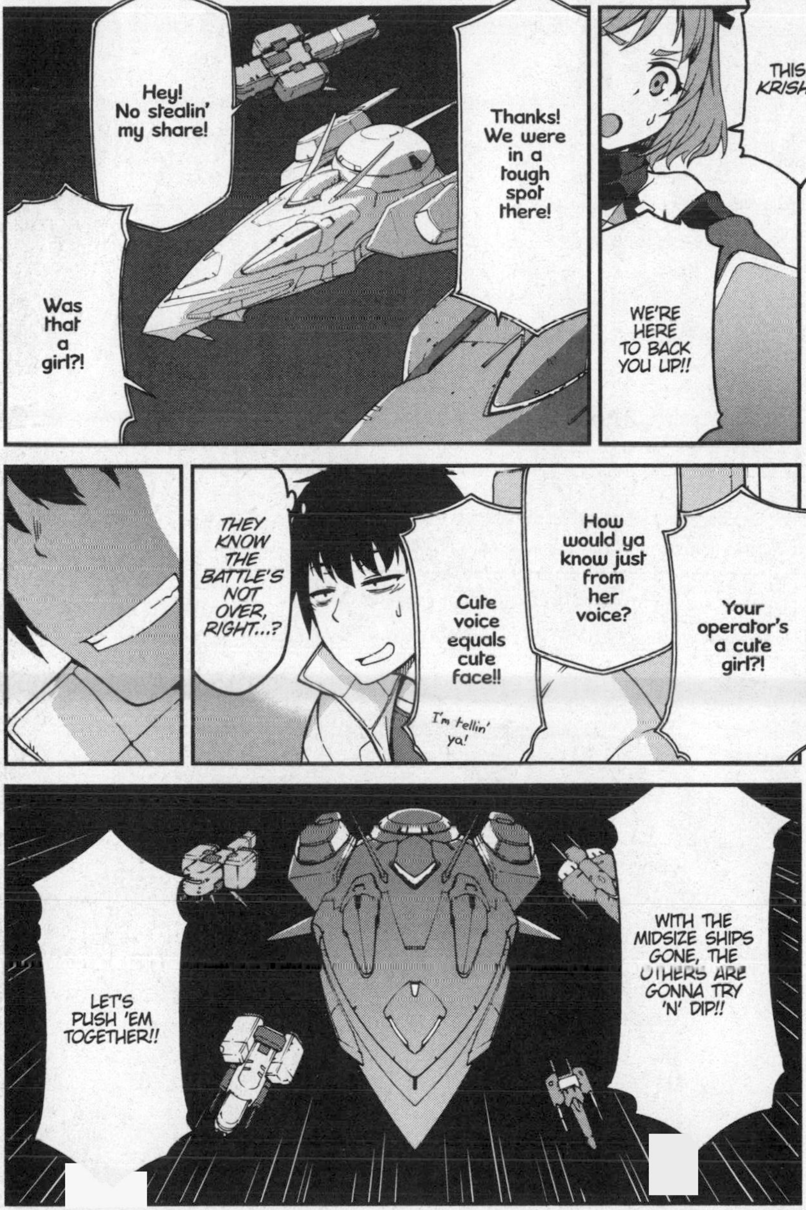
THIS IS KRISHNA!
WE'RE HERE TO BACK YOU UP!!
Thanks! We were in a tough spot there!
Hey! No stealin' my share!
Was that a girl?!
Your operator's a cute girl?!
How would ya know just from her voice?
Cute voice equals cute face!!
I'm tellin' ya!
THEY KNOW THE BATTLE'S NOT OVER, RIGHT...?
WITH THE MIDSIZE SHIPS GONE, THE OTHERS ARE GONNA TRY 'N' DIP!!
LET'S PUSH 'EM TOGETHER!!

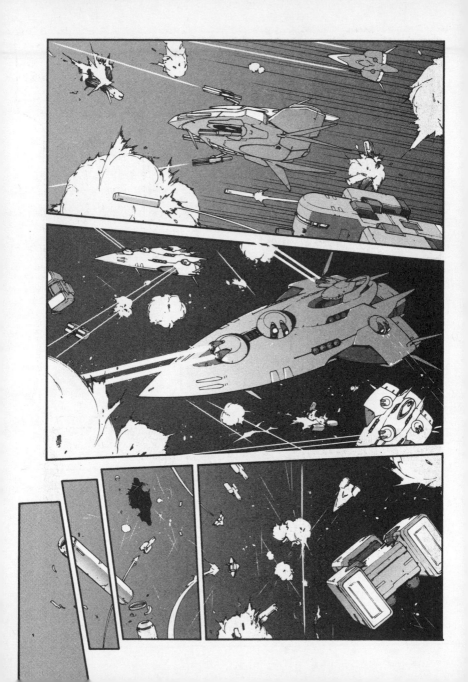

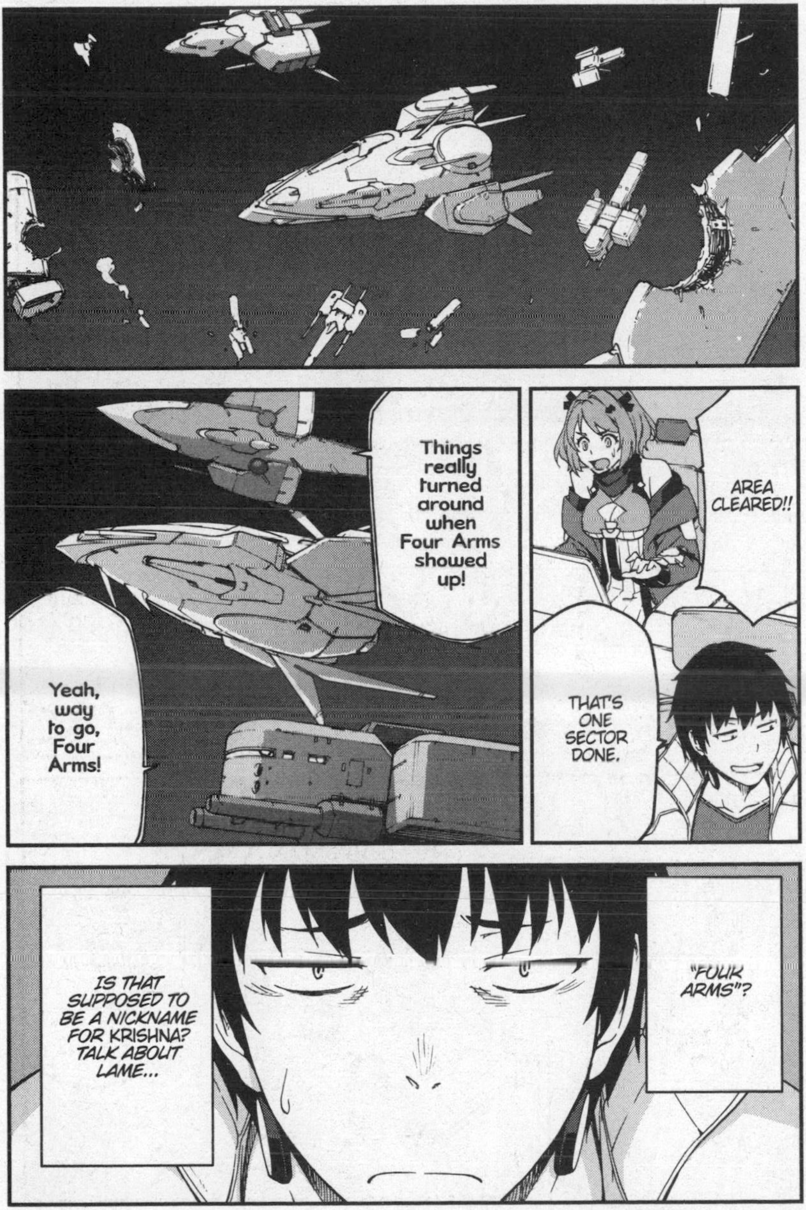
AREA CLEARED!!
THAT'S ONE SECTOR DONE.
Things really turned around when Four Arms showed up!
Yeah, way to go, Four Arms!
"FOUR ARMS"?
IS THAT SUPPOSED TO BE A NICKNAME FOR KRISHNA? TALK ABOUT LAME...

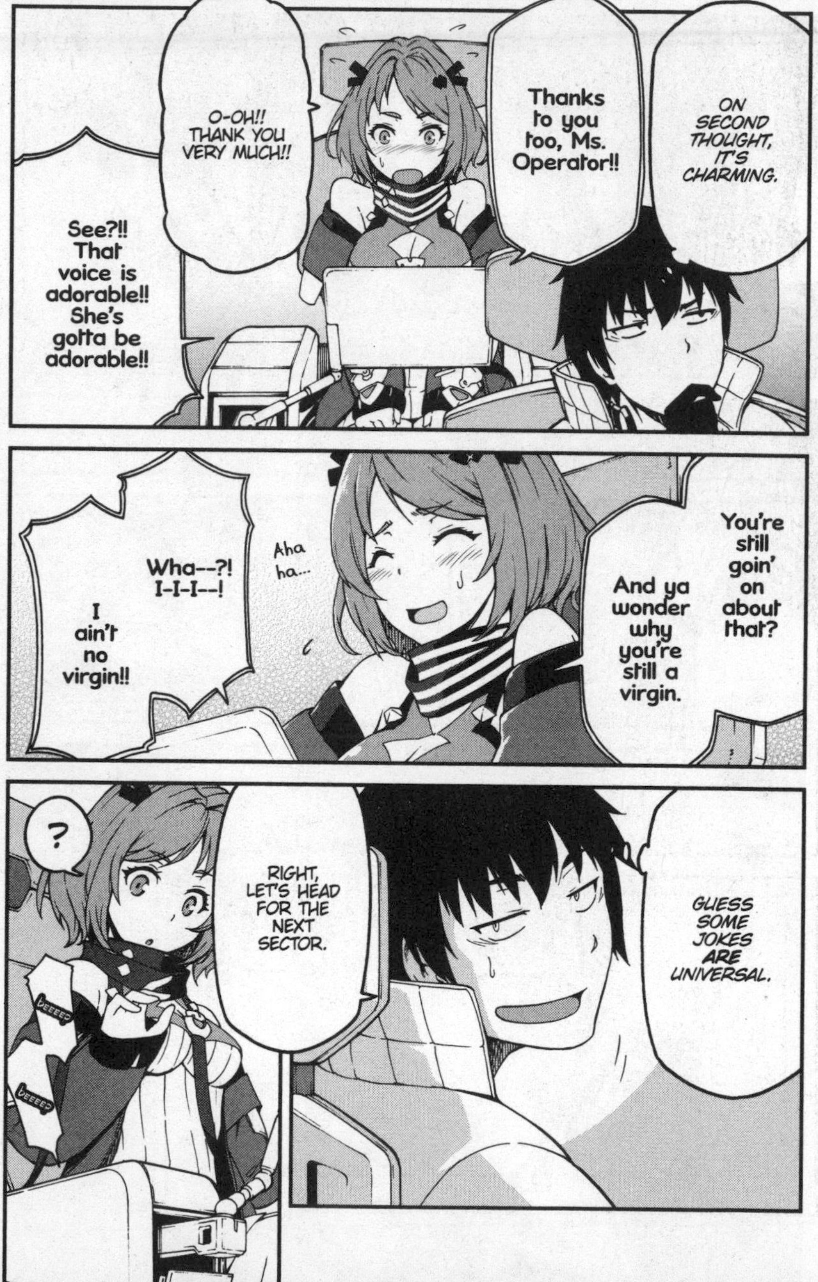
ON SECOND THOUGHT, IT'S CHARMING.
Thanks to you too, Ms. Operator!!
O-OH!! THANK YOU VERY MUCH!!
See?!! That voice is adorable!! She's gotta be adorable!!
You're still goin' on about that?
And ya wonder why you're still a virgin.
Aha ha...
Wha--?! I-I-I--!
I ain't no virgin!!
GUESS SOME JOKES ARE UNIVERSAL.
RIGHT, LET'S HEAD FOR THE NEXT SECTOR.
?
beeeep
beeeep

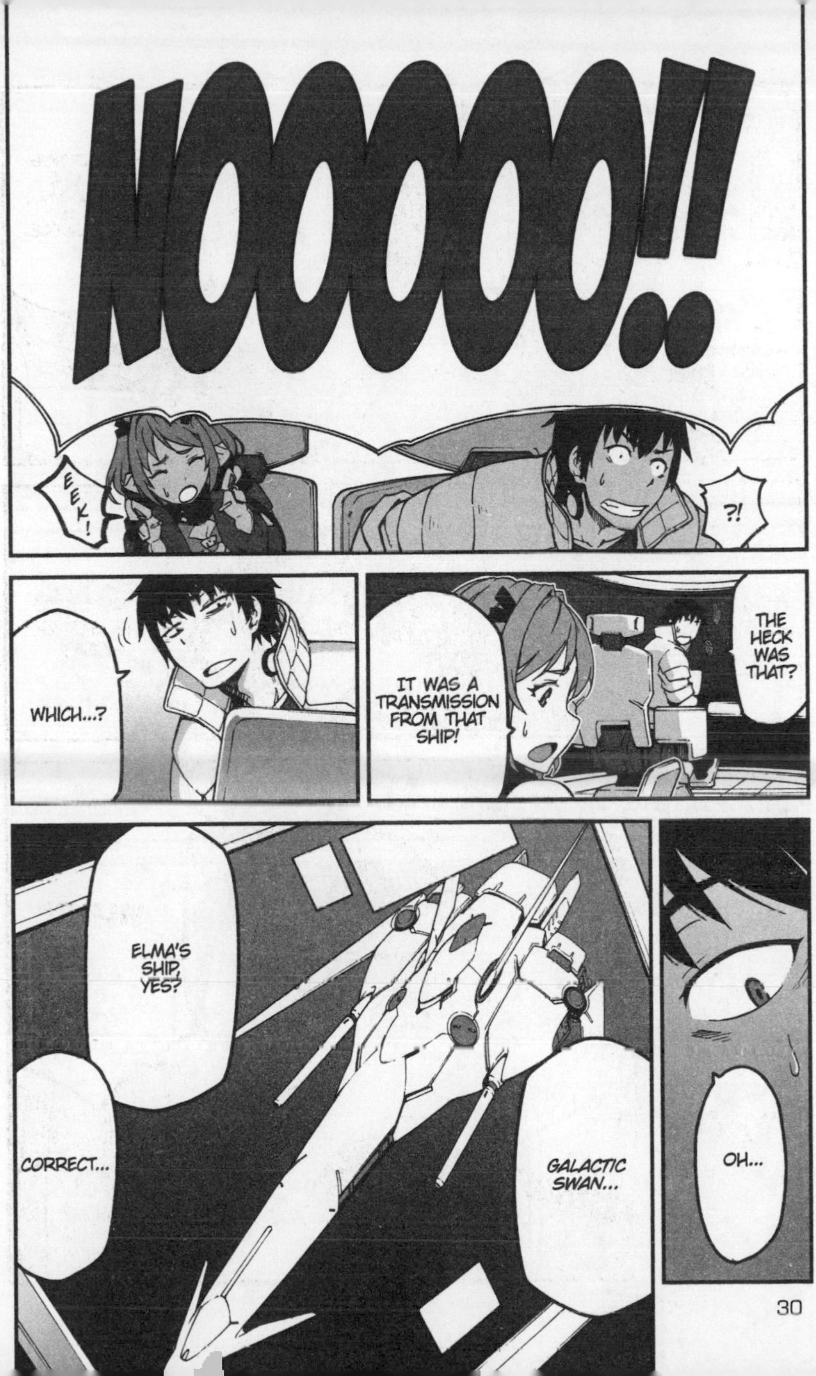
NOOOOO!!
?!
EEK!
THE HECK WAS THAT?
IT WAS A TRANSMISSION FROM THAT SHIP!
WHICH...?
OH...
ELMA'S SHIP, YES?
GALACTIC SWAN...
CORRECT...

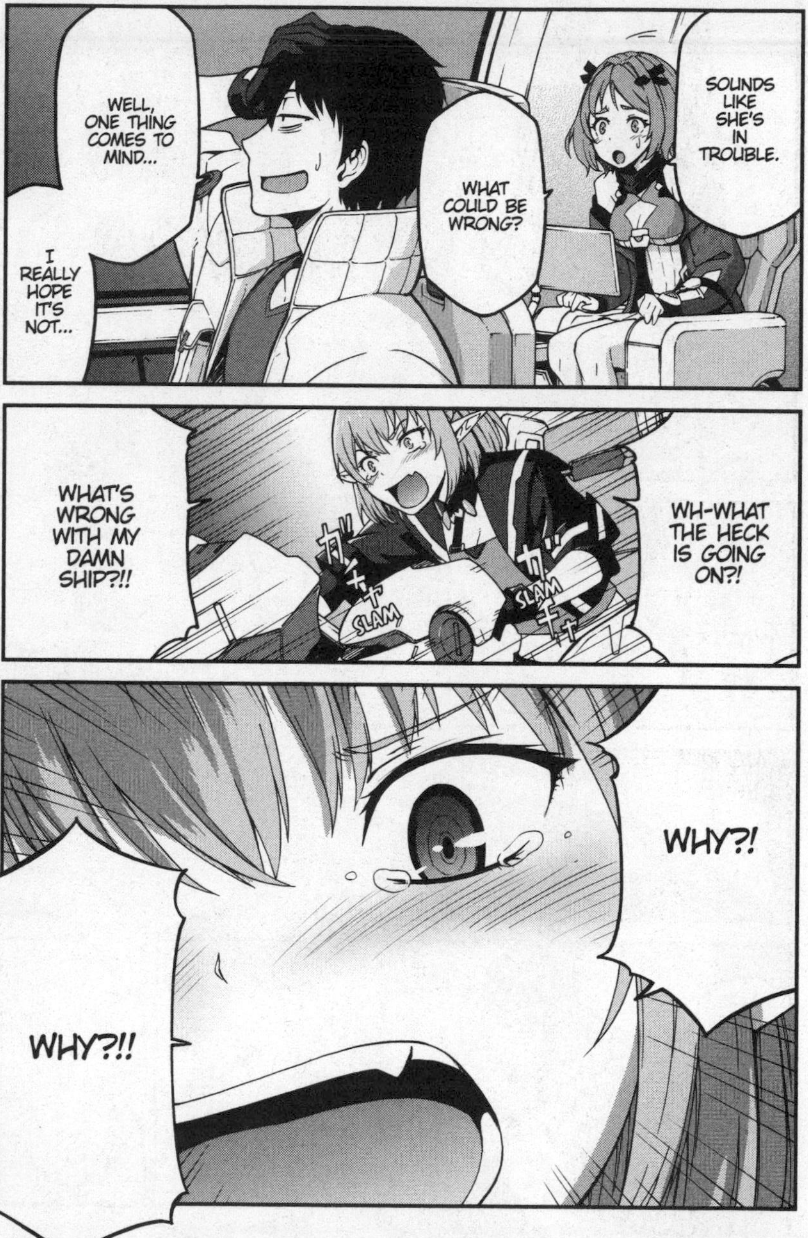
SOUNDS LIKE SHE'S IN TROUBLE.
WHAT COULD BE WRONG?
WELL, ONE THING COMES TO MIND...
I REALLY HOPE IT'S NOT...
WH-WHAT THE HECK IS GOING ON?!
SLAM
SLAM
WHAT'S WRONG WITH MY DAMN SHIP?!!
WHY?!
WHY?!!

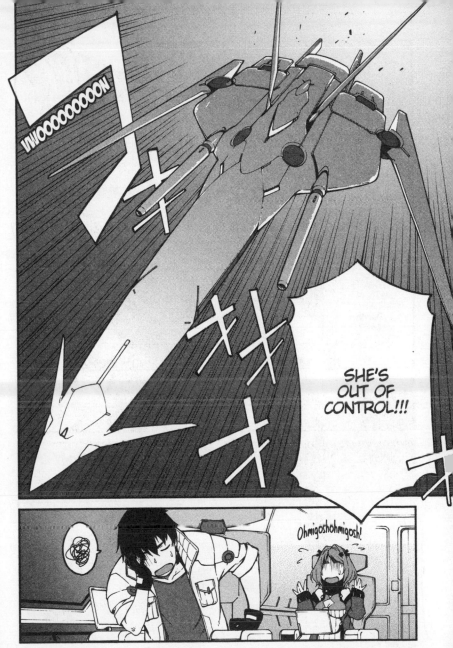

VWOOOOOOOOON

SHE'S OUT OF CONTROL!!!

Ohmigoshohmigosh!

32

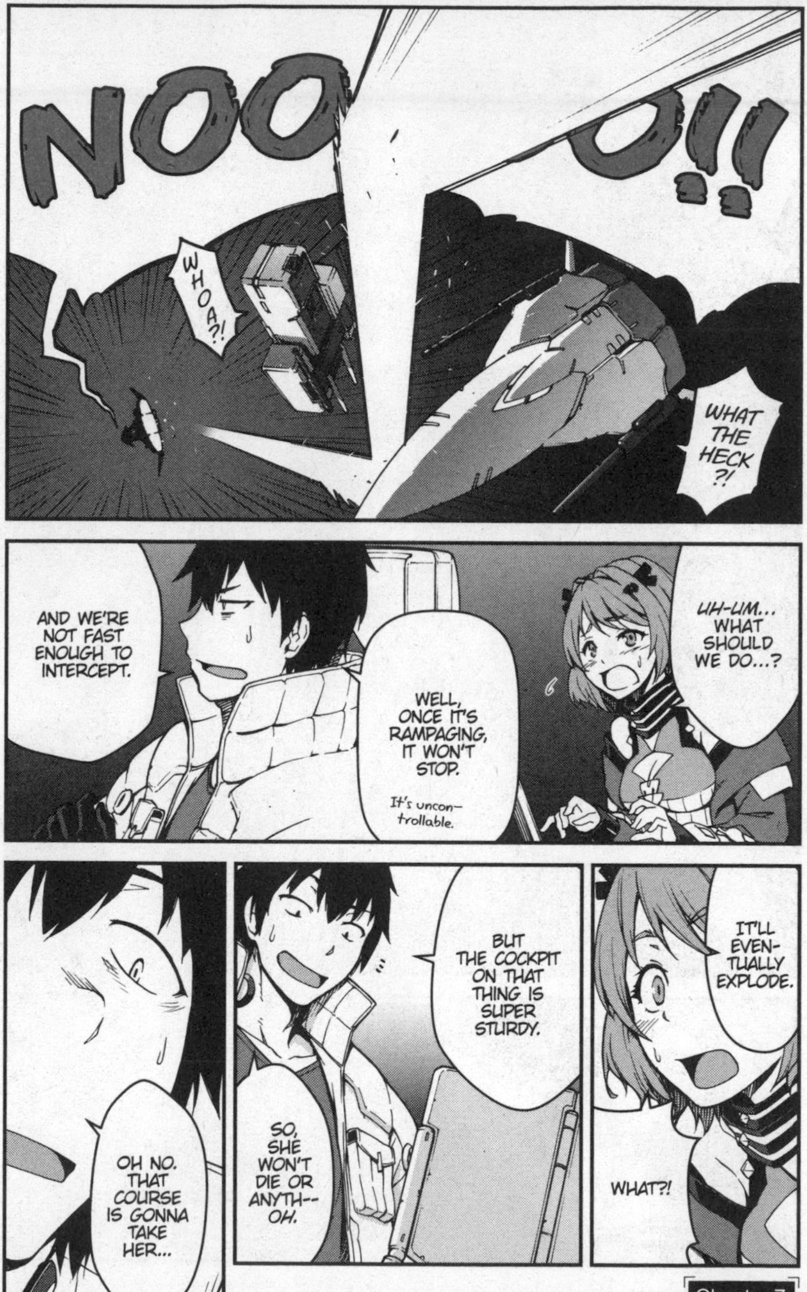
NOO O!!
WHAT THE HECK?!
WHOA?!
UH-UM... WHAT SHOULD WE DO...?
WELL, ONCE IT'S RAMPAGING, IT WON'T STOP.
It's uncon-trollable.
AND WE'RE NOT FAST ENOUGH TO INTERCEPT.
IT'LL EVEN-TUALLY EXPLODE.
WHAT?!
BUT THE COCKPIT ON THAT THING IS SUPER STURDY.
SO, SHE WON'T DIE OR ANYTH-- OH.
OH NO. THAT COURSE IS GONNA TAKE HER...

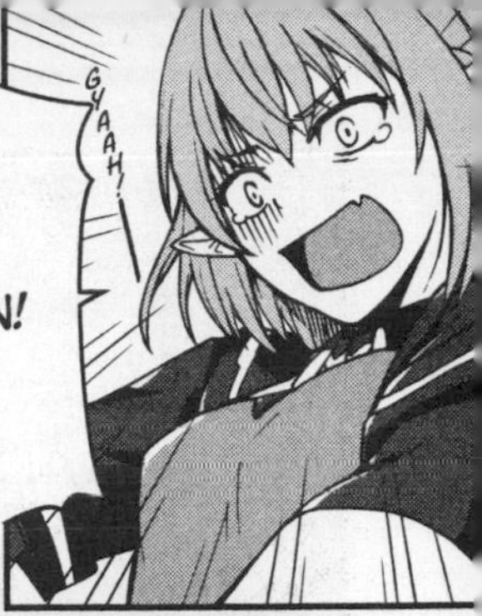
GYAAH!
TURN!
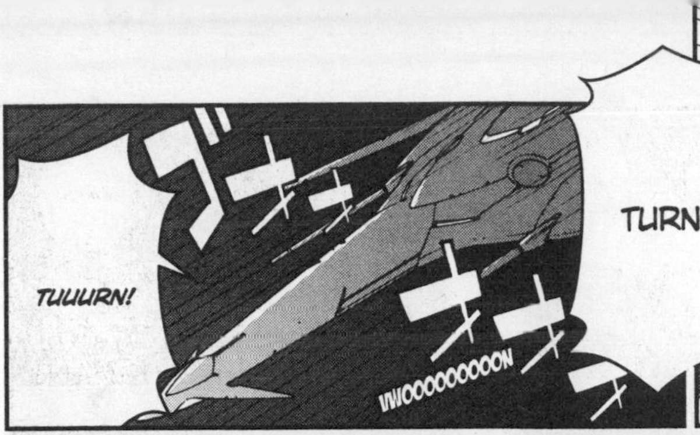
TUUURN!
VWOOOOOOOOOON
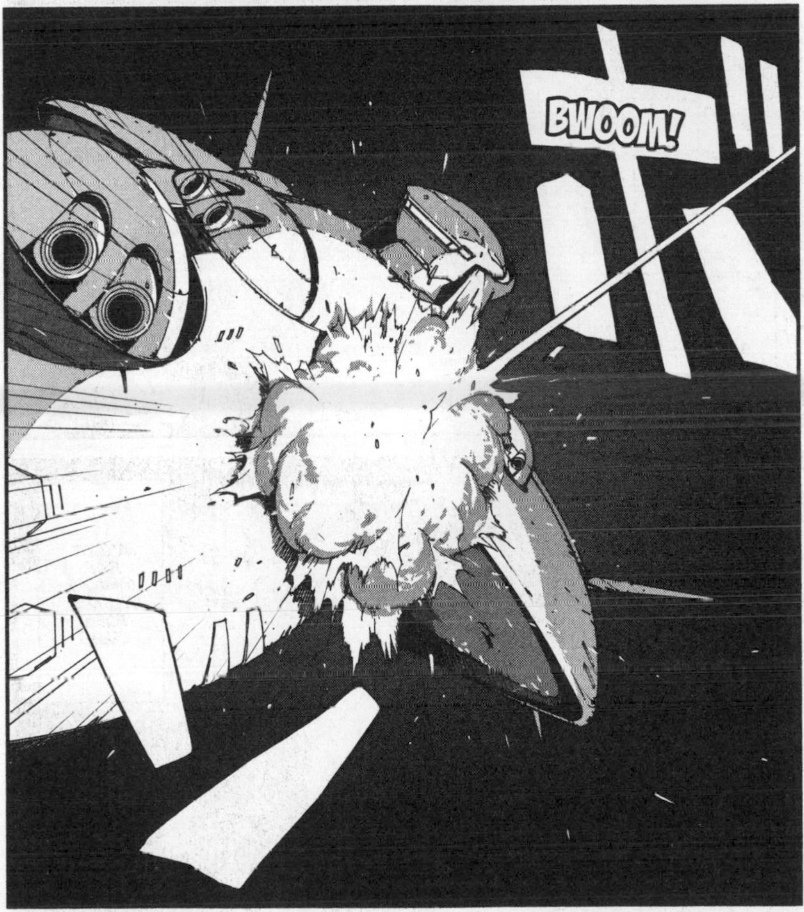
BWOOM!

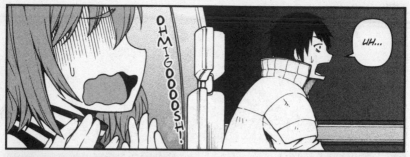

OHMIGOOOSH!

UH...

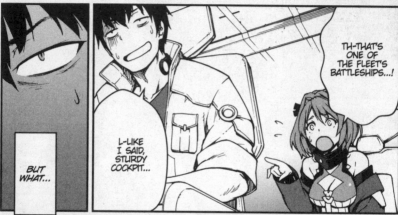

TH-THAT'S ONE OF THE FLEET'S BATTLESHIPS...!

L-LIKE I SAID, STURDY COCKPIT...

BUT WHAT...

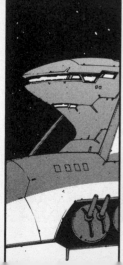

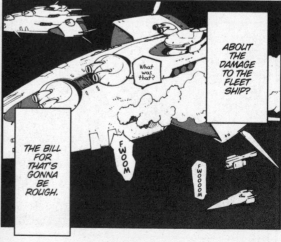

What was that?

ABOUT THE DAMAGE TO THE FLEET SHIP?

THE BILL FOR THAT'S GONNA BE ROUGH.

FWOOM

FWOOOOM

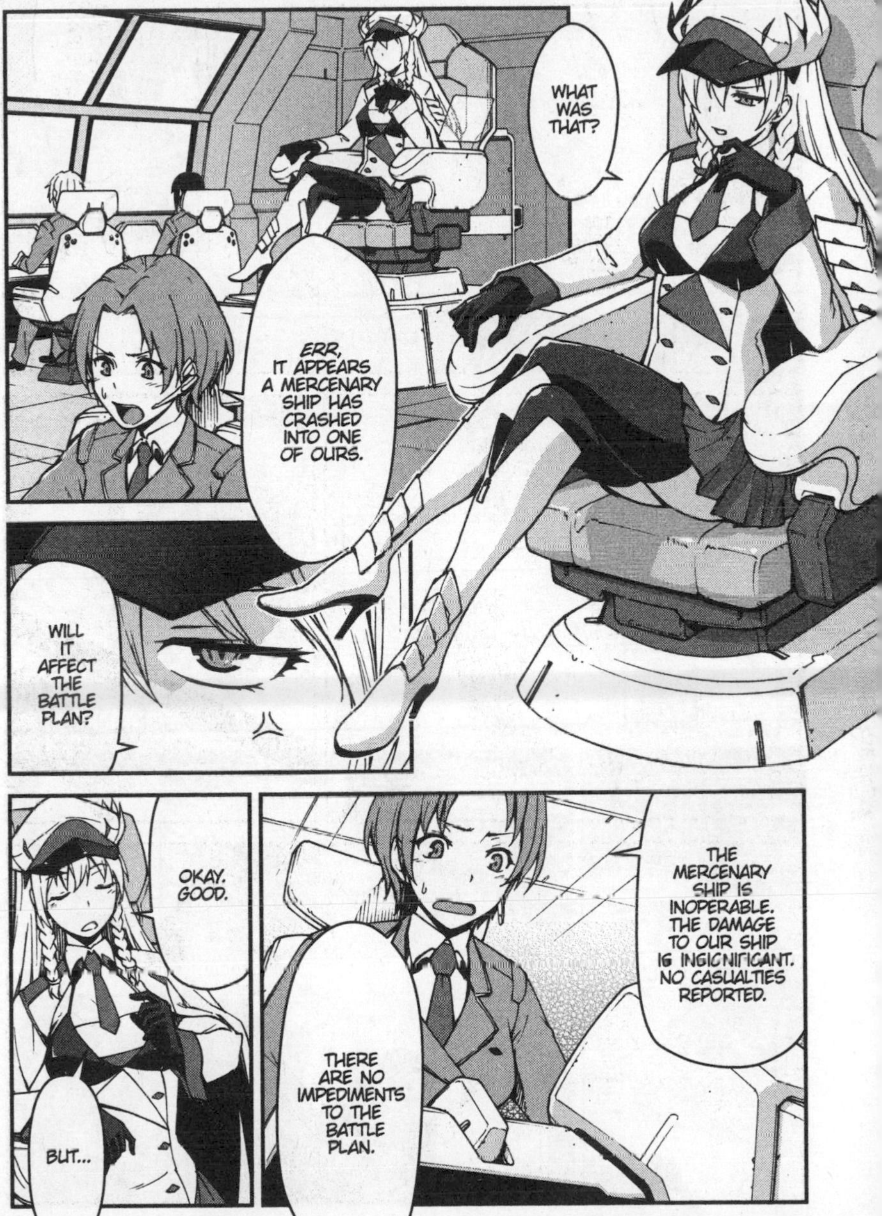
WHAT WAS THAT?
ERR, IT APPEARS A MERCENARY SHIP HAS CRASHED INTO ONE OF OURS.
WILL IT AFFECT THE BATTLE PLAN?
THE MERCENARY SHIP IS INOPERABLE. THE DAMAGE TO OUR SHIP IS INSIGNIFICANT. NO CASUALTIES REPORTED.
THERE ARE NO IMPEDIMENTS TO THE BATTLE PLAN.
OKAY. GOOD.
BUT...

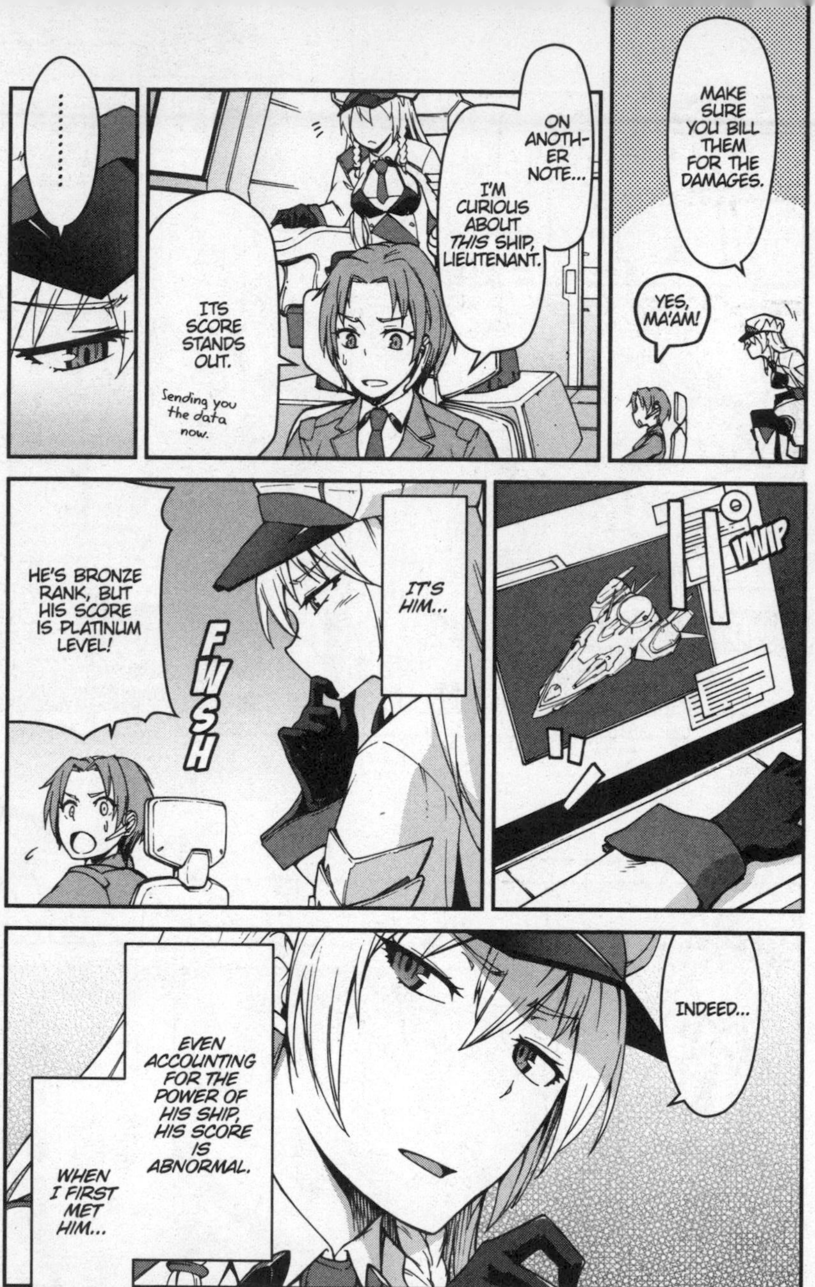
MAKE SURE YOU BILL THEM FOR THE DAMAGES.
YES, MA'AM!
ON ANOTHER-ER NOTE...
I'M CURIOUS ABOUT *THIS* SHIP, LIEUTENANT.
ITS SCORE STANDS OUT.
Sending you the data now.
......
VWIP
IT'S HIM...
HE'S BRONZE RANK, BUT HIS SCORE IS PLATINUM LEVEL!
FWSH
INDEED...
EVEN ACCOUNTING FOR THE POWER OF HIS SHIP, HIS SCORE IS ABNORMAL.
WHEN I FIRST MET HIM...

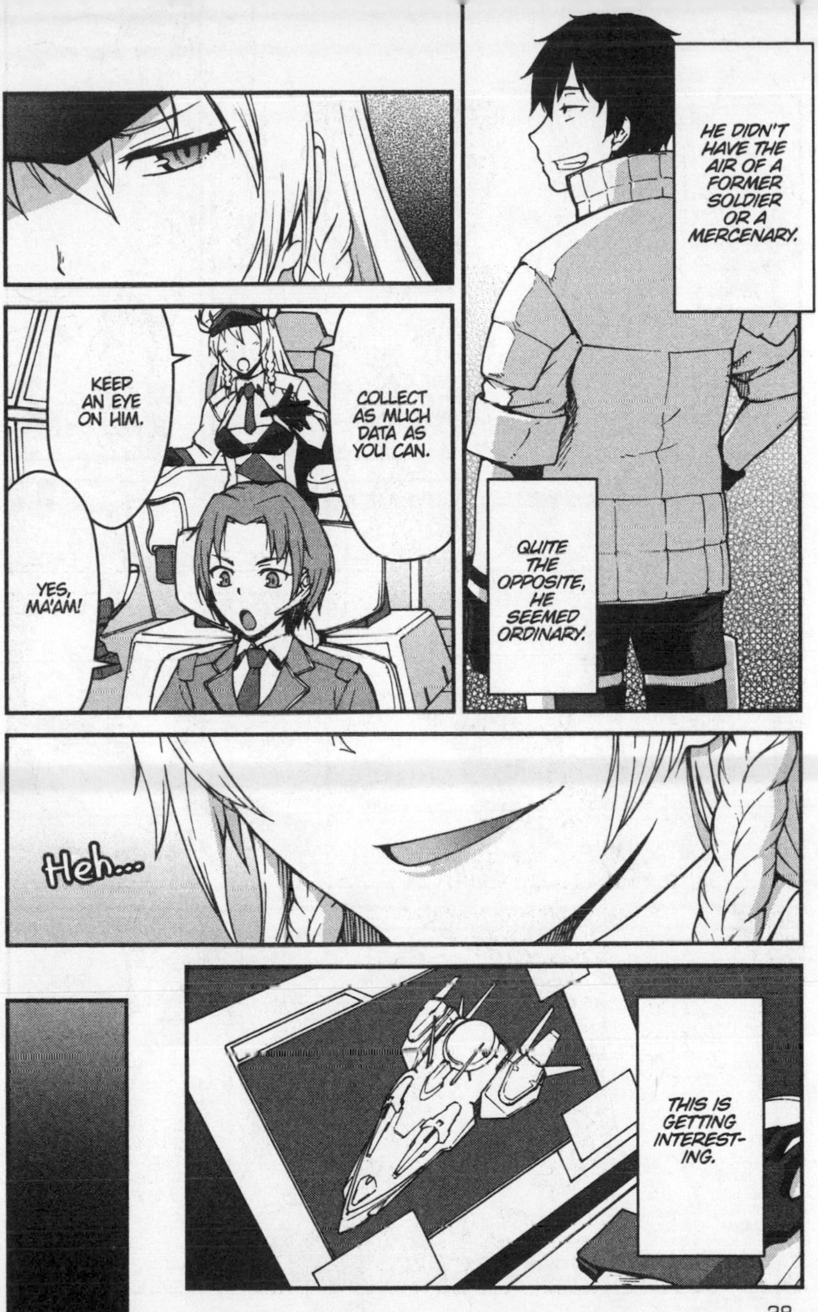
HE DIDN'T HAVE THE AIR OF A FORMER SOLDIER OR A MERCENARY.
QUITE THE OPPOSITE, HE SEEMED ORDINARY.
COLLECT AS MUCH DATA AS YOU CAN.
KEEP AN EYE ON HIM.
YES, MA'AM!
Heh...
THIS IS GETTING INTEREST-ING.

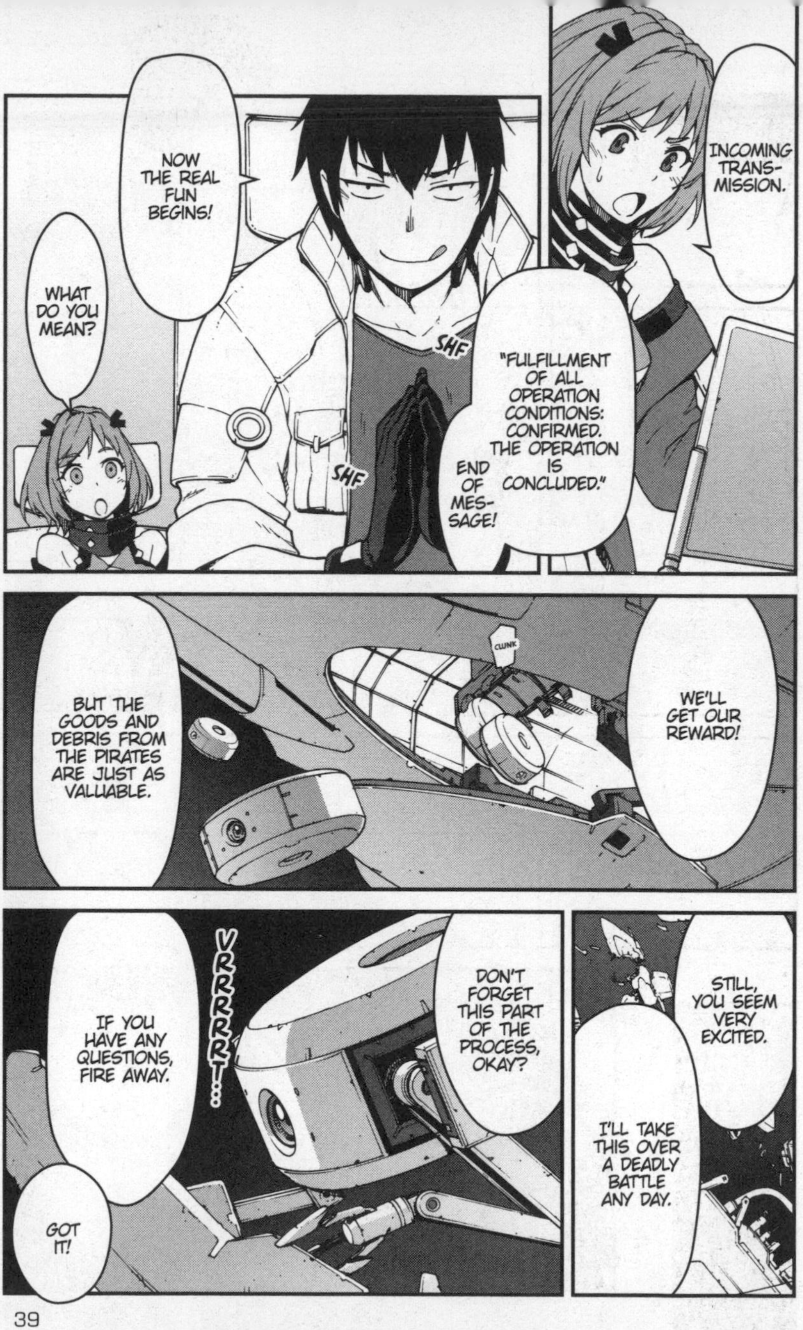
INCOMING TRANSMISSION.
"FULFILLMENT OF ALL OPERATION CONDITIONS: CONFIRMED. THE OPERATION IS CONCLUDED."
END OF MES-SAGE!
SHF
SHF
NOW THE REAL FUN BEGINS!
WHAT DO YOU MEAN?
WE'LL GET OUR REWARD!
CLUNK
BUT THE GOODS AND DEBRIS FROM THE PIRATES ARE JUST AS VALUABLE.
STILL, YOU SEEM VERY EXCITED.
I'LL TAKE THIS OVER A DEADLY BATTLE ANY DAY.
DON'T FORGET THIS PART OF THE PROCESS, OKAY?
VRRRRRT...
IF YOU HAVE ANY QUESTIONS, FIRE AWAY.
GOT IT!

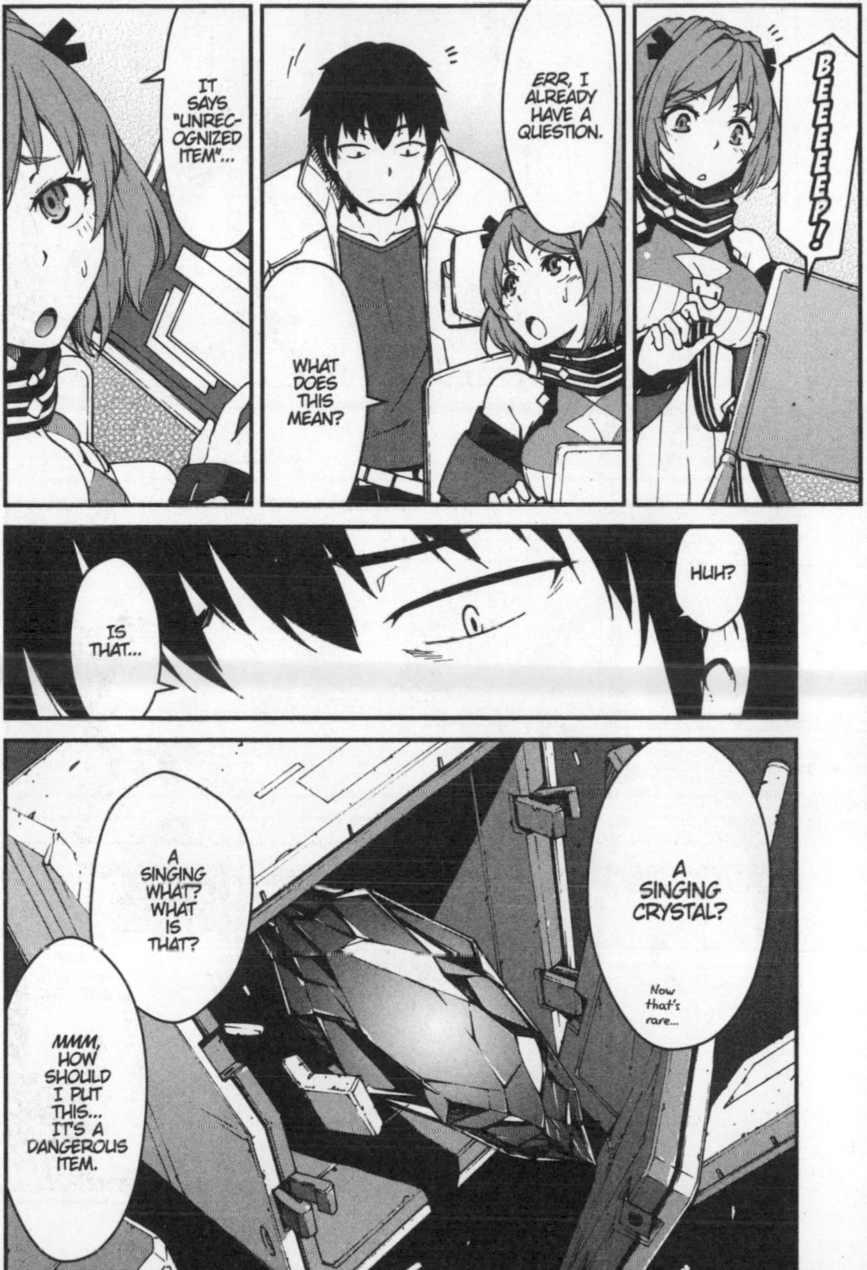
BEEEEEP!
ERR, I ALREADY HAVE A QUESTION.
WHAT DOES THIS MEAN?
IT SAYS "UNRECOGNIZED ITEM"...
HUH?
IS THAT...
A SINGING CRYSTAL?
Now that's rare...
A SINGING WHAT? WHAT IS THAT?
MMM, HOW SHOULD I PUT THIS... IT'S A DANGEROUS ITEM.

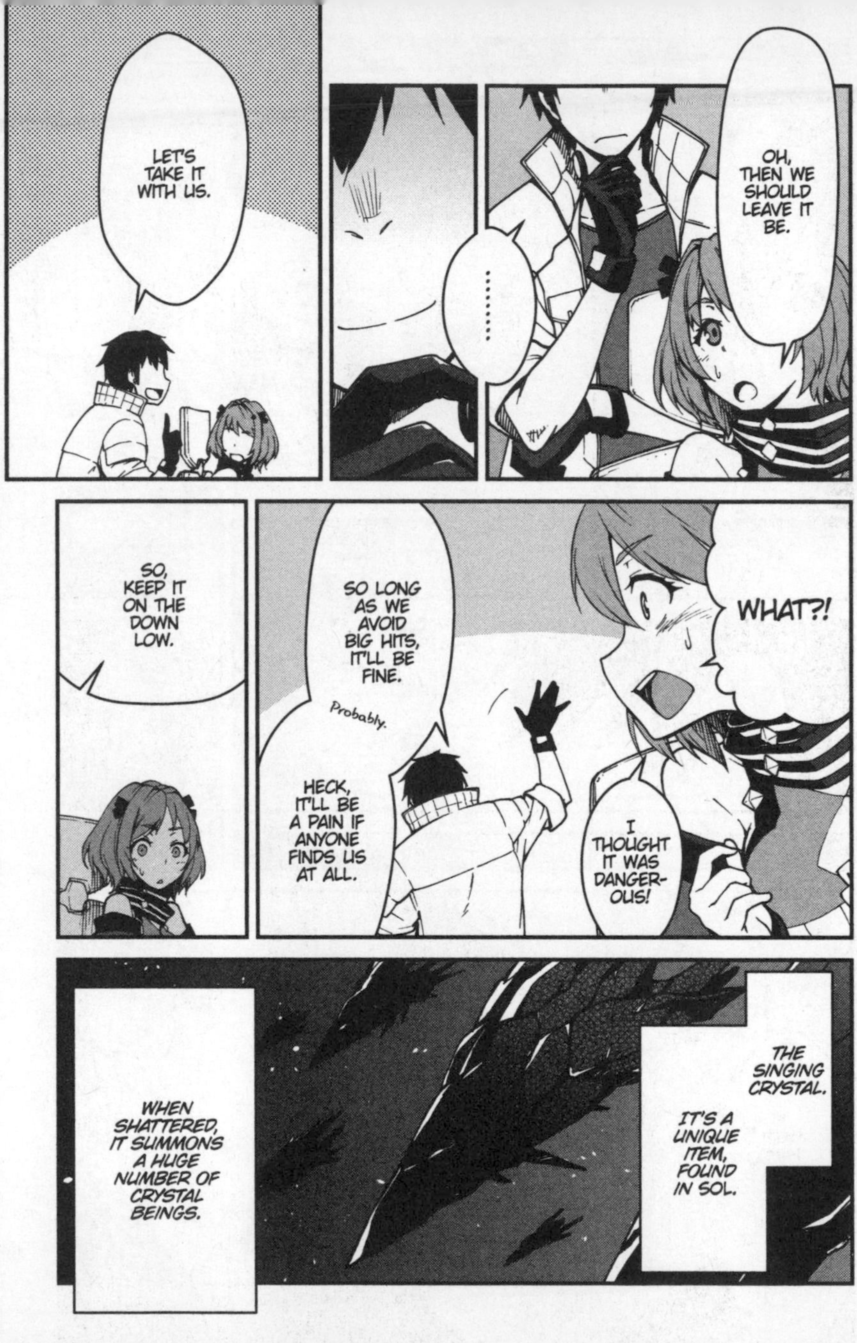
OH, THEN WE SHOULD LEAVE IT BE.
……
LET'S TAKE IT WITH US.
WHAT?!
I THOUGHT IT WAS DANGER-OUS!
SO LONG AS WE AVOID BIG HITS, IT'LL BE FINE.
Probably.
HECK, IT'LL BE A PAIN IF ANYONE FINDS US AT ALL.
SO, KEEP IT ON THE DOWN LOW.
THE SINGING CRYSTAL.
IT'S A UNIQUE ITEM, FOUND IN SOL.
WHEN SHATTERED, IT SUMMONS A HUGE NUMBER OF CRYSTAL BEINGS.

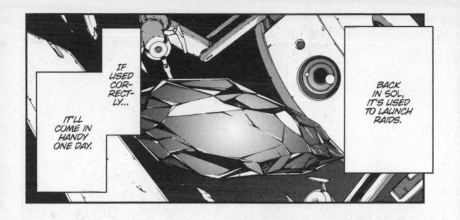

BACK IN SOL, IT'S USED TO LAUNCH RAIDS.
IF USED CORRECTLY...
IT'LL COME IN HANDY ONE DAY.
BWAHN
SO, CAPTAIN, WHAT'S NEXT?
BWAHN
WHADDYA MEAN?
UHHH, WE'LL JUST TAKE A BREAK.
I'm pretty tired.
ERR, I MEANT MORE LIKE...
WHERE WILL WE GO, AND DO?
Our next "goal."

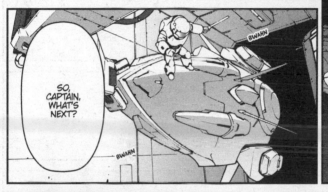

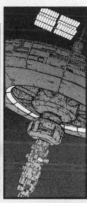

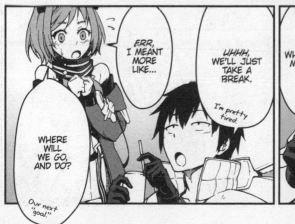

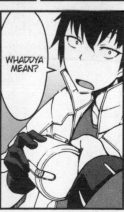

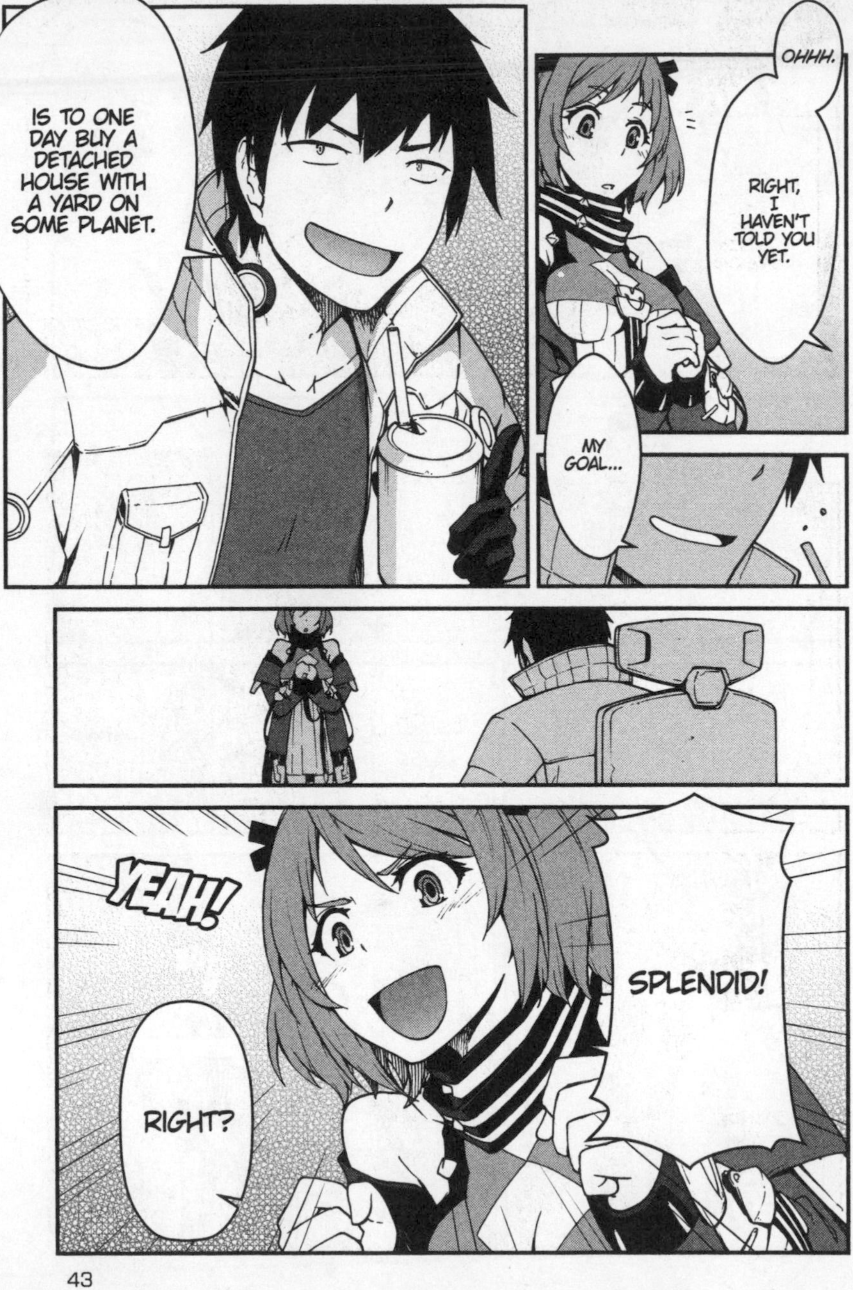
OHHH.
RIGHT, I HAVEN'T TOLD YOU YET.
MY GOAL...
IS TO ONE DAY BUY A DETACHED HOUSE WITH A YARD ON SOME PLANET.
SPLENDID!
YEAH!
RIGHT?

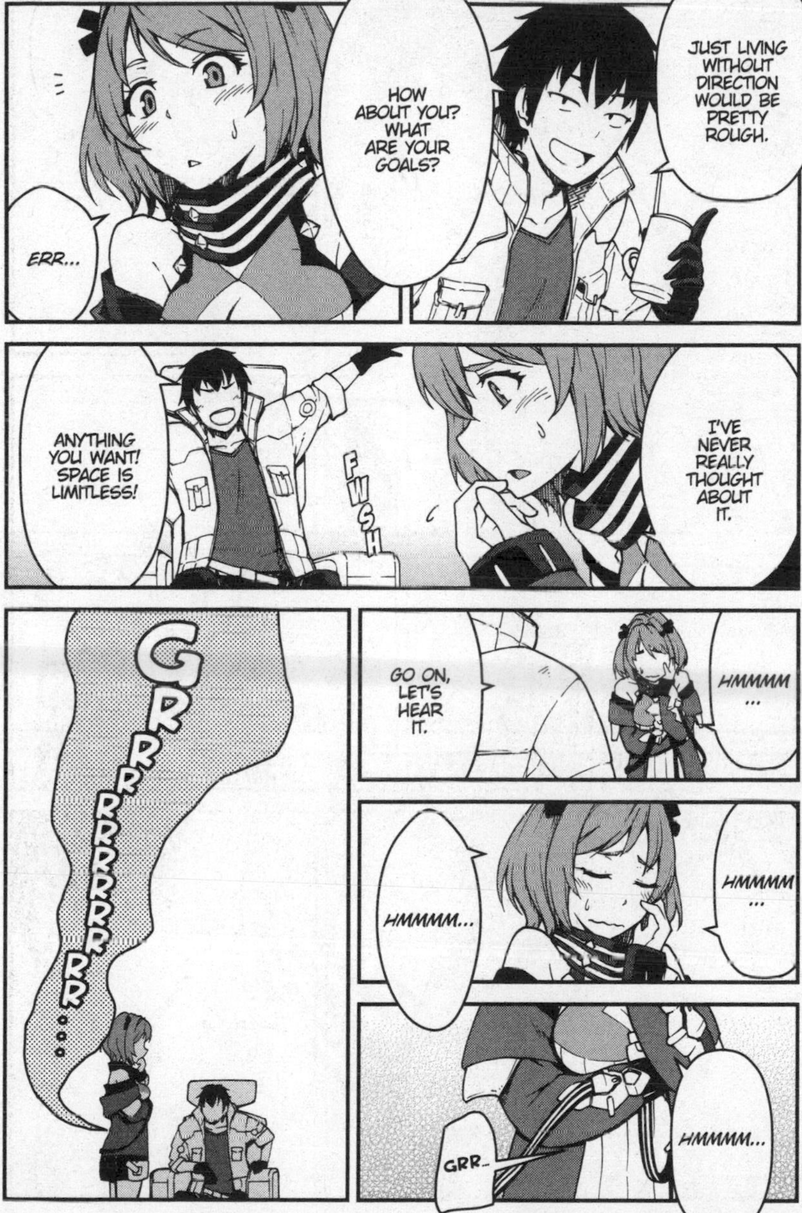
JUST LIVING WITHOUT DIRECTION WOULD BE PRETTY ROUGH.
HOW ABOUT YOU? WHAT ARE YOUR GOALS?
ERR...
I'VE NEVER REALLY THOUGHT ABOUT IT.
ANYTHING YOU WANT! SPACE IS LIMITLESS!
FWSH
HMMMM ...
GO ON, LET'S HEAR IT.
HMMMM ...
HMMMM...
HMMMM...
GRR...
GRRRRRRRRRRRRRR...

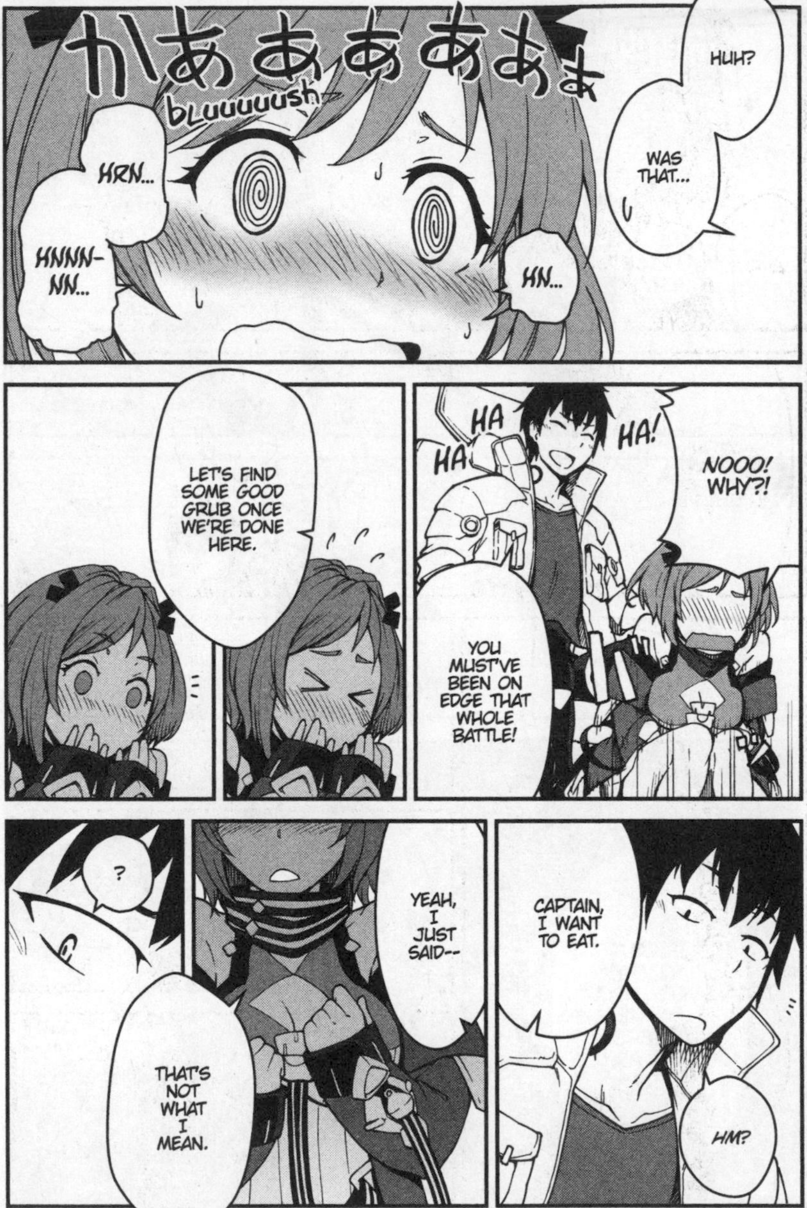
HUH?
WAS THAT...
かあああああぁ
bluuuush
HRN...
HNNN-NN...
HN...
HA HA HA!
NOOO! WHY?!
YOU MUST'VE BEEN ON EDGE THAT WHOLE BATTLE!
LET'S FIND SOME GOOD GRUB ONCE WE'RE DONE HERE.
CAPTAIN, I WANT TO EAT.
HM?
YEAH, I JUST SAID--
THAT'S NOT WHAT I MEAN.
?

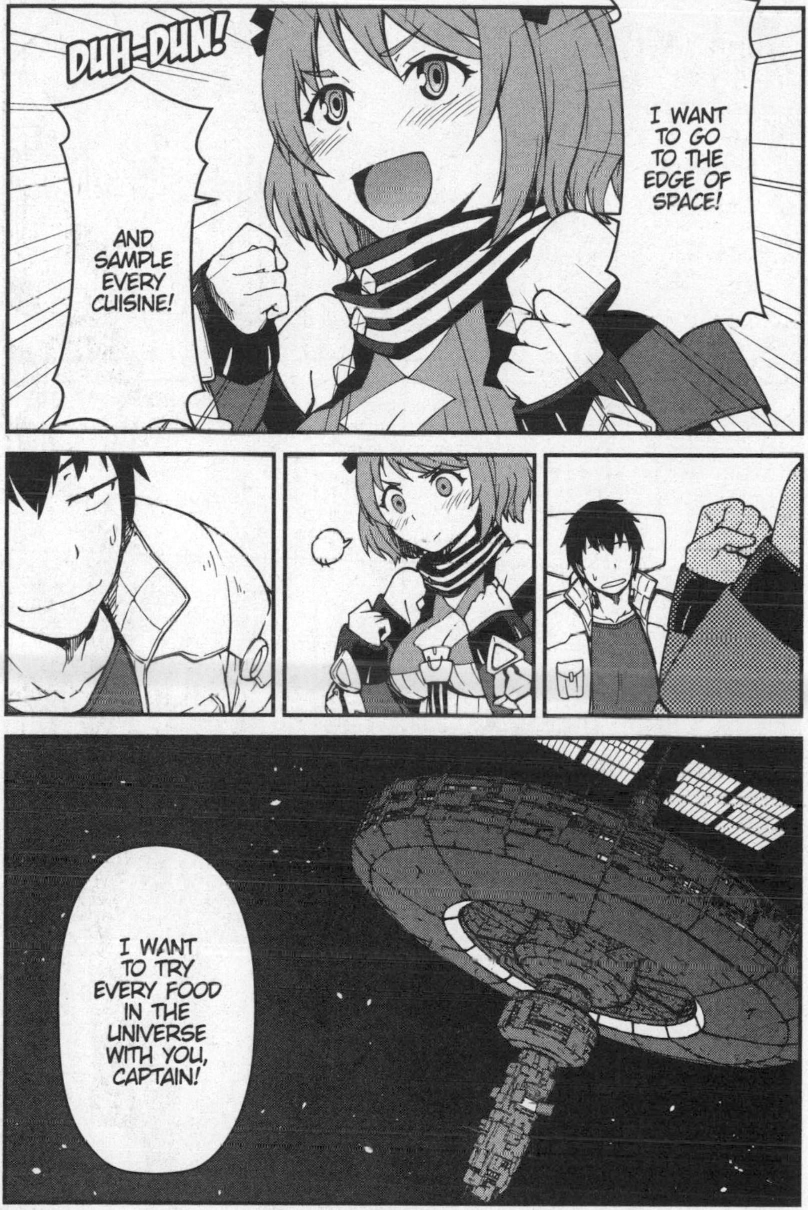
I WANT TO GO TO THE EDGE OF SPACE!
DUH-DUN!
AND SAMPLE EVERY CUISINE!
I WANT TO TRY EVERY FOOD IN THE UNIVERSE WITH YOU, CAPTAIN!

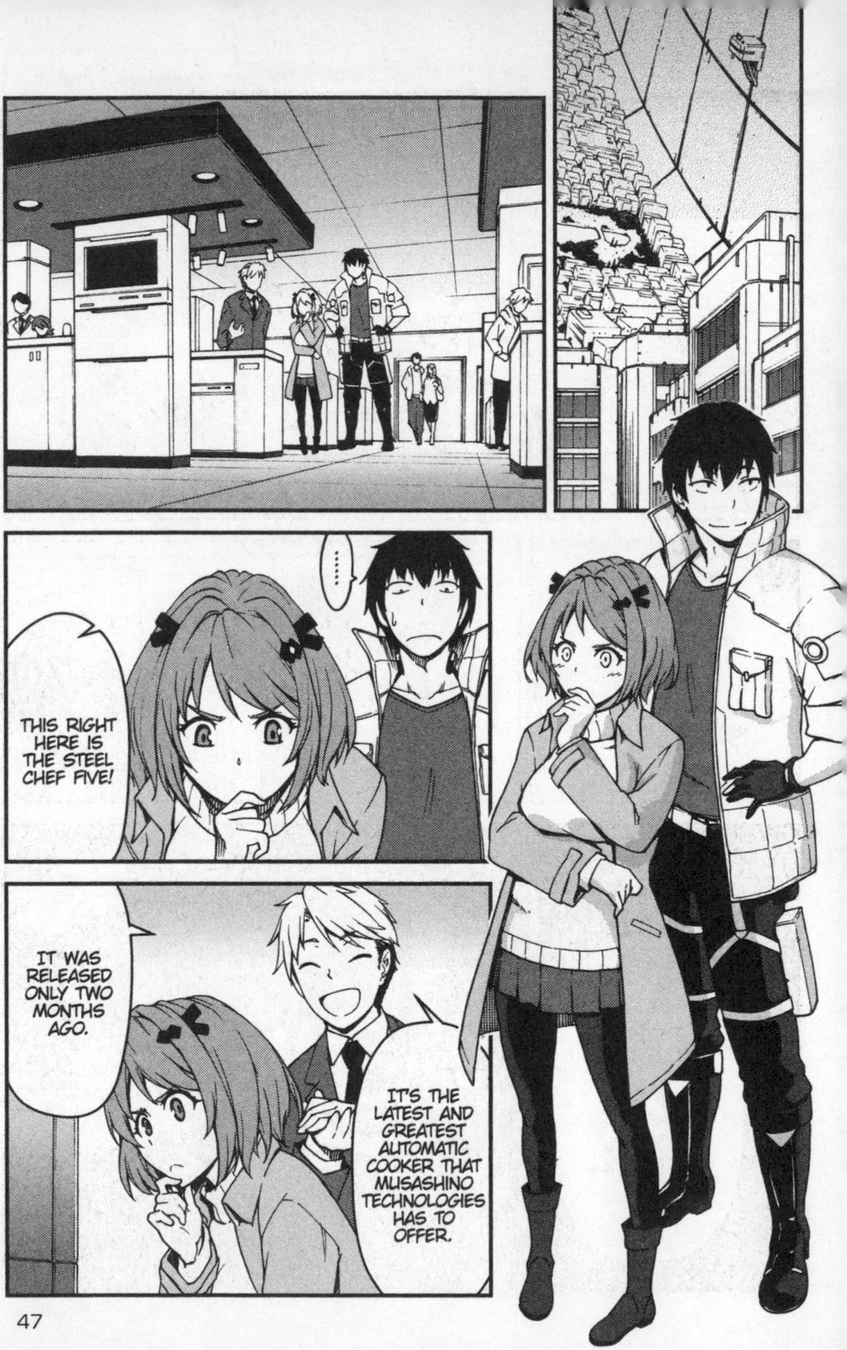
......
THIS RIGHT HERE IS THE STEEL CHEF FIVE!
IT WAS RELEASED ONLY TWO MONTHS AGO.
IT'S THE LATEST AND GREATEST AUTOMATIC COOKER THAT MUSASHINO TECHNOLOGIES HAS TO OFFER.

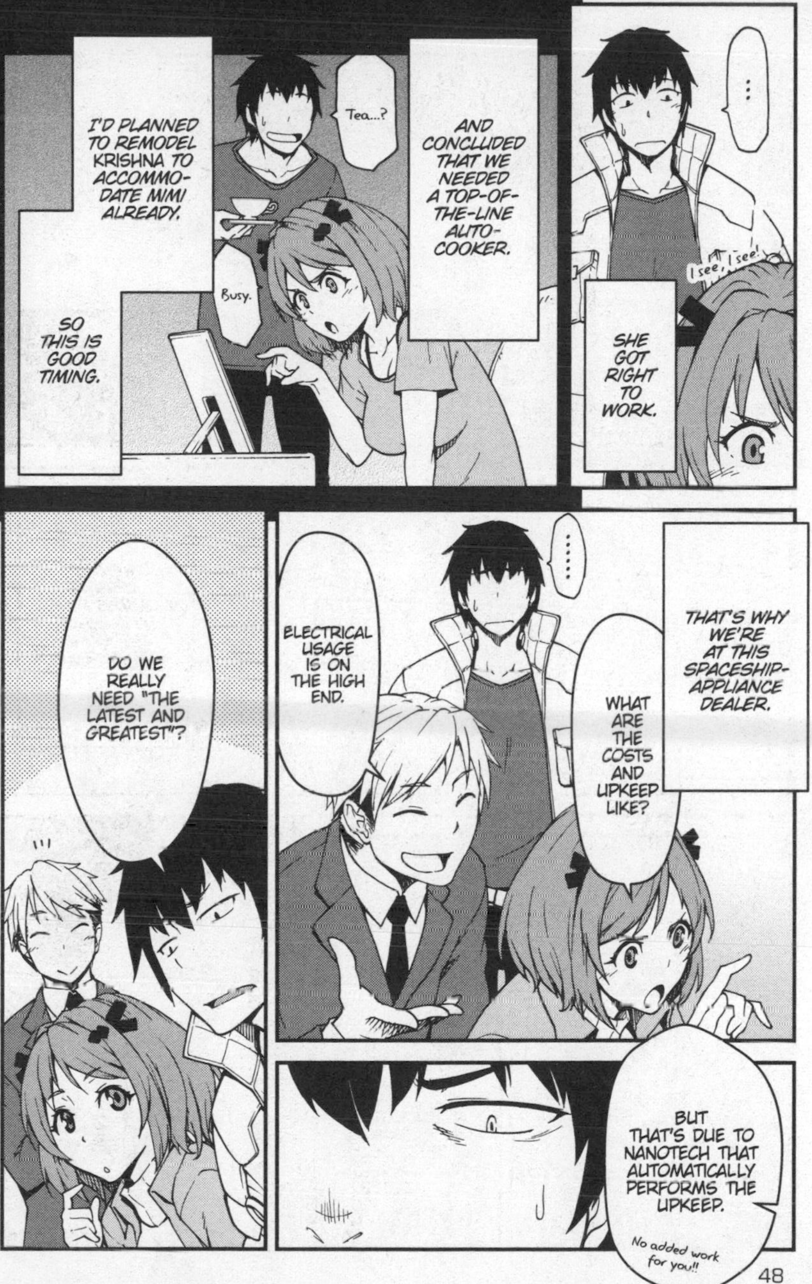
...
I see, I see!
SHE GOT RIGHT TO WORK.
AND CONCLUDED THAT WE NEEDED A TOP-OF-THE-LINE AUTO-COOKER.
Tea...?
I'D PLANNED TO REMODEL KRISHNA TO ACCOMMODATE MIMI ALREADY.
Busy.
SO THIS IS GOOD TIMING.
THAT'S WHY WE'RE AT THIS SPACESHIP-APPLIANCE DEALER.
......
WHAT ARE THE COSTS AND UPKEEP LIKE?
ELECTRICAL USAGE IS ON THE HIGH END.
BUT THAT'S DUE TO NANOTECH THAT AUTOMATICALLY PERFORMS THE UPKEEP.
No added work for you!!
DO WE REALLY NEED "THE LATEST AND GREATEST"?

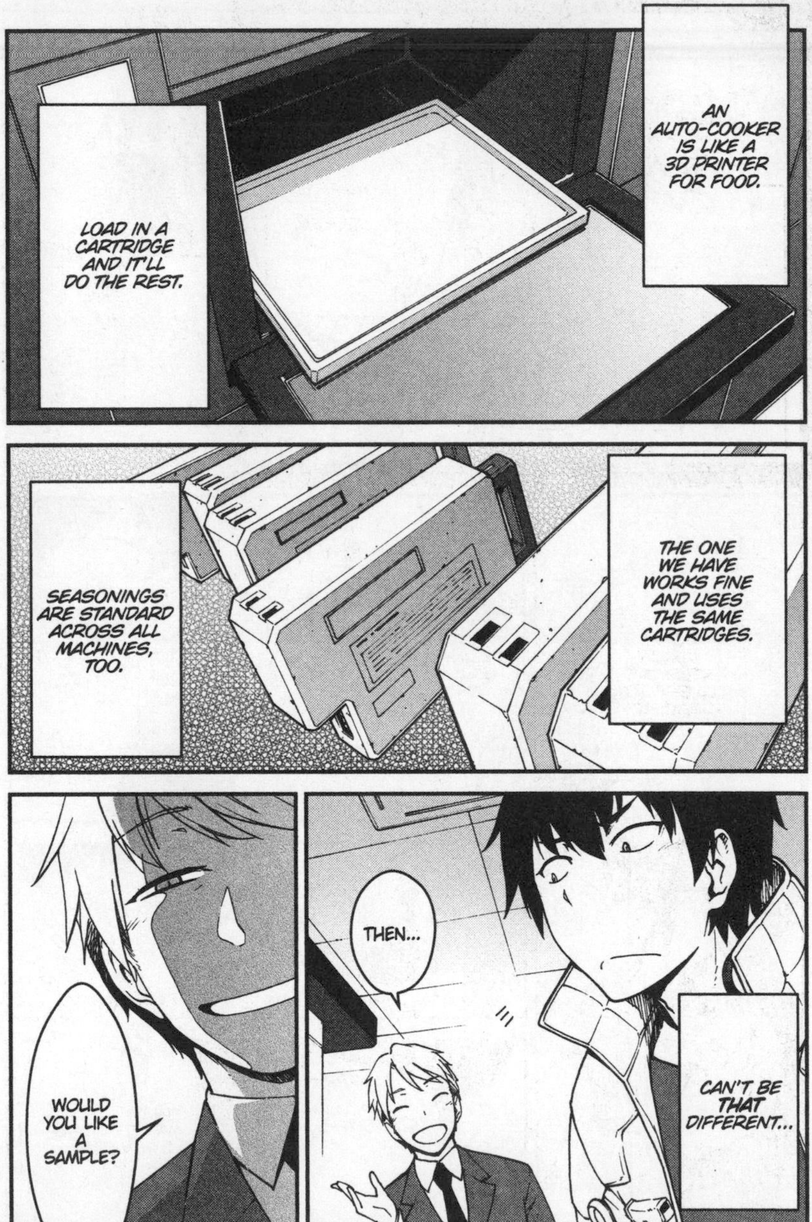
AN AUTO-COOKER IS LIKE A 3D PRINTER FOR FOOD.
LOAD IN A CARTRIDGE AND IT'LL DO THE REST.
THE ONE WE HAVE WORKS FINE AND USES THE SAME CARTRIDGES.
SEASONINGS ARE STANDARD ACROSS ALL MACHINES, TOO.
CAN'T BE THAT DIFFERENT...
THEN...
WOULD YOU LIKE A SAMPLE?

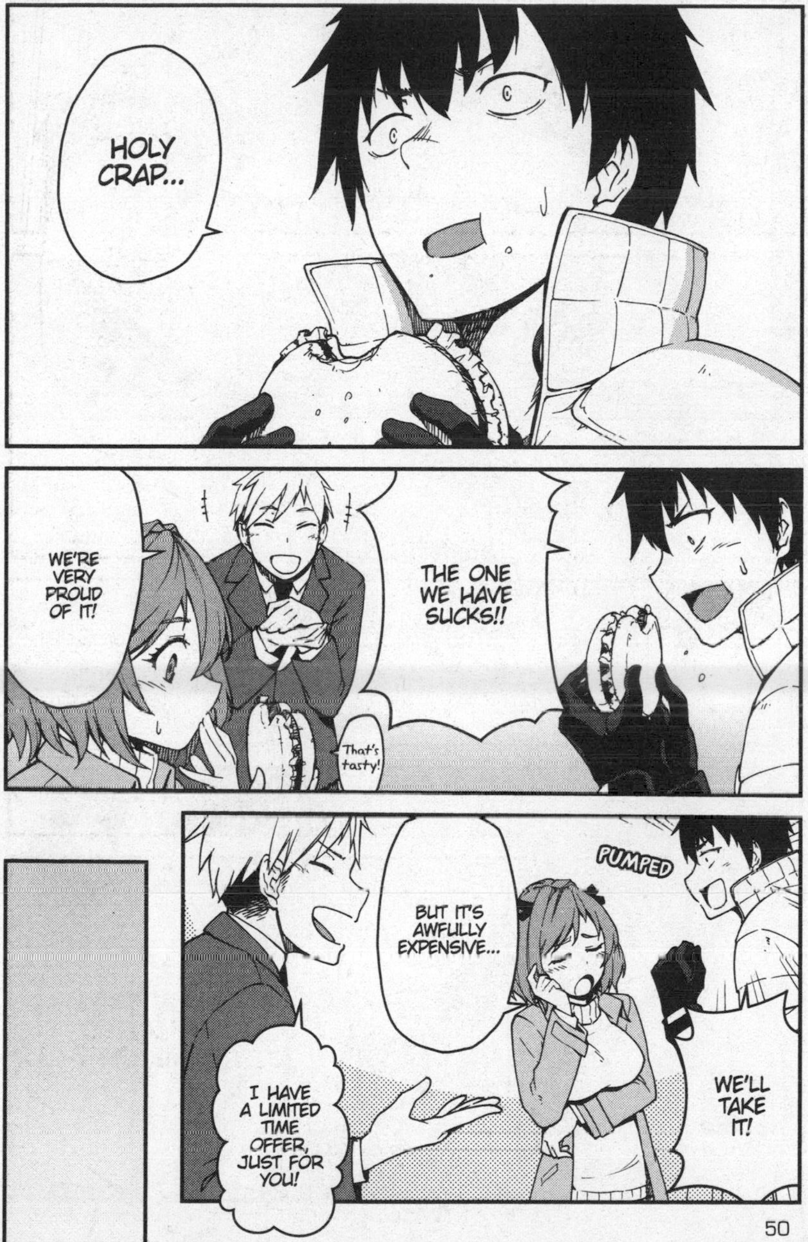
HOLY CRAP...
THE ONE WE HAVE SUCKS!!
WE'RE VERY PROUD OF IT!
That's tasty!
PUMPED
WE'LL TAKE IT!
BUT IT'S AWFULLY EXPENSIVE...
I HAVE A LIMITED TIME OFFER, JUST FOR YOU!

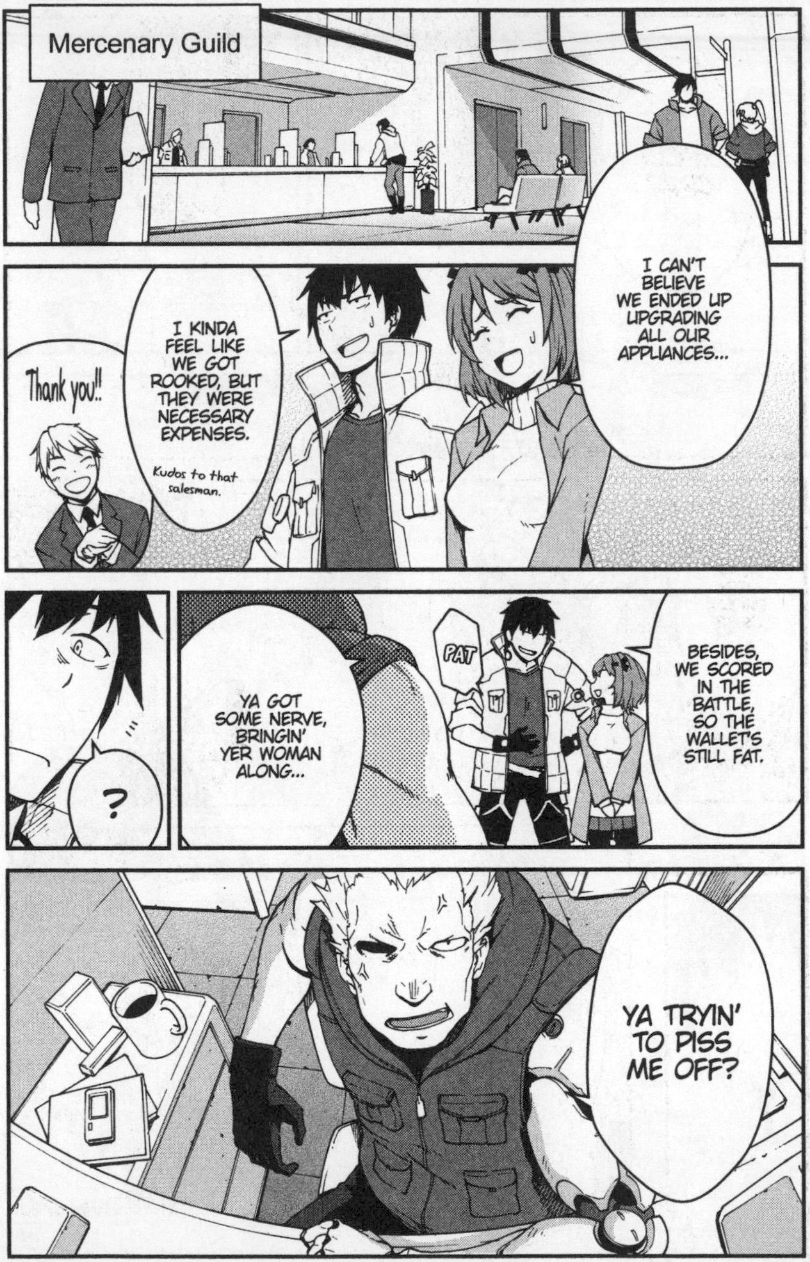
Mercenary Guild
I CAN'T BELIEVE WE ENDED UP UPGRADING ALL OUR APPLIANCES...
I KINDA FEEL LIKE WE GOT ROOKED, BUT THEY WERE NECESSARY EXPENSES.
Kudos to that salesman.
Thank you!!
BESIDES, WE SCORED IN THE BATTLE, SO THE WALLET'S STILL FAT.
PAT
YA GOT SOME NERVE, BRINGIN' YER WOMAN ALONG...
?
YA TRYIN' TO PISS ME OFF?

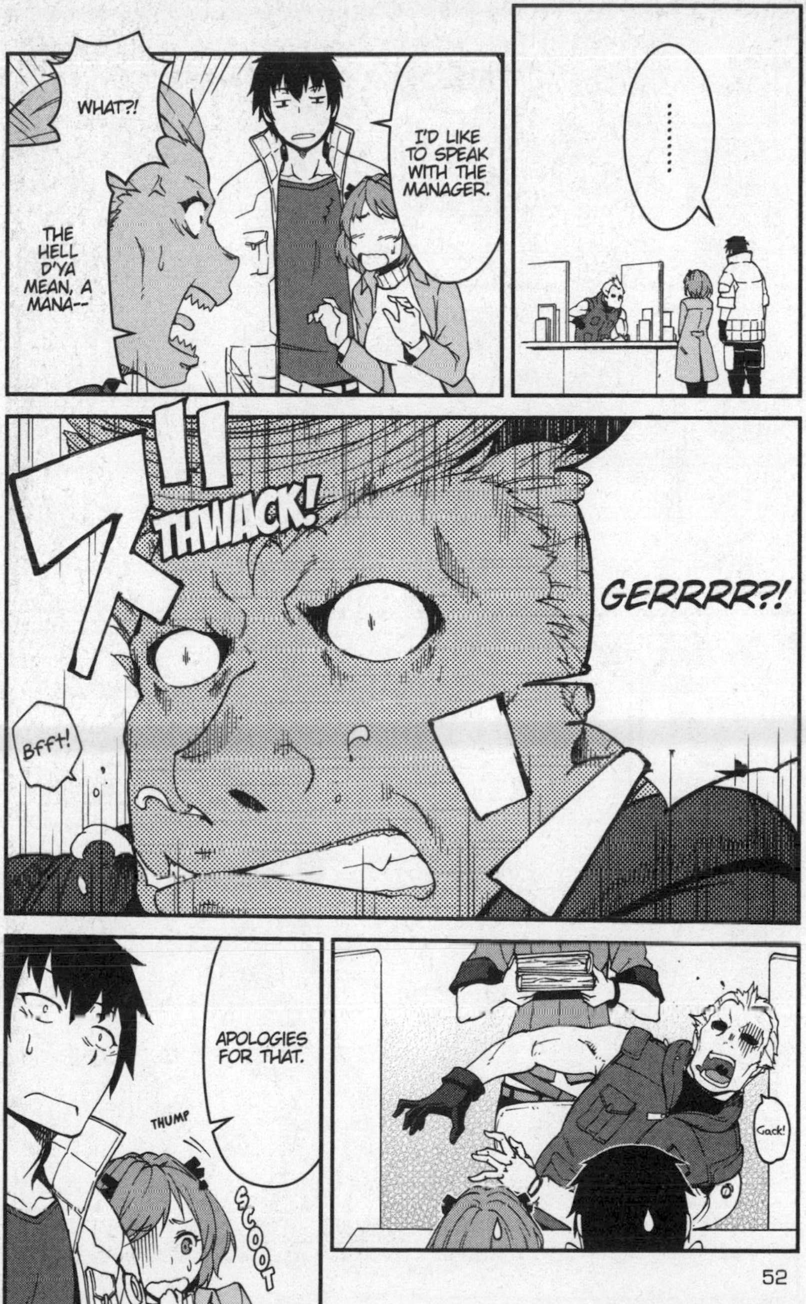
……
I'D LIKE TO SPEAK WITH THE MANAGER.
WHAT?!
THE HELL D'YA MEAN, A MANA--
THWACK!
GERRRR?!
Bfft!
Gack!
APOLOGIES FOR THAT.
THUMP
SCOOT

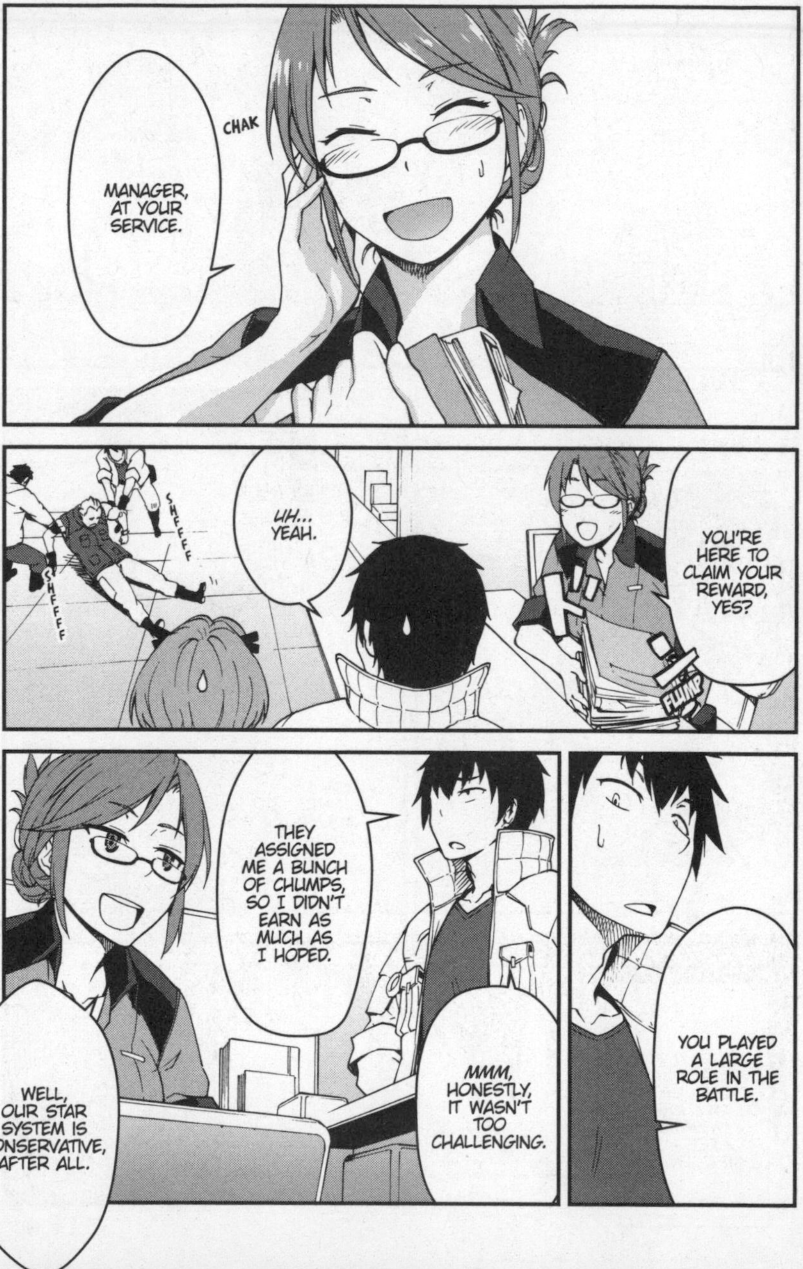
CHAK
MANAGER, AT YOUR SERVICE.
YOU'RE HERE TO CLAIM YOUR REWARD, YES?
FLUMP
UH... YEAH.
SHFFFF
SHFFFF
YOU PLAYED A LARGE ROLE IN THE BATTLE.
MMM, HONESTLY, IT WASN'T TOO CHALLENGING.
THEY ASSIGNED ME A BUNCH OF CHUMPS, SO I DIDN'T EARN AS MUCH AS I HOPED.
WELL, OUR STAR SYSTEM IS CONSERVATIVE, AFTER ALL.

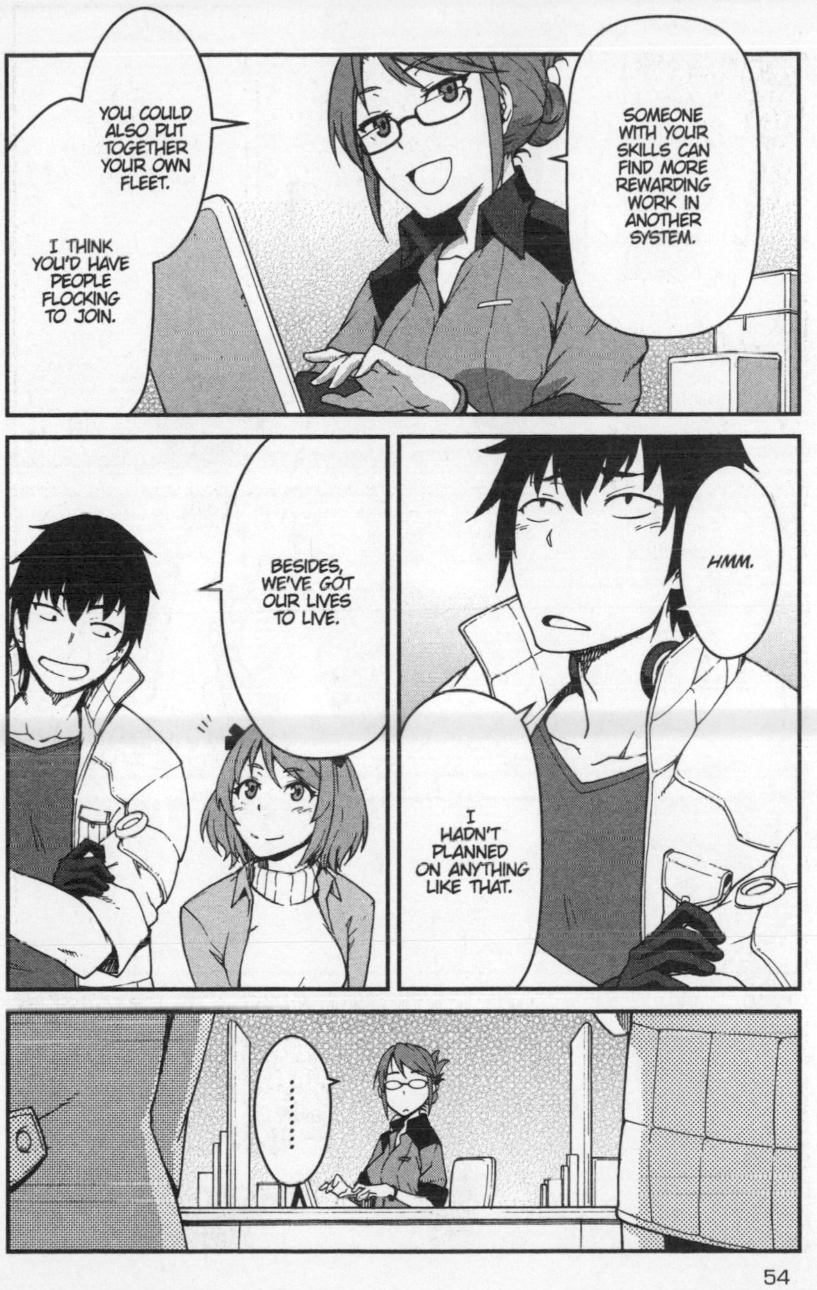
SOMEONE WITH YOUR SKILLS CAN FIND MORE REWARDING WORK IN ANOTHER SYSTEM.
YOU COULD ALSO PUT TOGETHER YOUR OWN FLEET.
I THINK YOU'D HAVE PEOPLE FLOCKING TO JOIN.
HMM.
I HADN'T PLANNED ON ANYTHING LIKE THAT.
BESIDES, WE'VE GOT OUR LIVES TO LIVE.
......

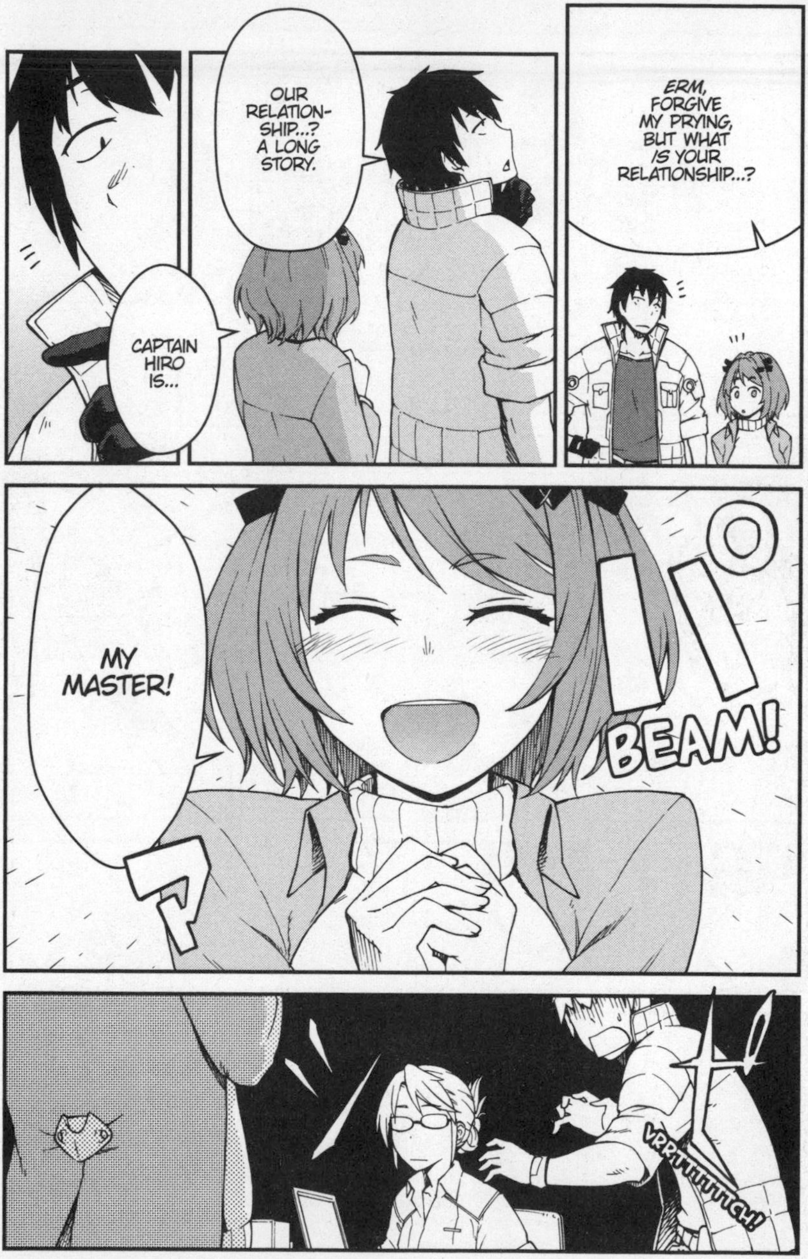
ERM, FORGIVE MY PRYING, BUT WHAT IS YOUR RELATIONSHIP...?
OUR RELATIONSHIP...? A LONG STORY.
CAPTAIN HIRO IS...
MY MASTER!
BEAM!
VRRTTTTTTTCH!

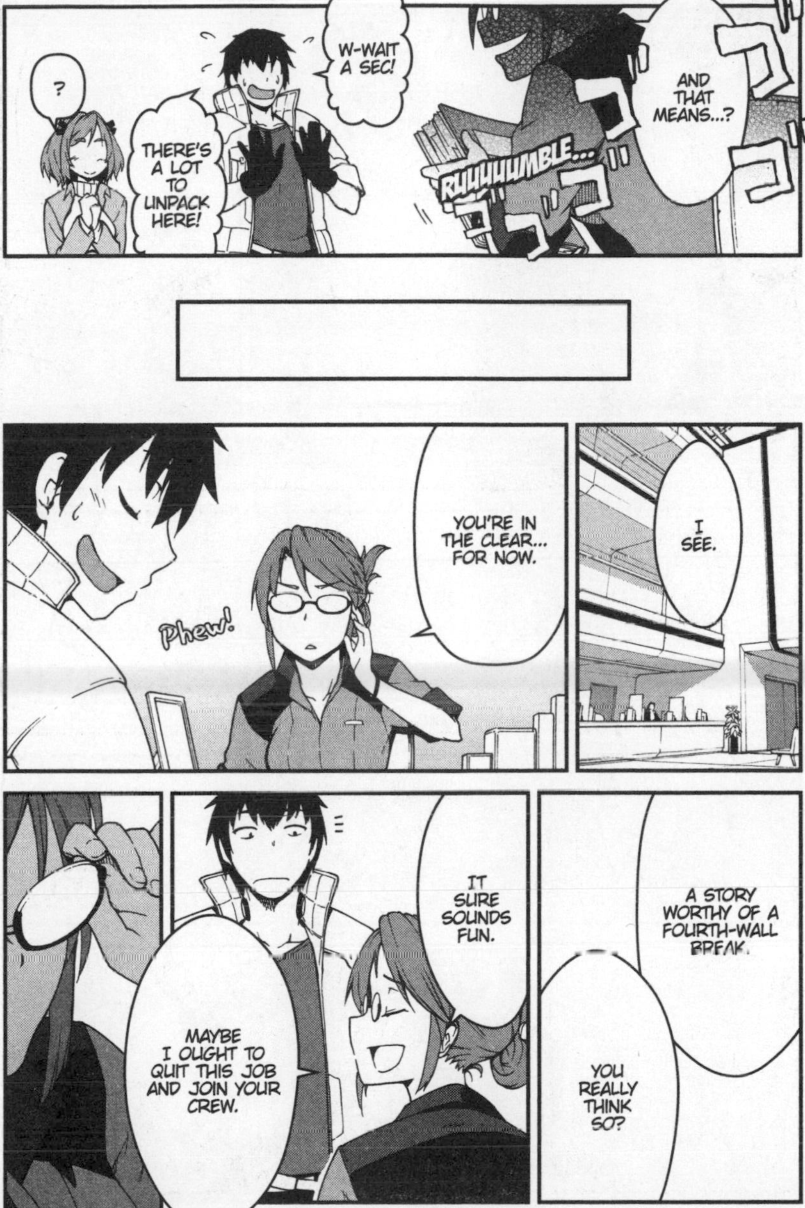
AND THAT MEANS...?
RUUUUUMBLE...
W-WAIT A SEC!
THERE'S A LOT TO UNPACK HERE!
?
I SEE.
YOU'RE IN THE CLEAR... FOR NOW.
Phew!
A STORY WORTHY OF A FOURTH-WALL BREAK.
YOU REALLY THINK SO?
IT SURE SOUNDS FUN.
MAYBE I OUGHT TO QUIT THIS JOB AND JOIN YOUR CREW.

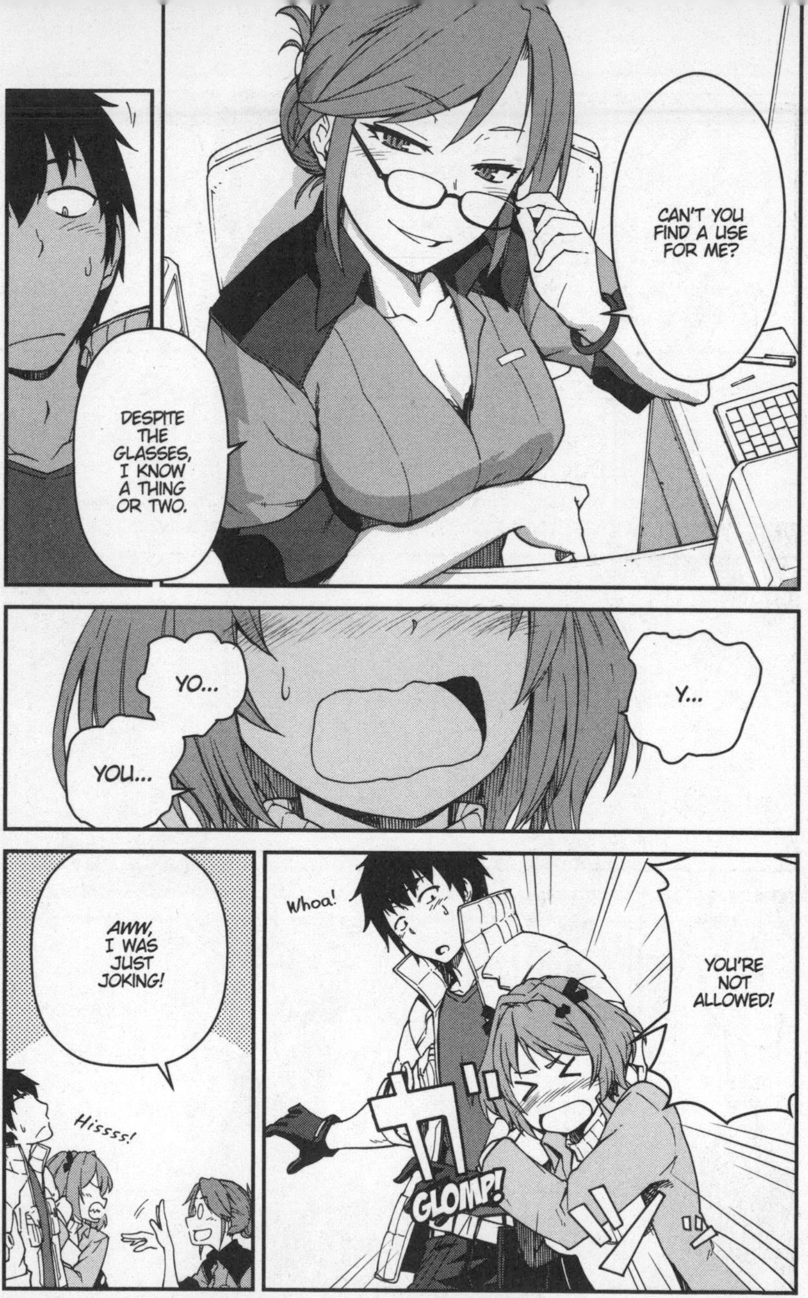
CAN'T YOU FIND A USE FOR ME?
DESPITE THE GLASSES, I KNOW A THING OR TWO.
Y...
YO...
YOU...
YOU'RE NOT ALLOWED!
Whoa!
GLOMP!
AWW, I WAS JUST JOKING!
Hissss!

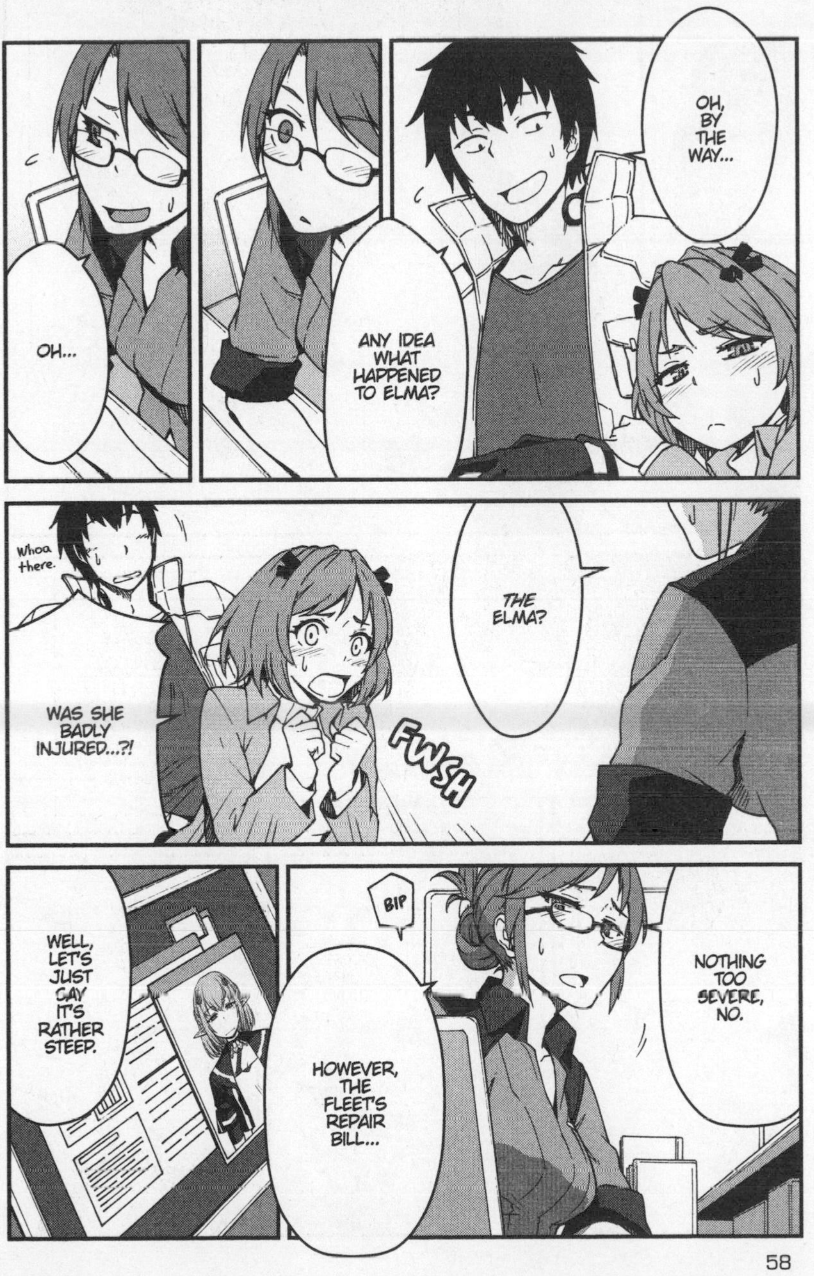
OH, BY THE WAY...
ANY IDEA WHAT HAPPENED TO ELMA?
OH...
THE ELMA?
Whoa there.
WAS SHE BADLY INJURED...?!
FWSH
BIP
NOTHING TOO SEVERE, NO.
HOWEVER, THE FLEET'S REPAIR BILL...
WELL, LET'S JUST SAY IT'S RATHER STEEP.

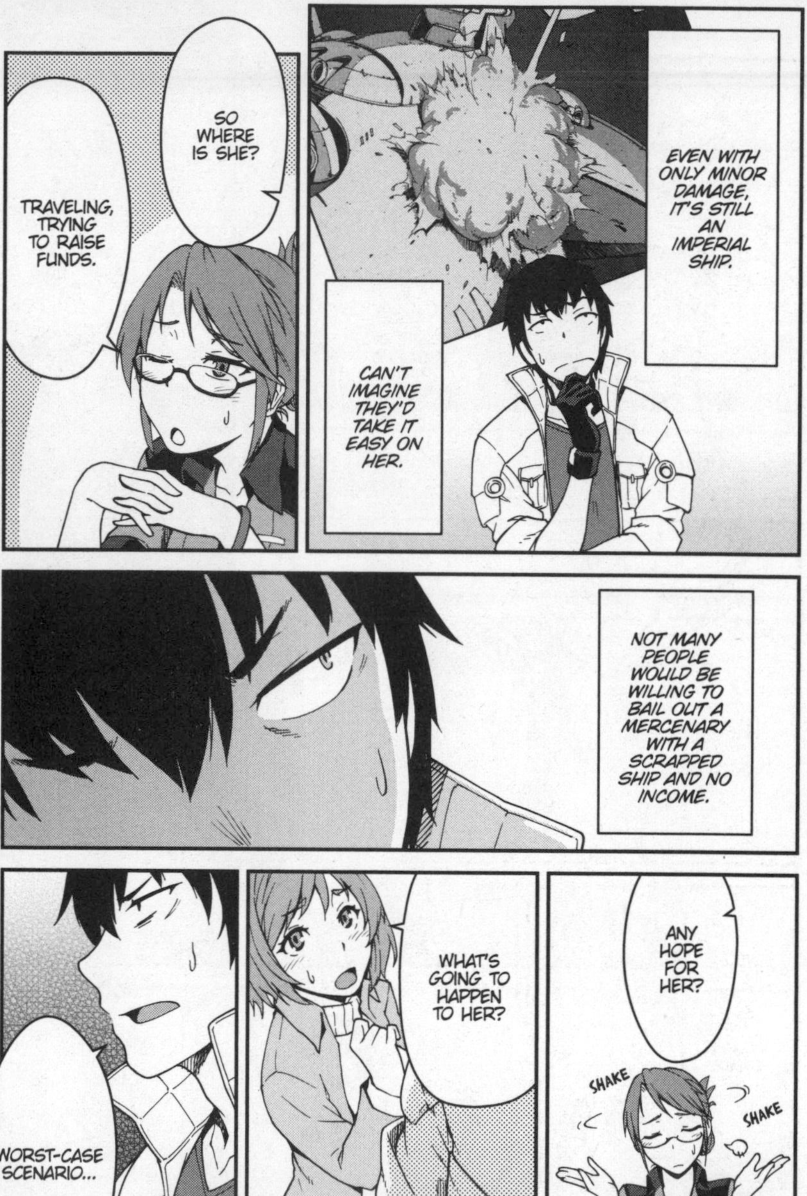
EVEN WITH ONLY MINOR DAMAGE, IT'S STILL AN IMPERIAL SHIP.
CAN'T IMAGINE THEY'D TAKE IT EASY ON HER.
SO WHERE IS SHE?
TRAVELING, TRYING TO RAISE FUNDS.
NOT MANY PEOPLE WOULD BE WILLING TO BAIL OUT A MERCENARY WITH A SCRAPPED SHIP AND NO INCOME.
ANY HOPE FOR HER?
SHAKE
SHAKE
WHAT'S GOING TO HAPPEN TO HER?
WORST-CASE SCENARIO...

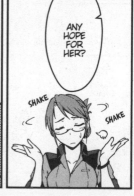

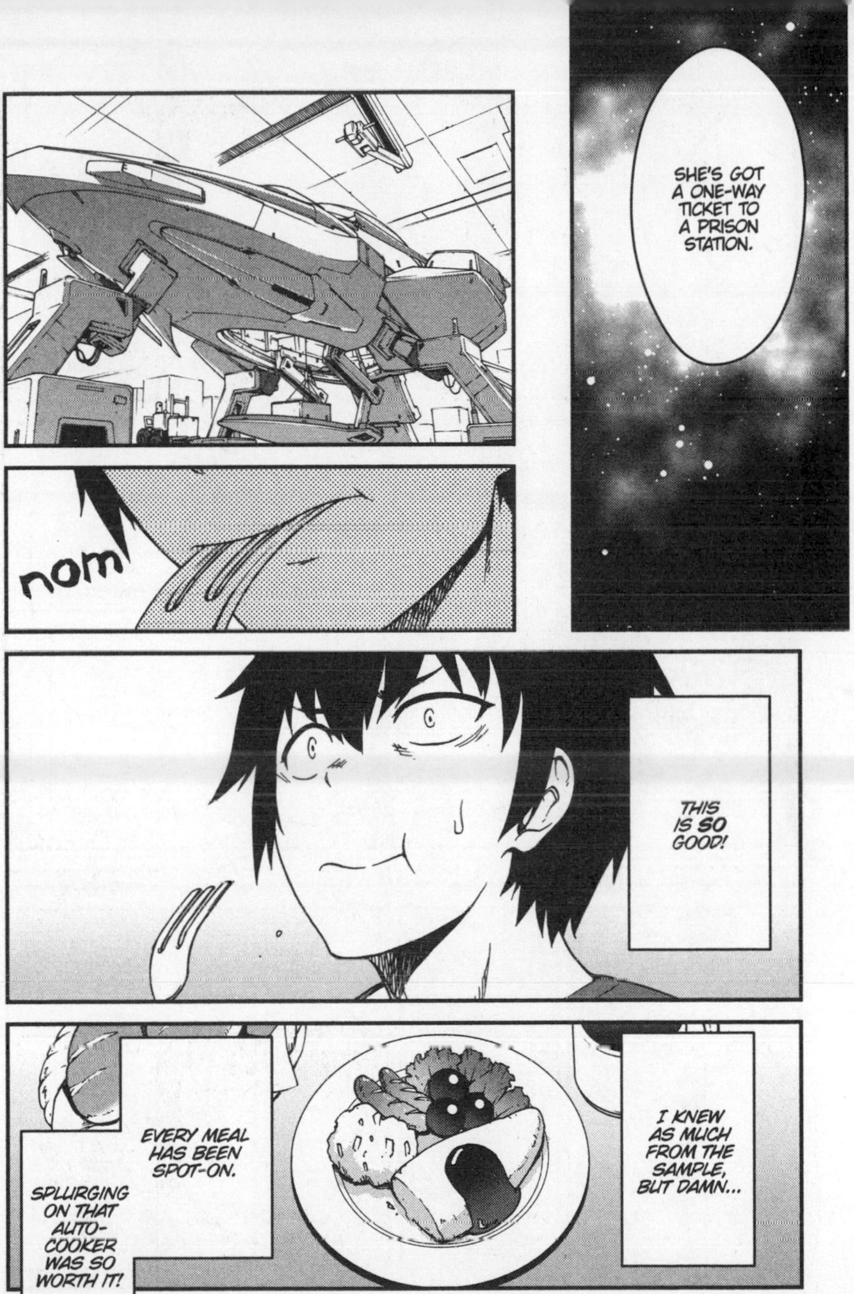
SHE'S GOT A ONE-WAY TICKET TO A PRISON STATION.
nom
THIS IS SO GOOD!
I KNEW AS MUCH FROM THE SAMPLE, BUT DAMN...
EVERY MEAL HAS BEEN SPOT-ON.
SPLURGING ON THAT AUTO-COOKER WAS SO WORTH IT!

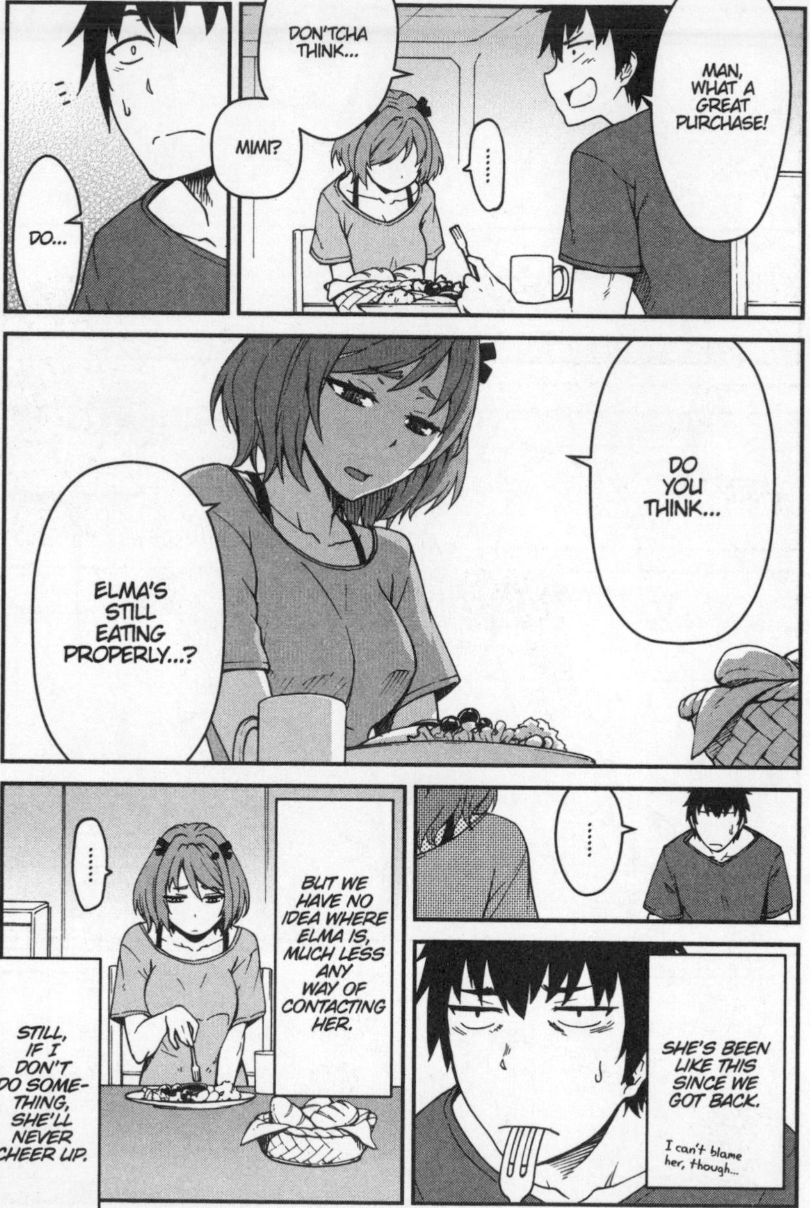
MAN, WHAT A GREAT PURCHASE!
DON'TCHA THINK...
MIMI?
......
DO...
DO YOU THINK...
ELMA'S STILL EATING PROPERLY...?
......
SHE'S BEEN LIKE THIS SINCE WE GOT BACK.
I can't blame her, though...
......
BUT WE HAVE NO IDEA WHERE ELMA IS, MUCH LESS ANY WAY OF CONTACTING HER.
STILL, IF I DON'T DO SOME-THING, SHE'LL NEVER CHEER UP.

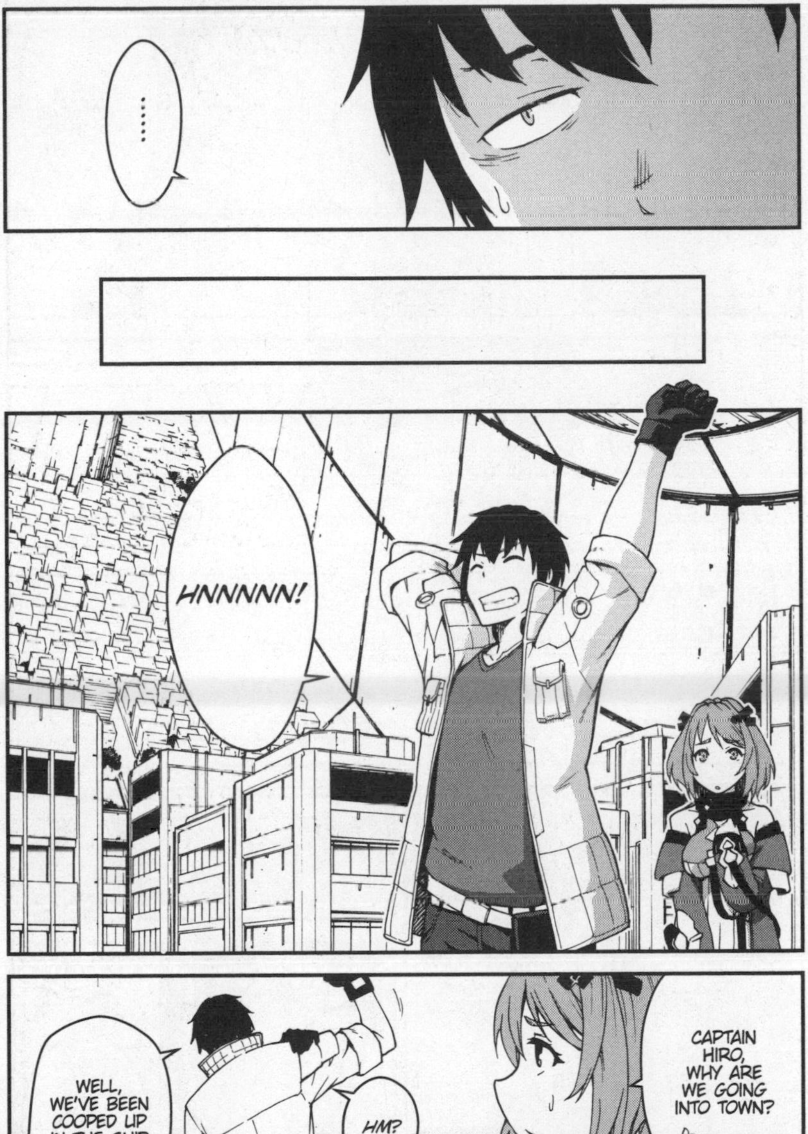
......
HNNNNN!
CAPTAIN HIRO, WHY ARE WE GOING INTO TOWN?
Do you still have errands?
HM?
WELL, WE'VE BEEN COOPED UP IN THE SHIP A LOT RECENTLY.

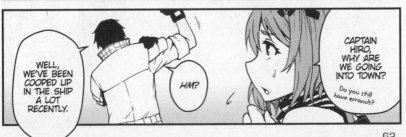

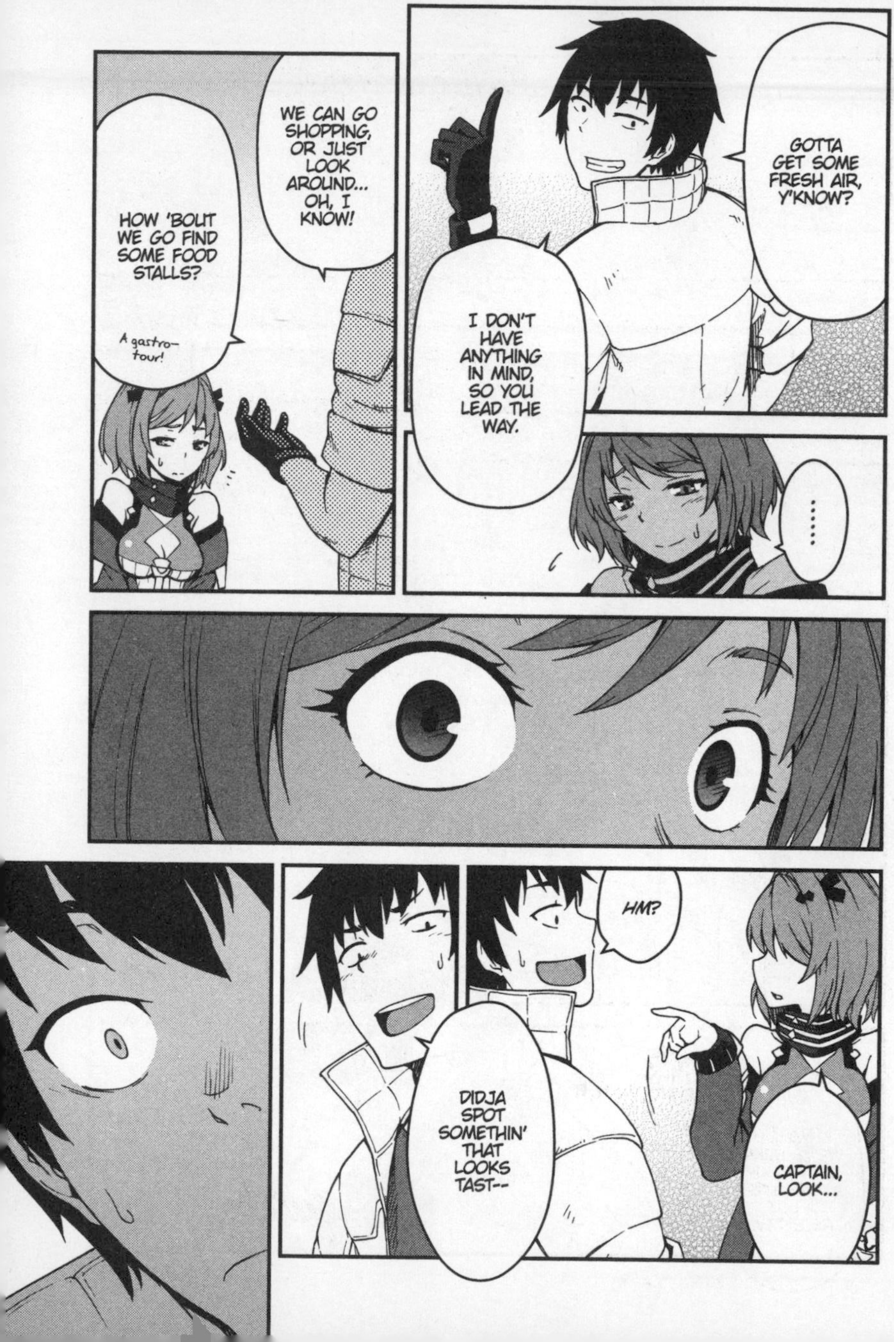
GOTTA GET SOME FRESH AIR, Y'KNOW?
I DON'T HAVE ANYTHING IN MIND, SO YOU LEAD THE WAY.
......
WE CAN GO SHOPPING, OR JUST LOOK AROUND... OH, I KNOW!
HOW 'BOUT WE GO FIND SOME FOOD STALLS?
A gastro-tour!
HM?
DIDJA SPOT SOMETHIN' THAT LOOKS TAST--
CAPTAIN, LOOK...

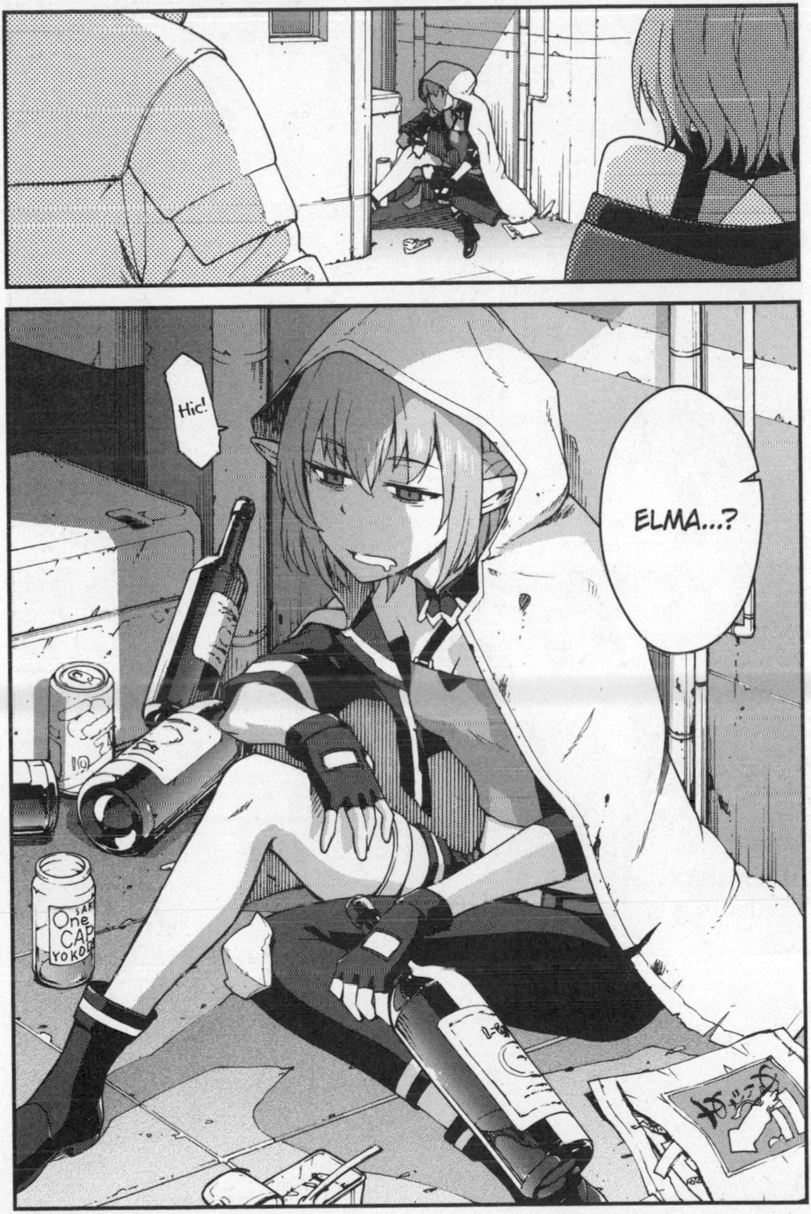
Hic!
ELMA...?

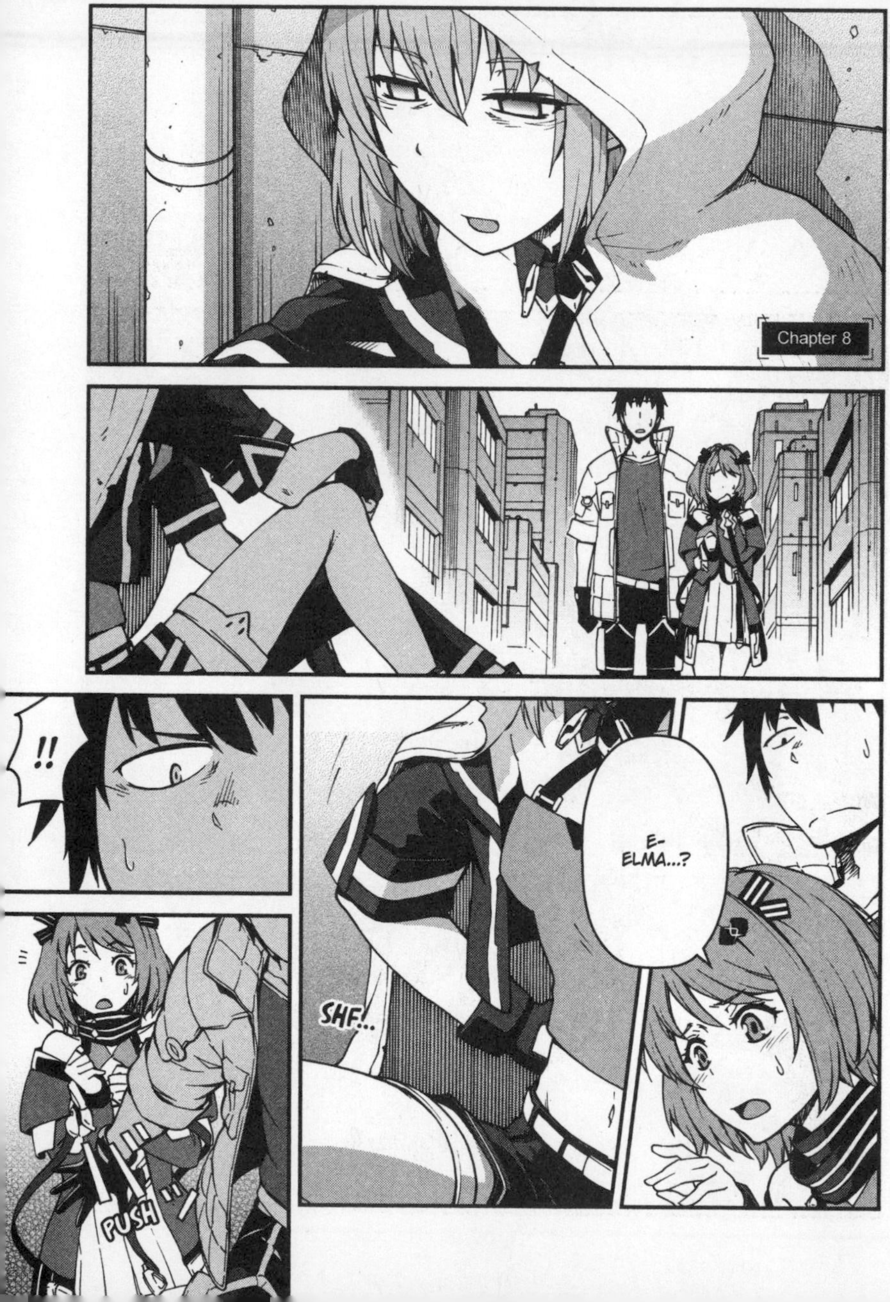
Chapter 8
E-ELMA...?
SHF...
!!
PUSH

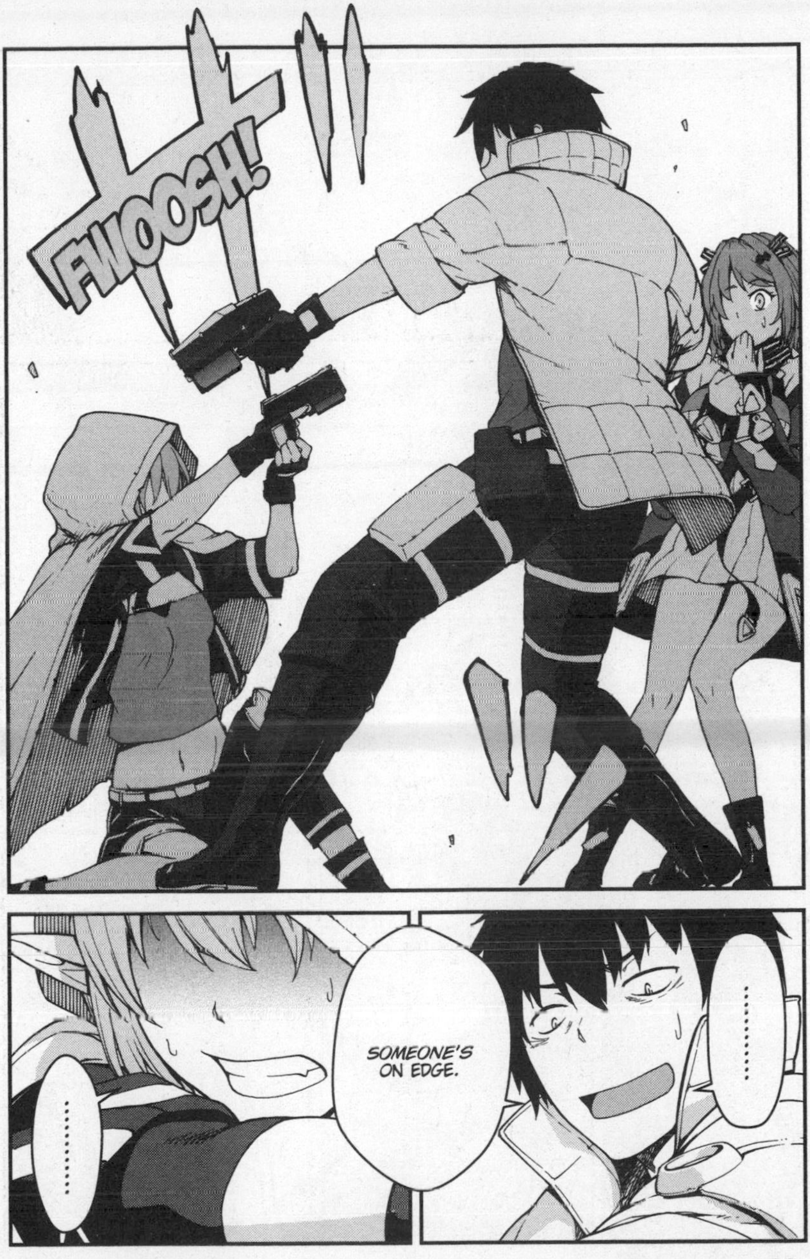
FWOOSH!
......
SOMEONE'S ON EDGE.
......

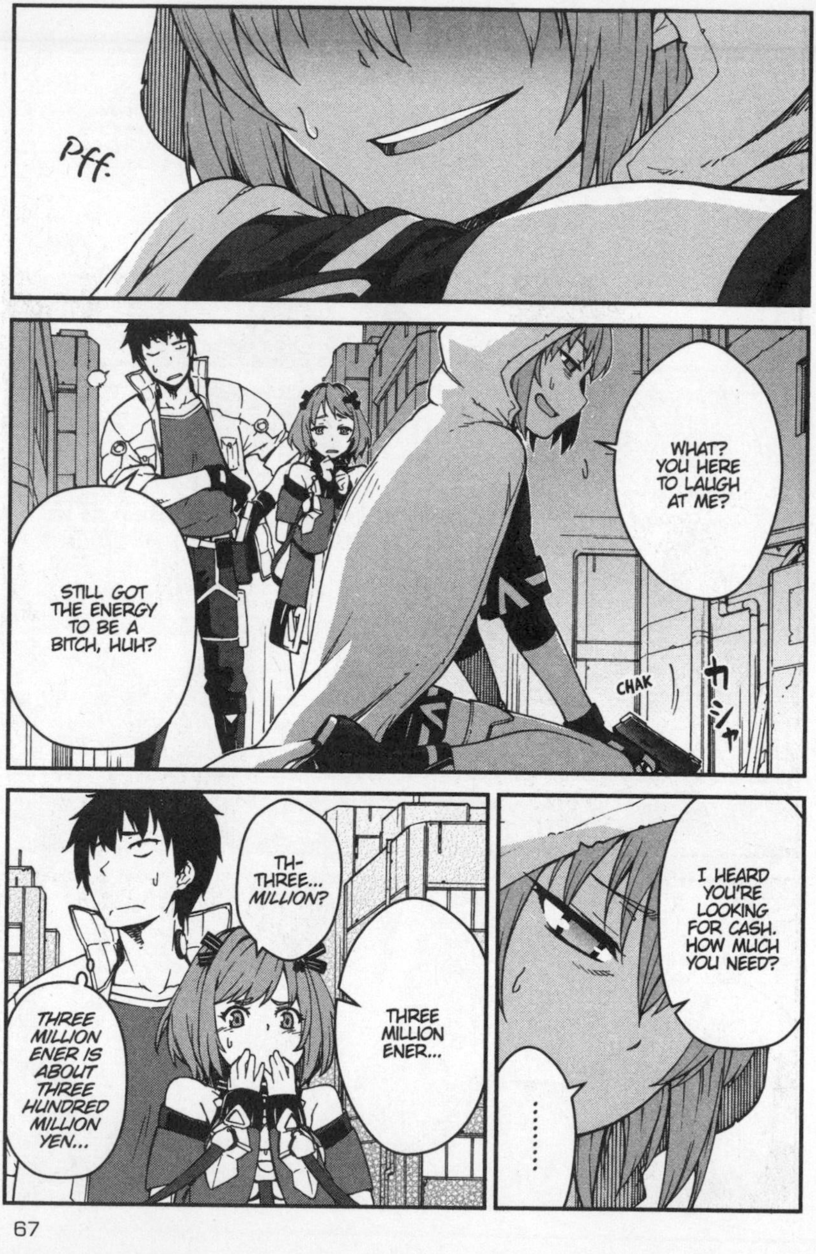
Pff.
WHAT? YOU HERE TO LAUGH AT ME?
CHAK
カシャ
STILL GOT THE ENERGY TO BE A BITCH, HUH?
I HEARD YOU'RE LOOKING FOR CASH. HOW MUCH YOU NEED?
......
THREE MILLION ENER...
TH-THREE... MILLION?
THREE MILLION ENER IS ABOUT THREE HUNDRED MILLION YEN...

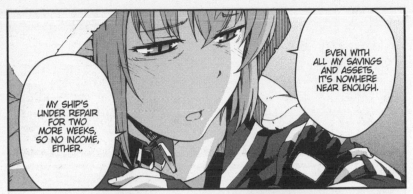

EVEN WITH ALL MY SAVINGS AND ASSETS, IT'S NOWHERE NEAR ENOUGH.
MY SHIP'S UNDER REPAIR FOR TWO MORE WEEKS, SO NO INCOME, EITHER.
GIVEN MY ACCIDENT, NO ONE WILL LEND ME A PENNY...
WHEN'S THE PAYMENT DUE?
TODAY.
IN TWO HOURS EXACTLY.
IF I CAN'T PAY UP, I'M DOOMED TO HARD LABOR ON A PRISON STATION NEAR TARMEIN III.
PLACE IS FULL OF PIRATES WHO GOT CAUGHT BY MERCS.

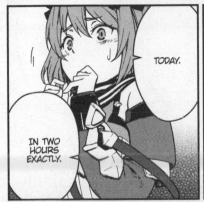

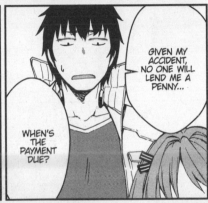

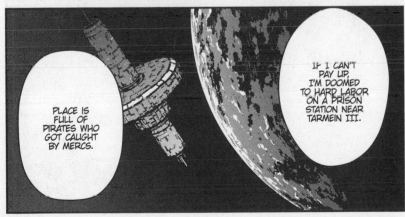

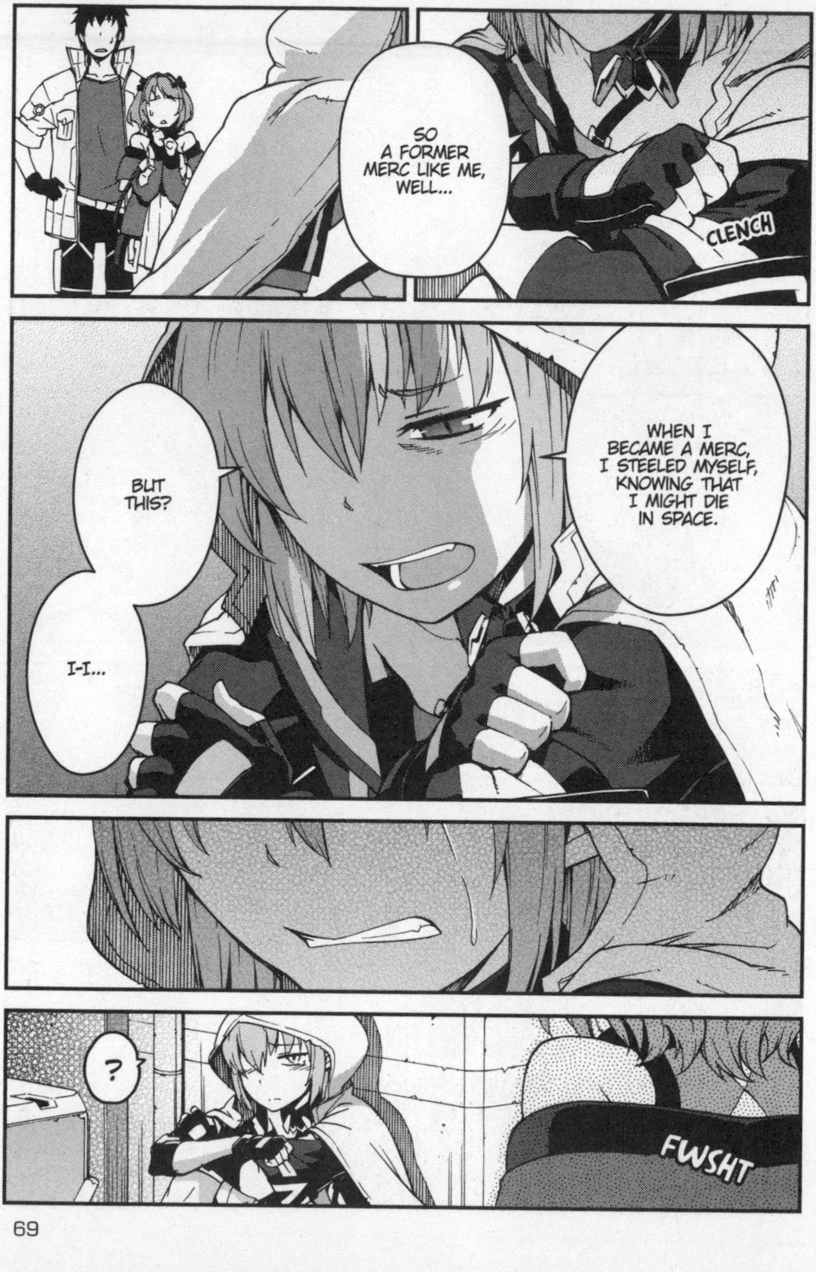
SO A FORMER MERC LIKE ME, WELL...
CLENCH
WHEN I BECAME A MERC, I STEELED MYSELF, KNOWING THAT I MIGHT DIE IN SPACE.
BUT THIS?
I-I...
FWSHT
?

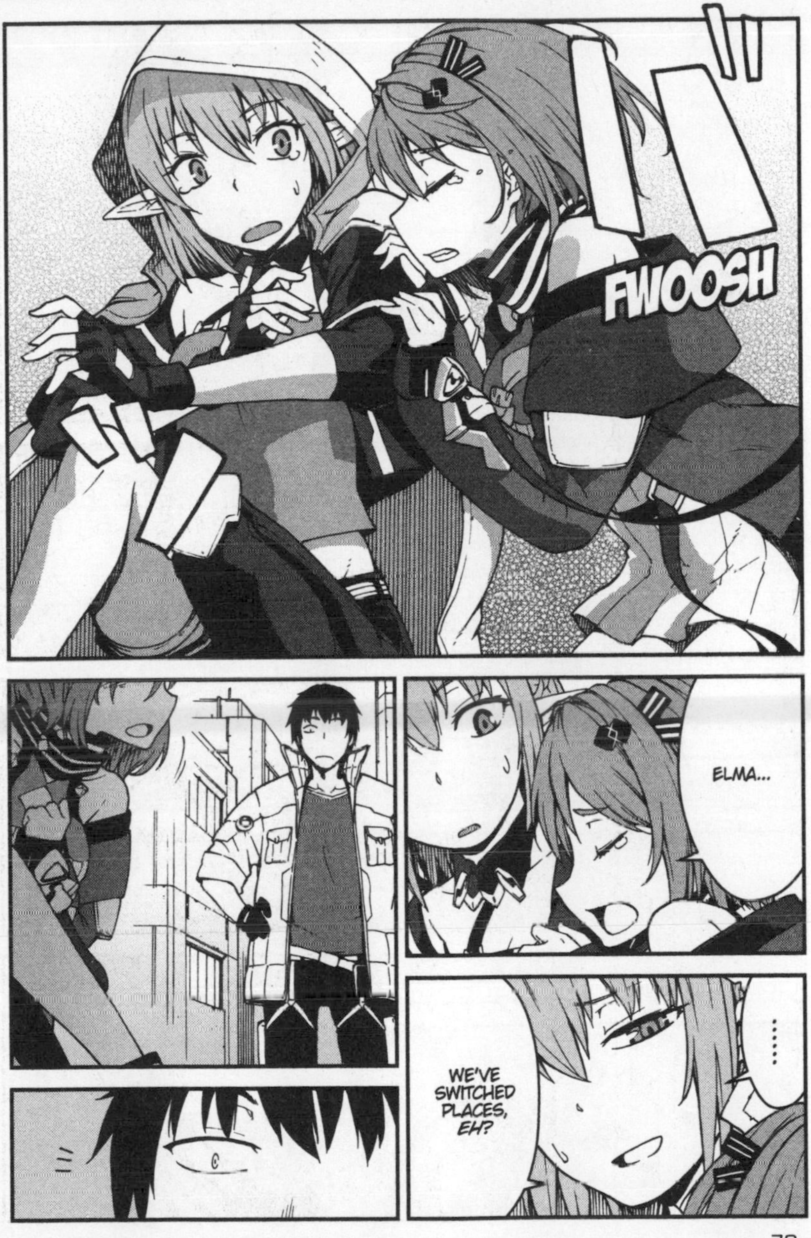
FWOOSH
ELMA...
......
WE'VE SWITCHED PLACES, EH?

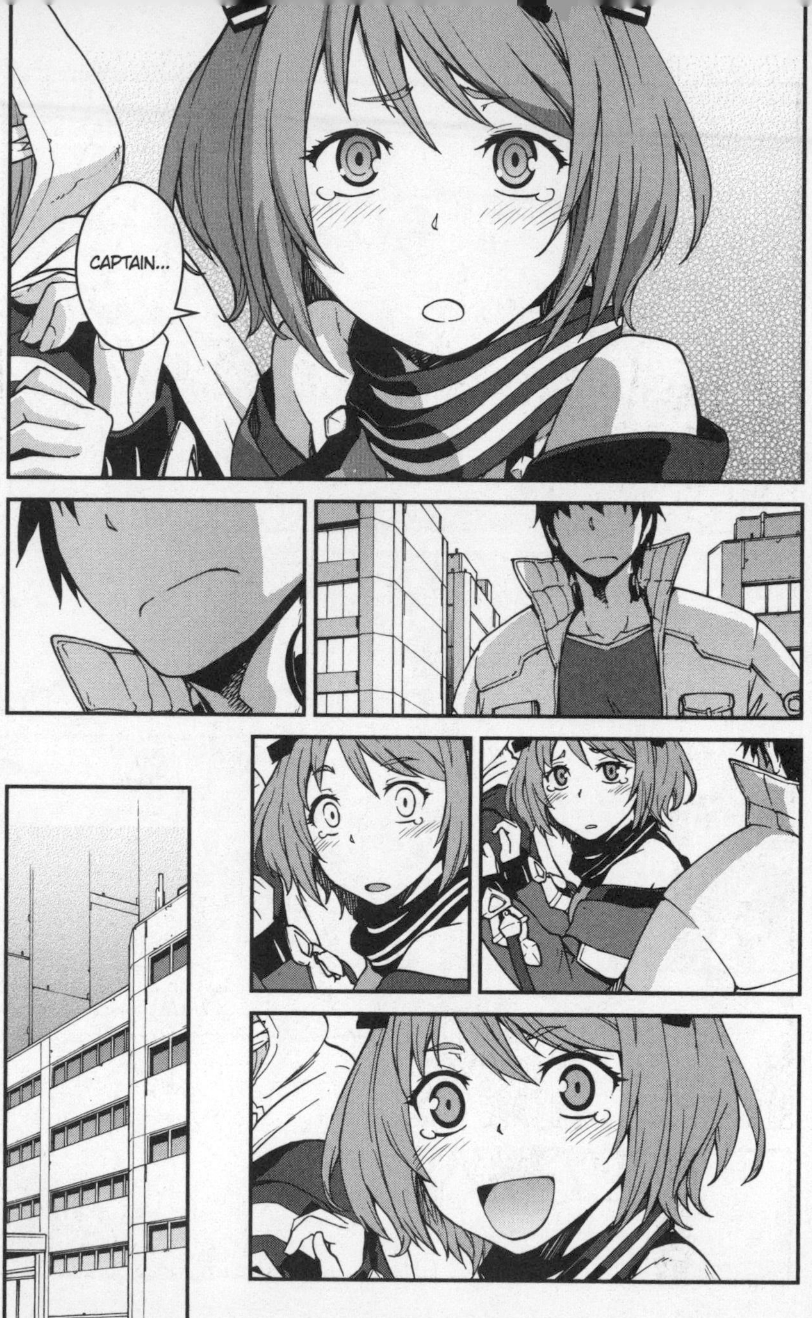
CAPTAIN...

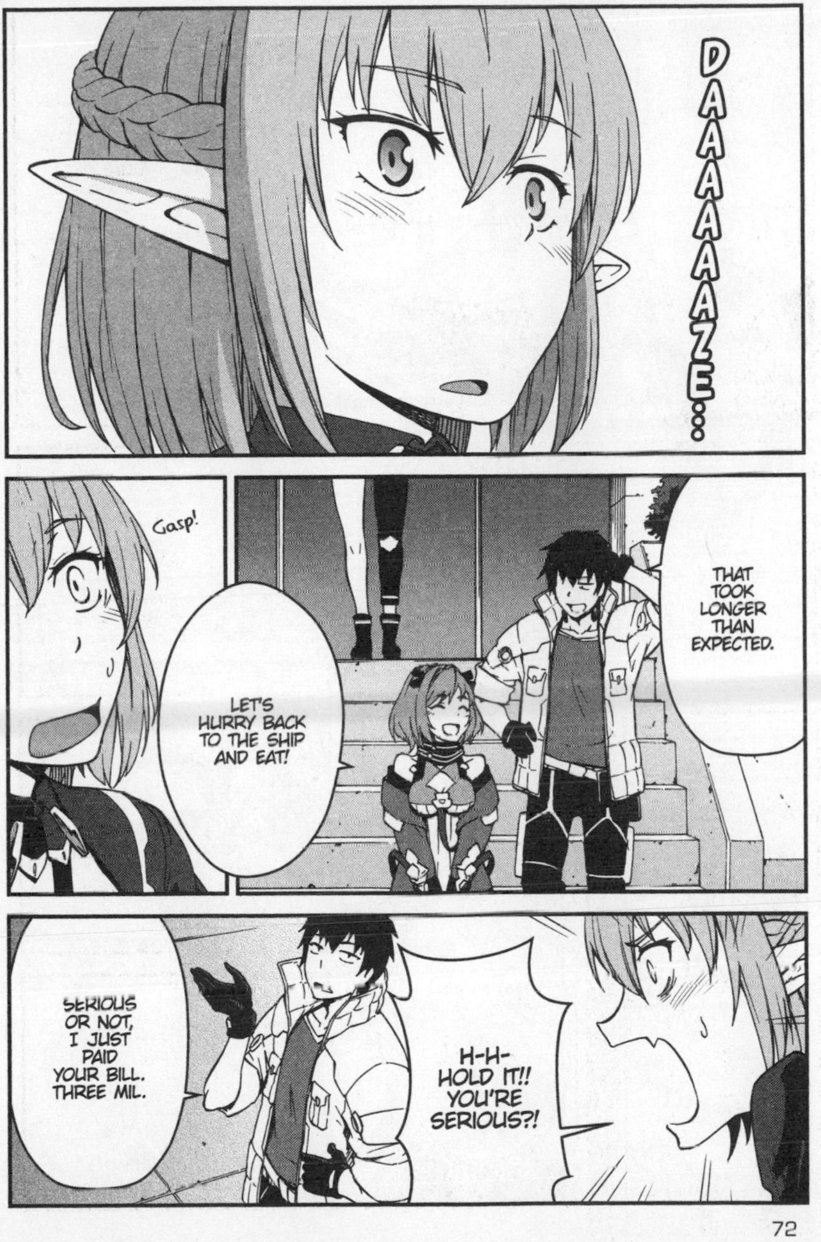
DAAAAAAAAZE...
THAT TOOK LONGER THAN EXPECTED.
LET'S HURRY BACK TO THE SHIP AND EAT!
Gasp!
H-H-HOLD IT!! YOU'RE SERIOUS?!
SERIOUS OR NOT, I JUST PAID YOUR BILL. THREE MIL.

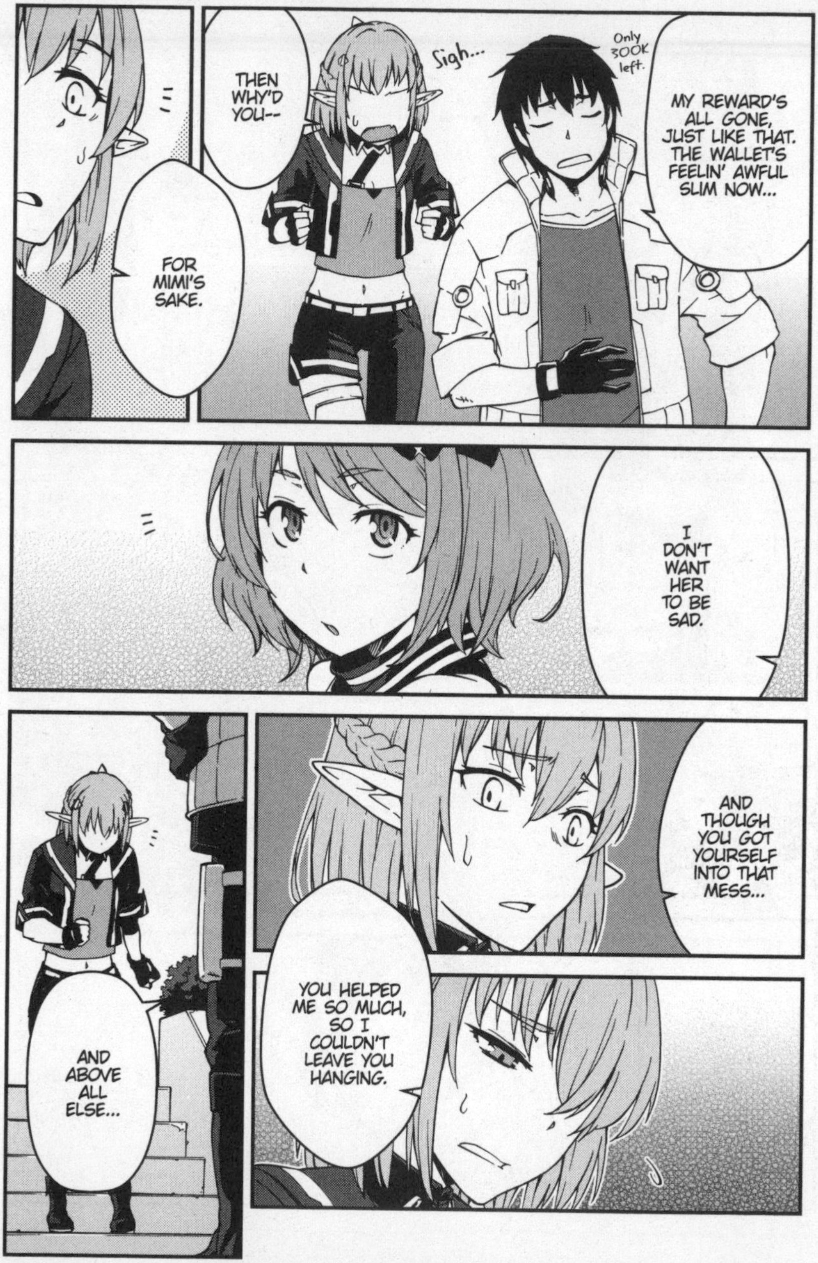
Only 300K left.
MY REWARD'S ALL GONE, JUST LIKE THAT. THE WALLET'S FEELIN' AWFUL SLIM NOW...
Sigh...
THEN WHY'D YOU--
FOR MIMI'S SAKE.
I DON'T WANT HER TO BE SAD.
AND THOUGH YOU GOT YOURSELF INTO THAT MESS...
YOU HELPED ME SO MUCH, SO I COULDN'T LEAVE YOU HANGING.
AND ABOVE ALL ELSE...

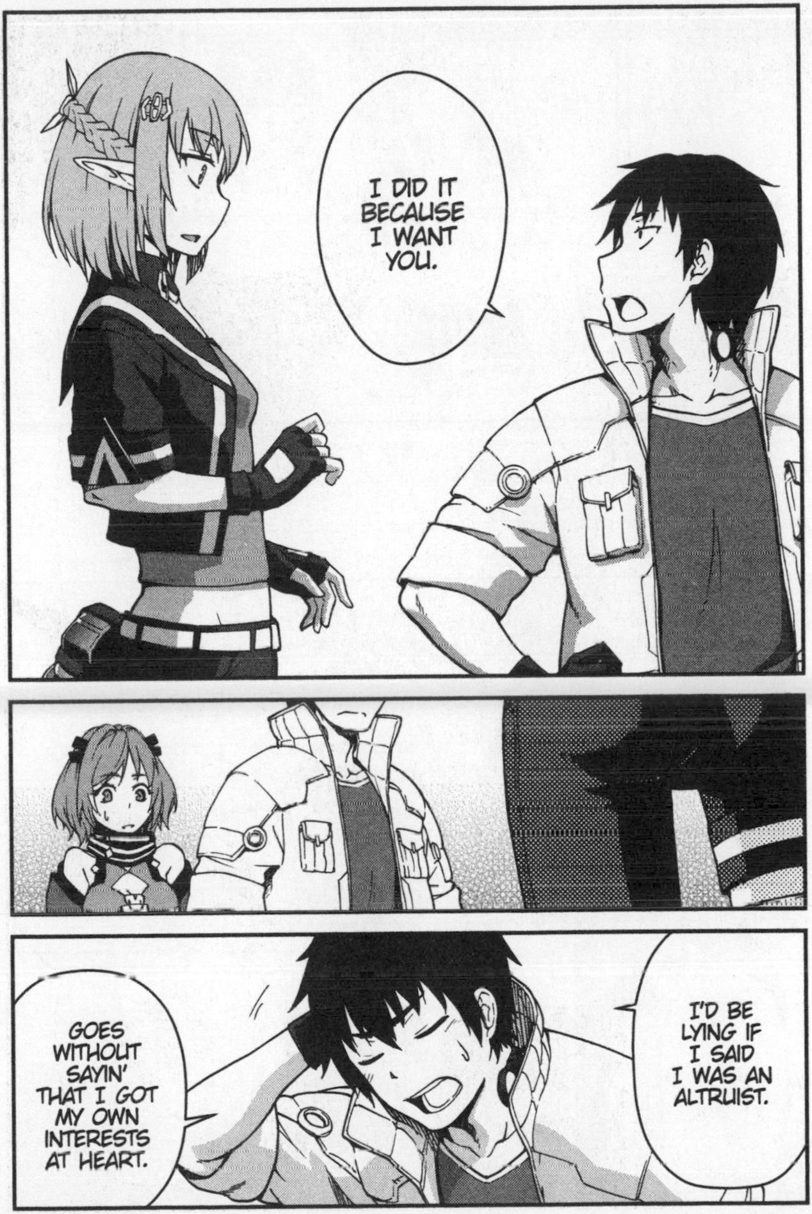
I DID IT BECAUSE I WANT YOU.
I'D BE LYING IF I SAID I WAS AN ALTRUIST.
GOES WITHOUT SAYIN' THAT I GOT MY OWN INTERESTS AT HEART.

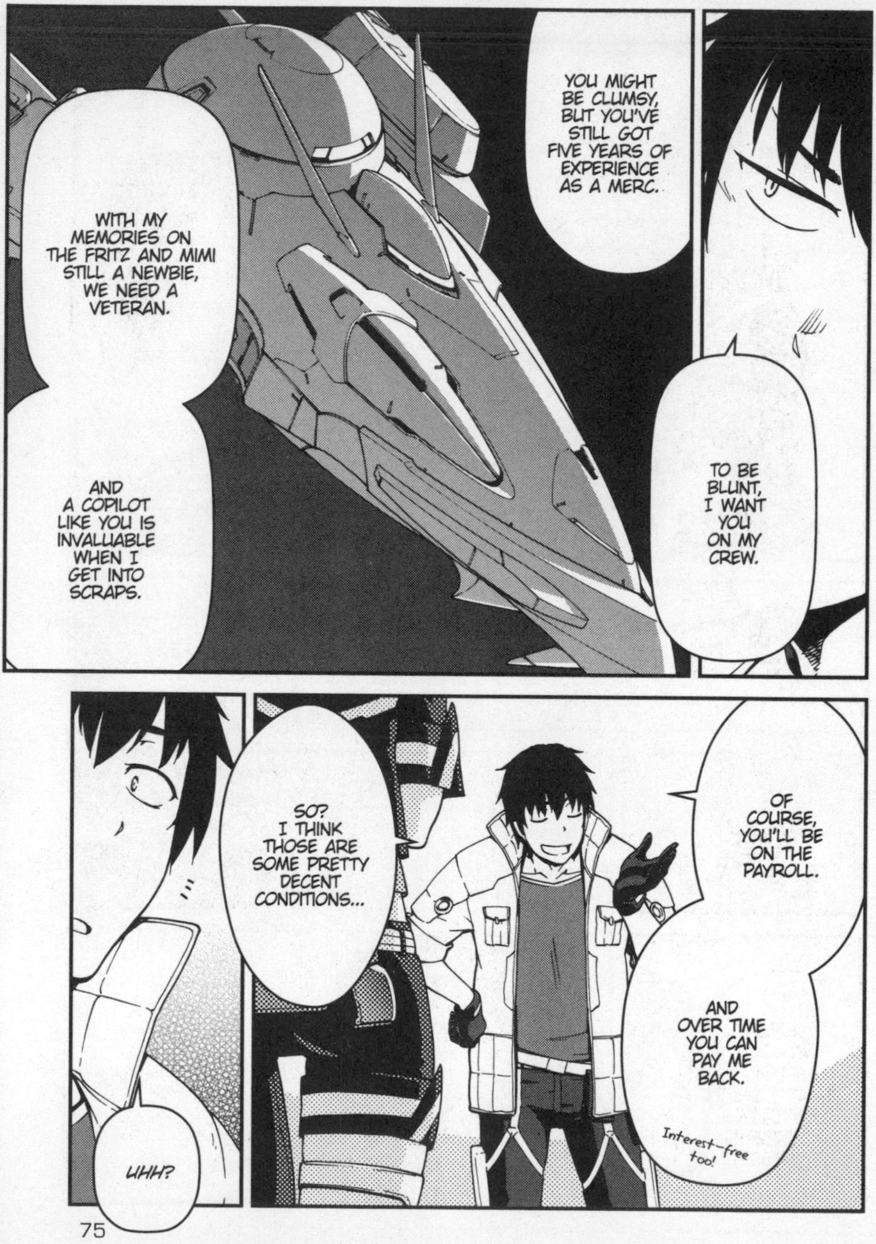
TO BE BLUNT, I WANT YOU ON MY CREW.
YOU MIGHT BE CLUMSY, BUT YOU'VE STILL GOT FIVE YEARS OF EXPERIENCE AS A MERC.
WITH MY MEMORIES ON THE FRITZ AND MIMI STILL A NEWBIE, WE NEED A VETERAN.
AND A COPILOT LIKE YOU IS INVALUABLE WHEN I GET INTO SCRAPS.
OF COURSE, YOU'LL BE ON THE PAYROLL.
AND OVER TIME YOU CAN PAY ME BACK.
Interest-free too!
SO? I THINK THOSE ARE SOME PRETTY DECENT CONDITIONS...
UHH?

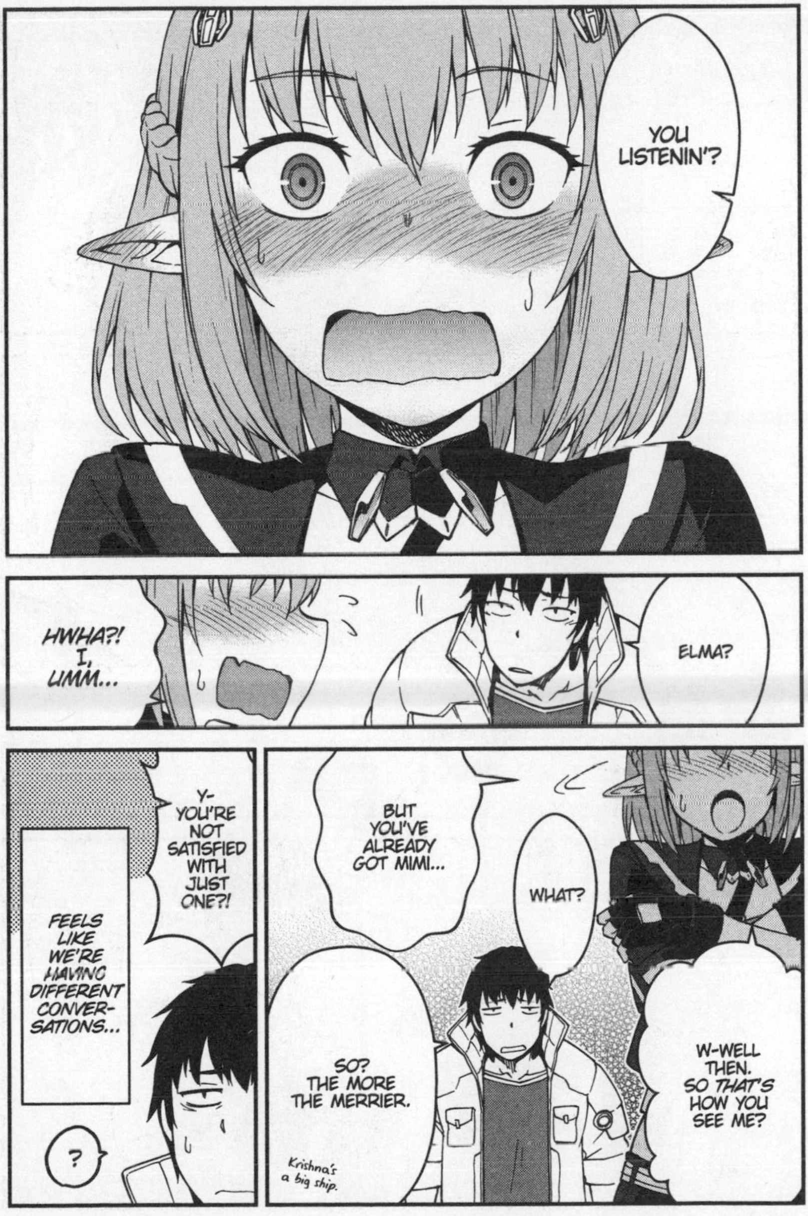

YOU LISTENIN'?
ELMA?
HWHA?! I, UMM...
BUT YOU'VE ALREADY GOT MIMI...
WHAT?
W-WELL THEN. SO THAT'S HOW YOU SEE ME?
SO? THE MORE THE MERRIER.
Krishna's a big ship.
Y-YOU'RE NOT SATISFIED WITH JUST ONE?!
FEELS LIKE WE'RE HAVING DIFFERENT CONVERSATIONS...
?

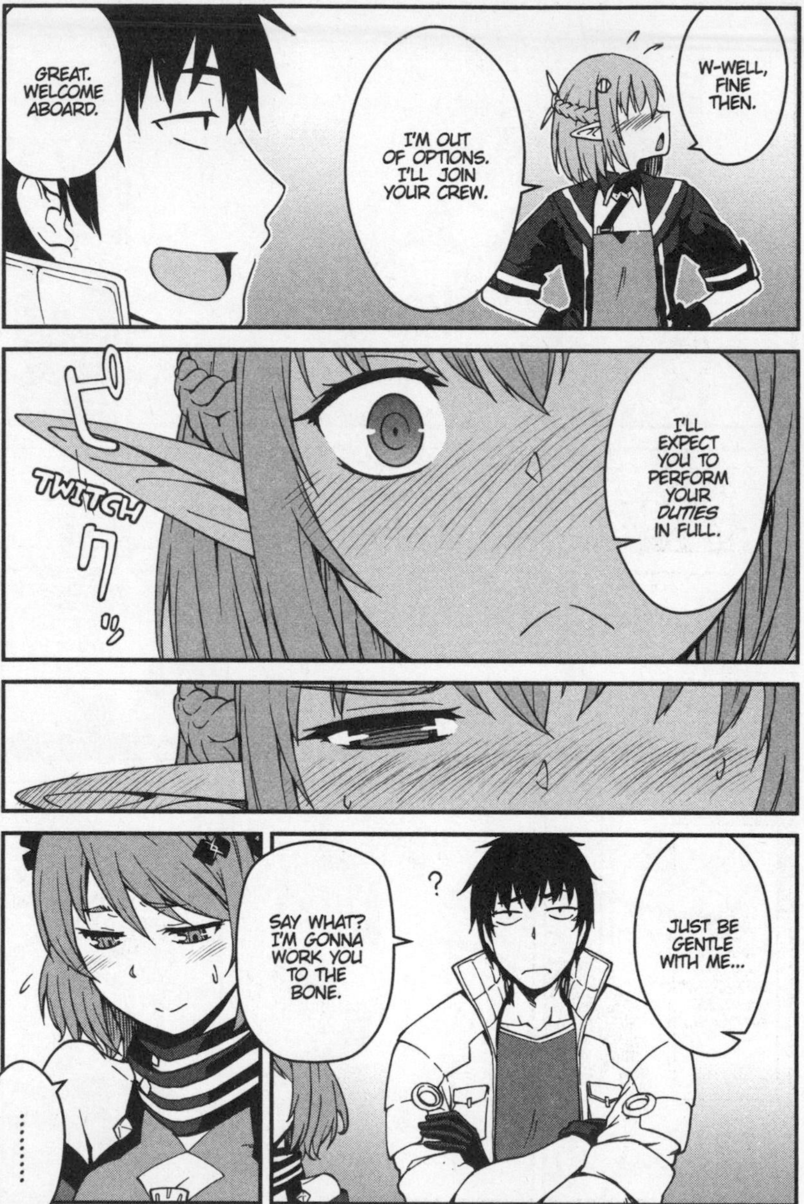
W-WELL, FINE THEN.
I'M OUT OF OPTIONS. I'LL JOIN YOUR CREW.
GREAT. WELCOME ABOARD.
I'LL EXPECT YOU TO PERFORM YOUR DUTIES IN FULL.
TWITCH
JUST BE GENTLE WITH ME...
?
SAY WHAT? I'M GONNA WORK YOU TO THE BONE.
......

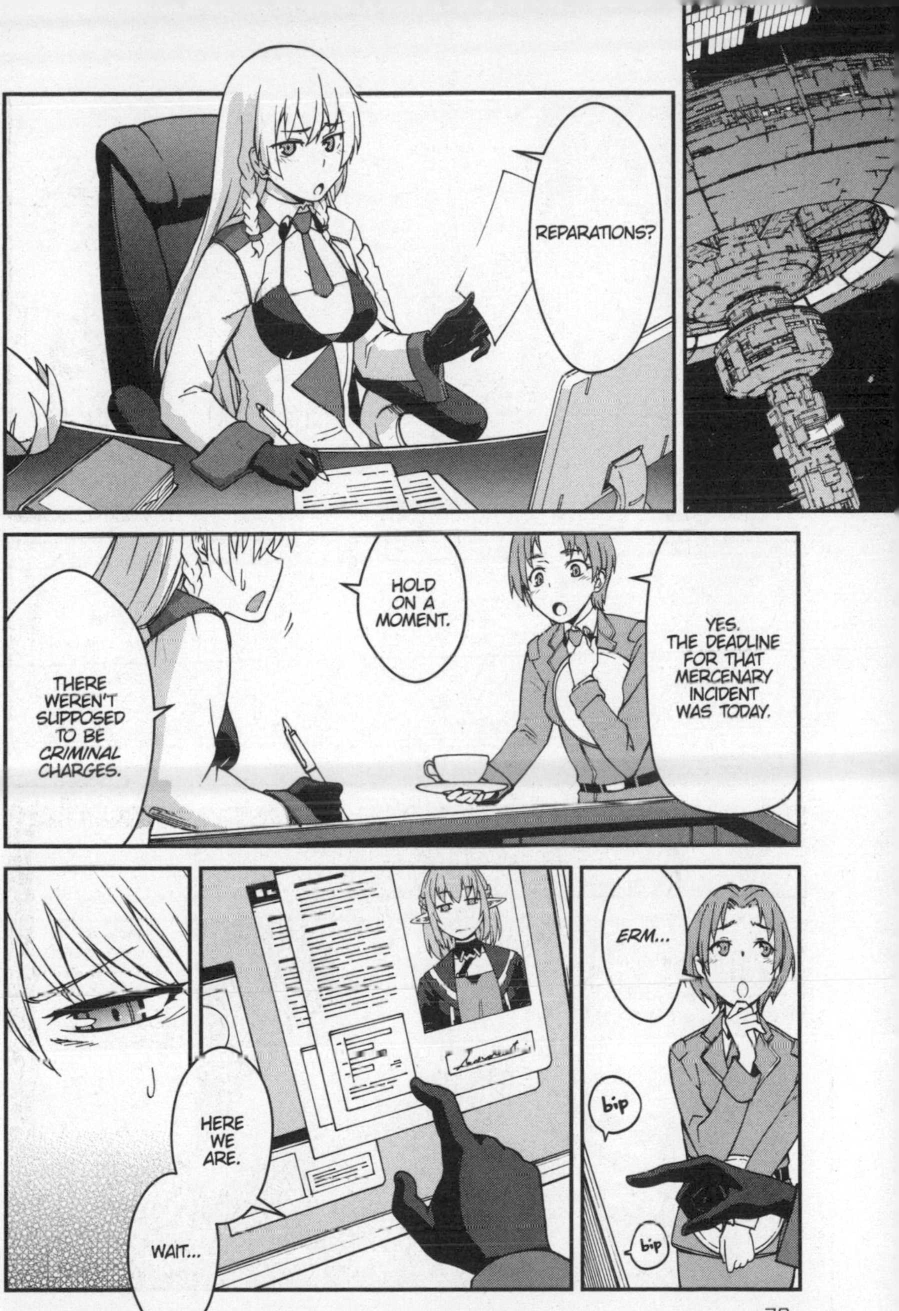
REPARATIONS?
YES. THE DEADLINE FOR THAT MERCENARY INCIDENT WAS TODAY.
HOLD ON A MOMENT.
THERE WEREN'T SUPPOSED TO BE *CRIMINAL* CHARGES.
ERM...
bip
bip
HERE WE ARE.
WAIT...

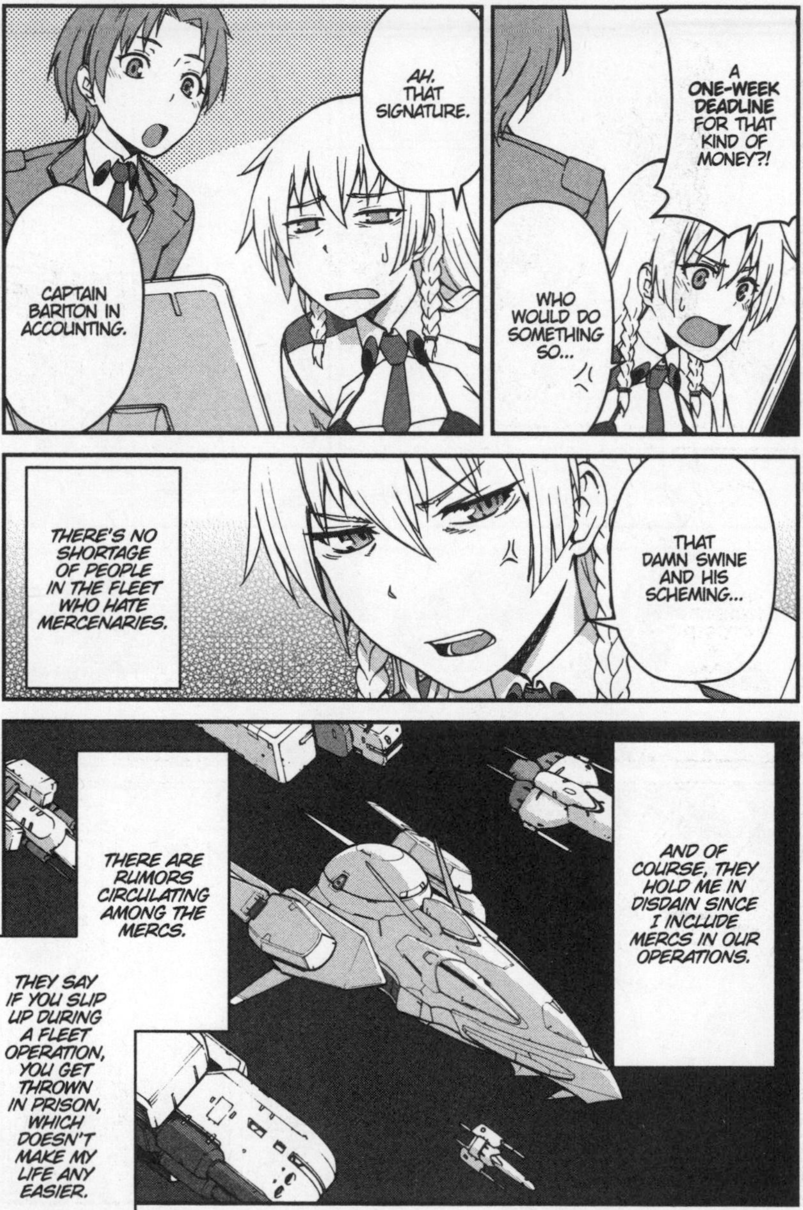
A ONE-WEEK DEADLINE FOR THAT KIND OF MONEY?!
WHO WOULD DO SOMETHING SO...
AH. THAT SIGNATURE.
CAPTAIN BARITON IN ACCOUNTING.
THAT DAMN SWINE AND HIS SCHEMING...
THERE'S NO SHORTAGE OF PEOPLE IN THE FLEET WHO HATE MERCENARIES.
AND OF COURSE, THEY HOLD ME IN DISDAIN SINCE I INCLUDE MERCS IN OUR OPERATIONS.
THERE ARE RUMORS CIRCULATING AMONG THE MERCS.
THEY SAY IF YOU SLIP UP DURING A FLEET OPERATION, YOU GET THROWN IN PRISON, WHICH DOESN'T MAKE MY LIFE ANY EASIER.

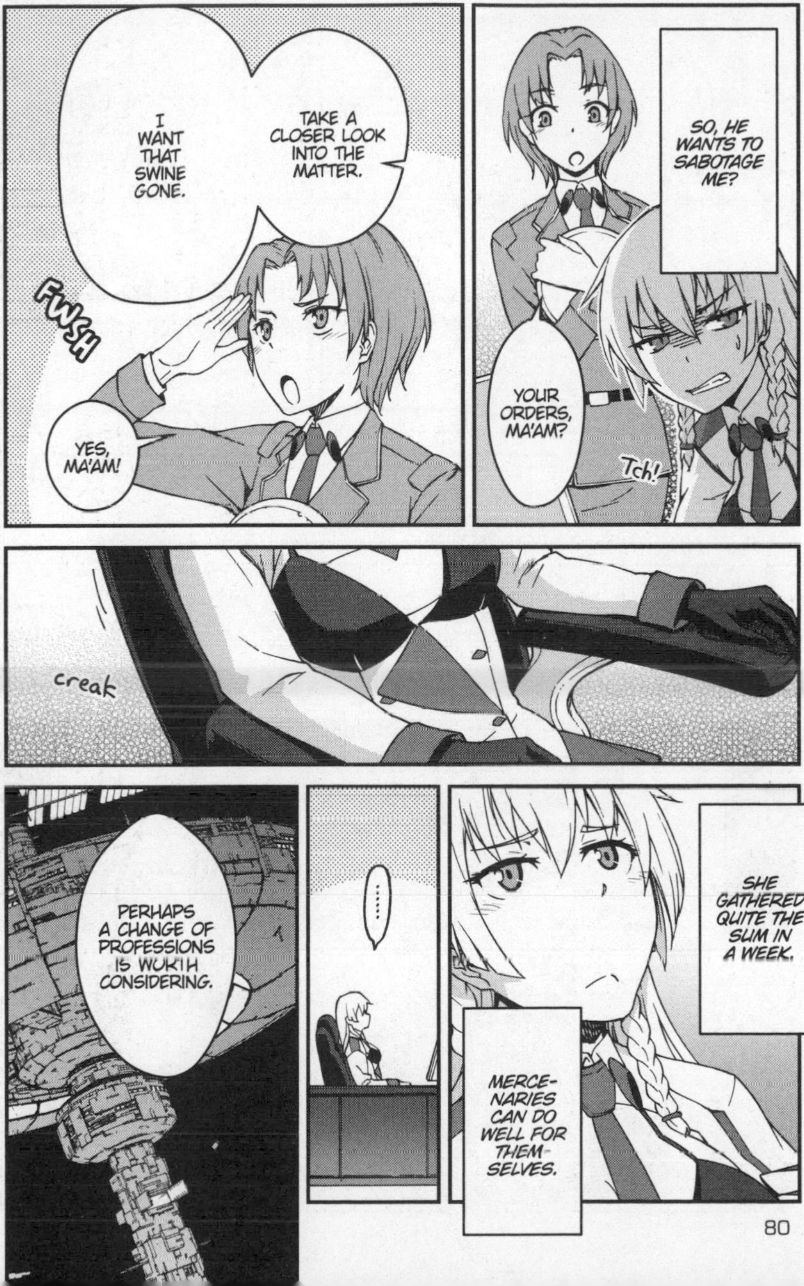

SO, HE WANTS TO SABOTAGE ME?
YOUR ORDERS, MA'AM?
Tch!
TAKE A CLOSER LOOK INTO THE MATTER.
I WANT THAT SWINE GONE.
FWSH
YES, MA'AM!
creak
SHE GATHERED QUITE THE SUM IN A WEEK.
MERCE-NARIES CAN DO WELL FOR THEM-SELVES.
......
PERHAPS A CHANGE OF PROFESSIONS IS WORTH CONSIDERING.

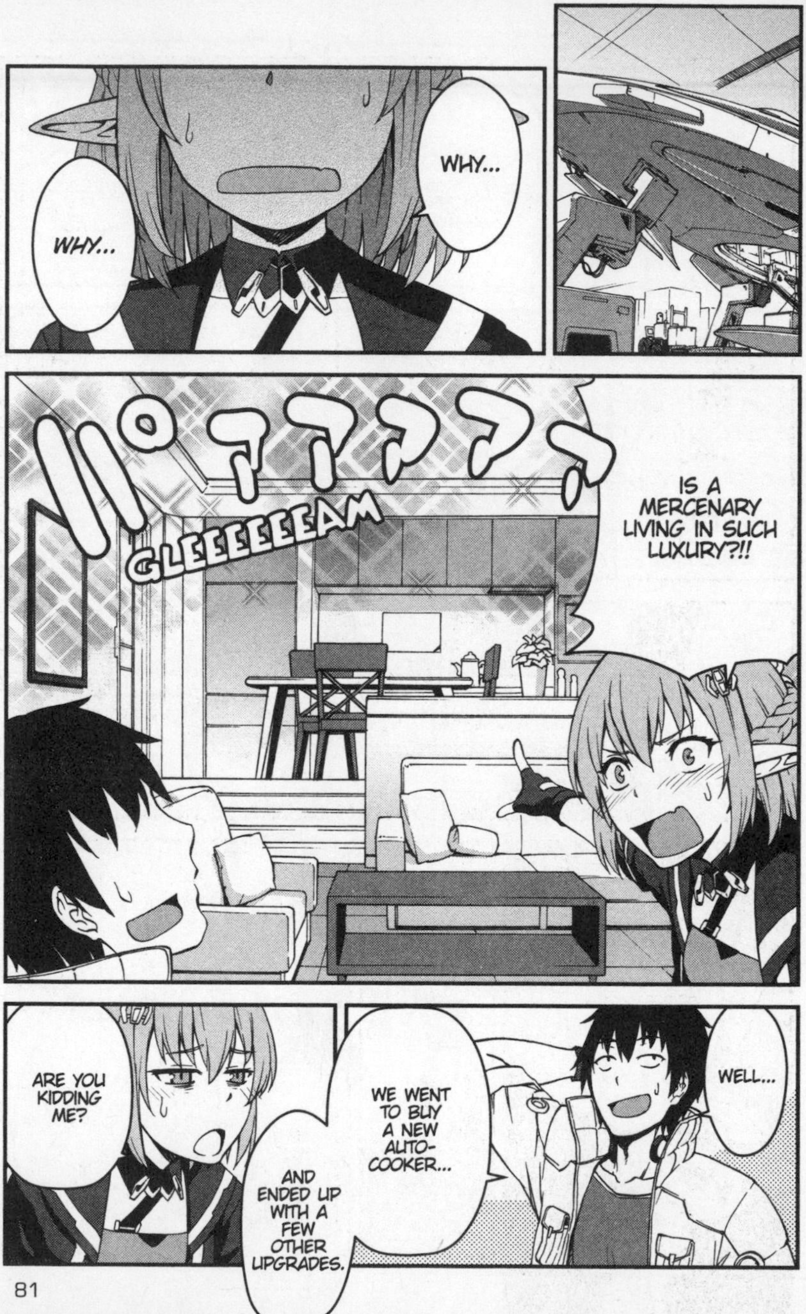
WHY...
WHY...
パアアアァ
GLEEEEEEAM
IS A MERCENARY LIVING IN SUCH LUXURY?!!
WELL...
WE WENT TO BUY A NEW AUTO-COOKER...
AND ENDED UP WITH A FEW OTHER UPGRADES.
ARE YOU KIDDING ME?

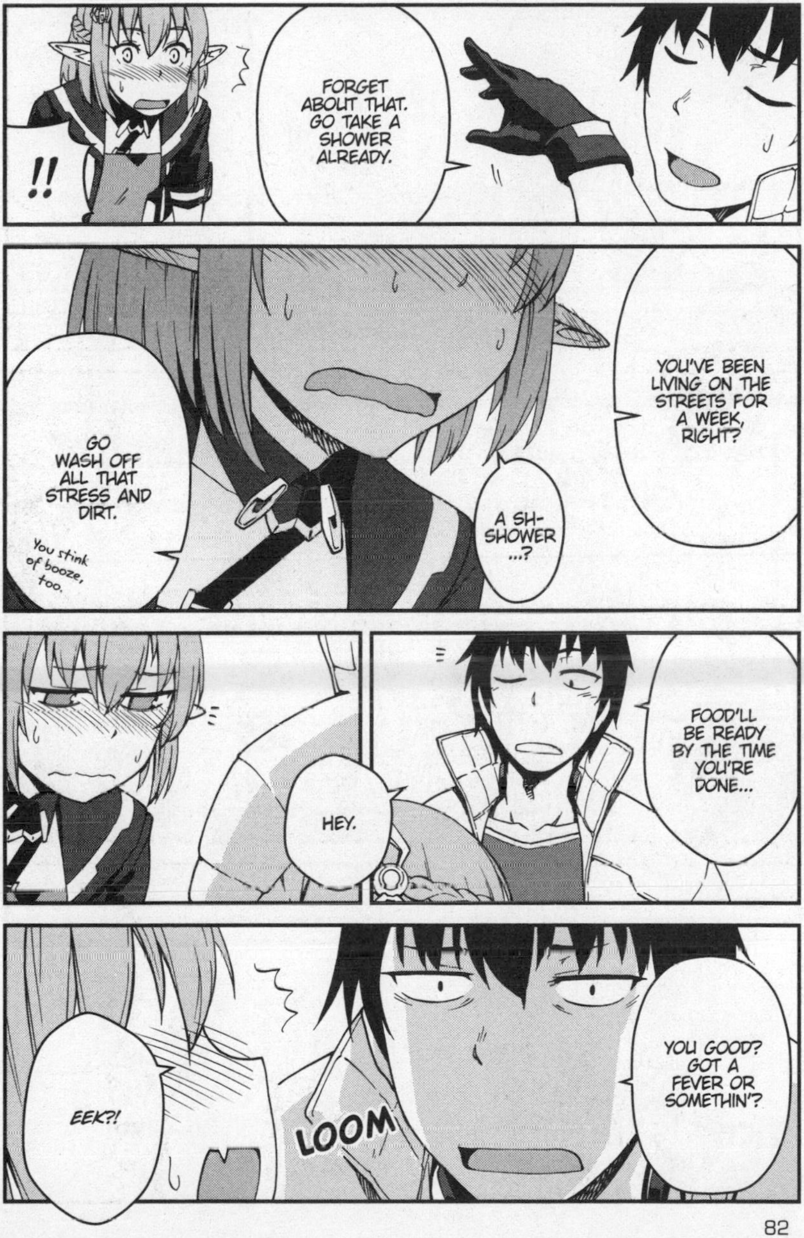
FORGET ABOUT THAT. GO TAKE A SHOWER ALREADY.
!!
YOU'VE BEEN LIVING ON THE STREETS FOR A WEEK, RIGHT?
A SH-SHOWER ...?
GO WASH OFF ALL THAT STRESS AND DIRT.
You stink of booze, too.
FOOD'LL BE READY BY THE TIME YOU'RE DONE...
HEY.
YOU GOOD? GOT A FEVER OR SOMETHIN'?
LOOM
EEK?!

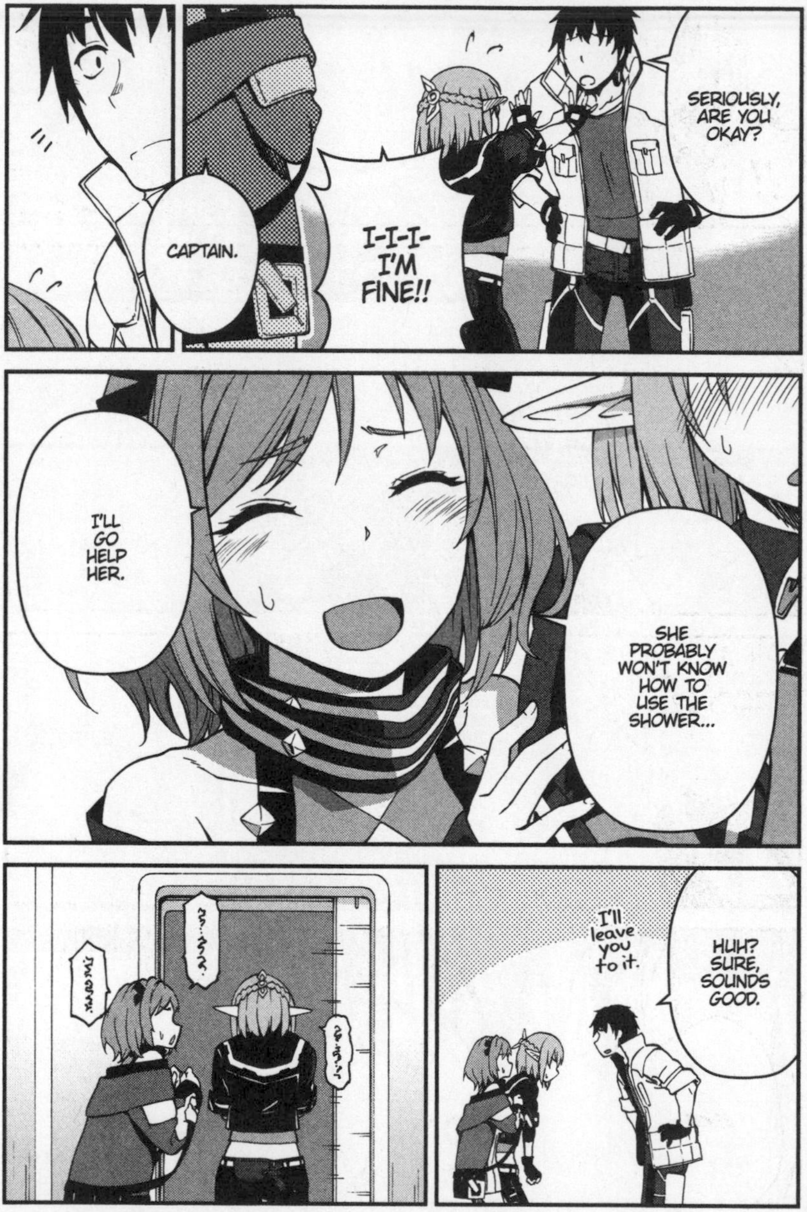
SERIOUSLY, ARE YOU OKAY?
I-I-I-I'M FINE!!
CAPTAIN.
SHE PROBABLY WON'T KNOW HOW TO USE THE SHOWER...
I'LL GO HELP HER.
HUH? SURE, SOUNDS GOOD.
I'll leave you to it.

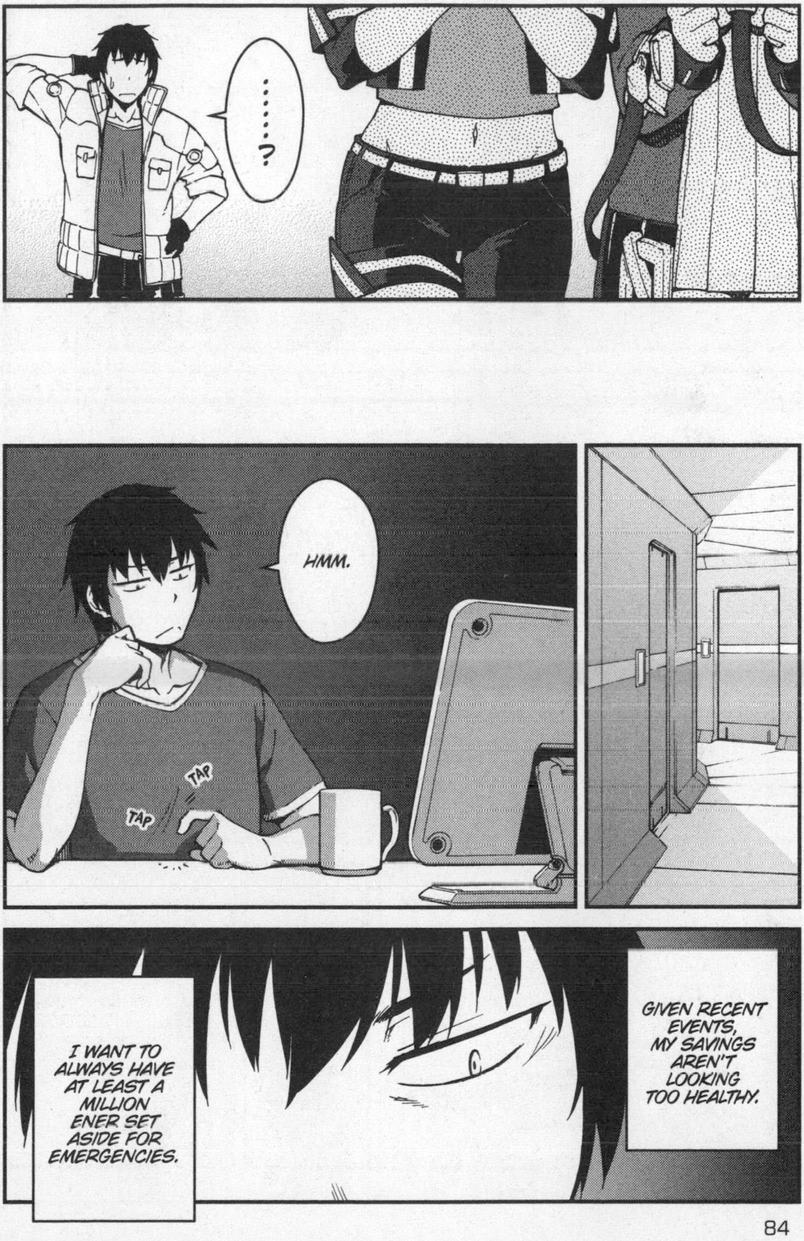
......?
HMM.
TAP
TAP
GIVEN RECENT EVENTS, MY SAVINGS AREN'T LOOKING TOO HEALTHY.
I WANT TO ALWAYS HAVE AT LEAST A MILLION ENER SET ASIDE FOR EMERGENCIES.

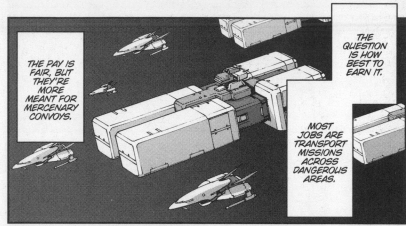

THE QUESTION IS HOW BEST TO EARN IT.
MOST JOBS ARE TRANSPORT MISSIONS ACROSS DANGEROUS AREAS.
THE PAY IS FAIR, BUT THEY'RE MORE MEANT FOR MERCENARY CONVOYS.
NOT FOR KRISHNA, WHICH DOESN'T HAVE THE BIGGEST HOLD.
THAT LEAVES BOUNTY HUNTING.
WE MIGHT'VE DESTROYED A PIRATE BASE, BUT THE SYSTEM ISN'T FREE OF THEM.
THERE'S PLENTY OF SMALLER GROUPS ALL OVER.
INDEPEN-DENT ONES, SKILLED AND WELL EQUIPPED.

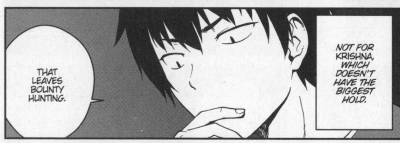

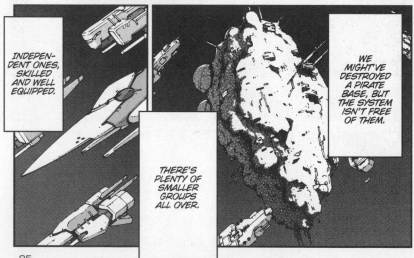

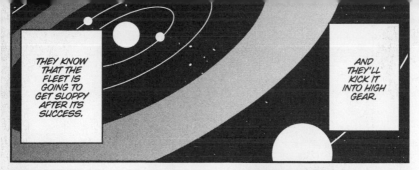

AND THEY'LL KICK IT INTO HIGH GEAR.
THEY KNOW THAT THE FLEET IS GOING TO GET SLOPPY AFTER ITS SUCCESS.
I BET THE PIRATES WILL BE GUNNING FOR THE ASTEROID BELT...
HUNTING FOR CIVILIAN MINING SHIPS LOADED WITH VALUABLE ORE.
OKAY! LET'S FIND THE MOST LIKELY TARGETS.
HMM, SO THERE'S HEAVY CIVILIAN TRAFFIC HERE...
AND THE FLEET'S DEFENSE IS PROBABLY THIN HERE...
...
PSSHT
?
?

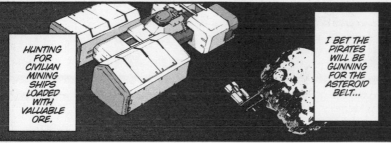

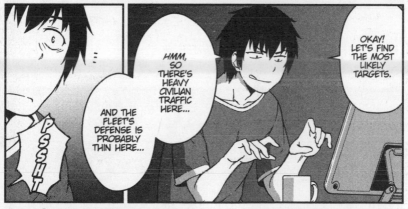

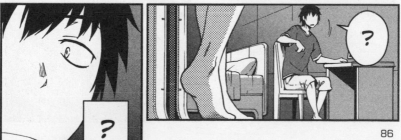

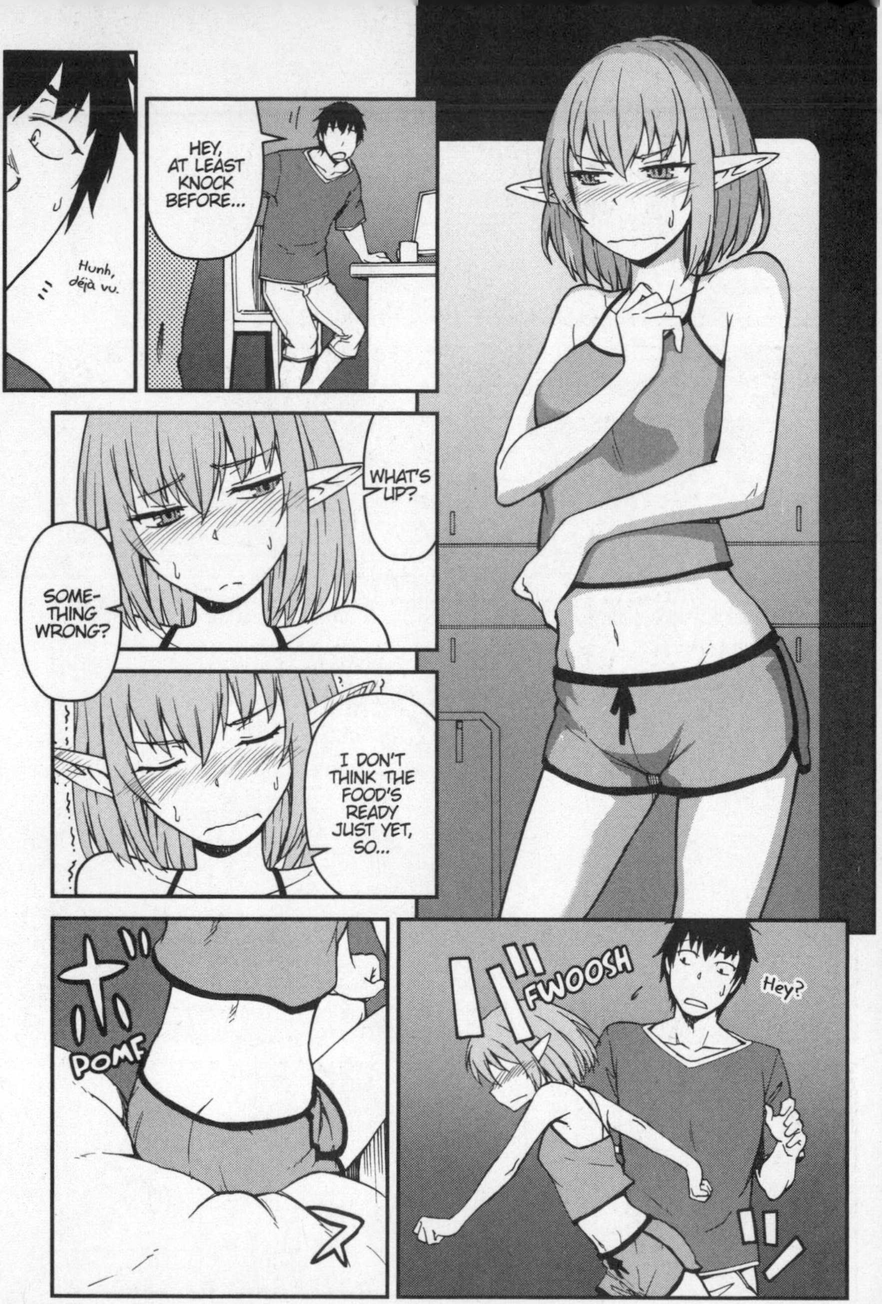
HEY, AT LEAST KNOCK BEFORE...
Hunh, déjà vu.
WHAT'S UP?
SOME-THING WRONG?
I DON'T THINK THE FOOD'S READY JUST YET, SO...
FWOOSH
Hey?
POMF

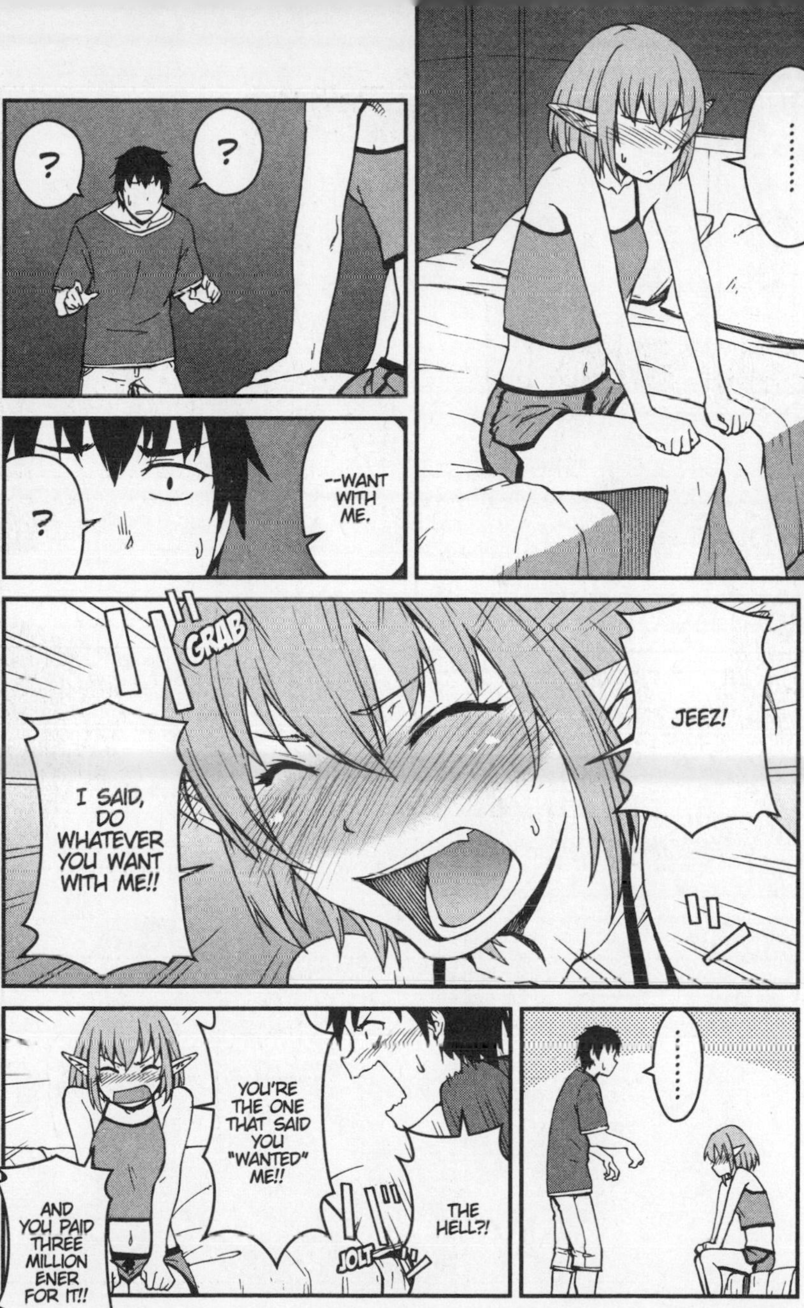
......
?
?
?
--WANT WITH ME.
GRAB
JEEZ!
I SAID, DO WHATEVER YOU WANT WITH ME!!
......
THE HELL?!
JOLT
YOU'RE THE ONE THAT SAID YOU "WANTED" ME!!
AND YOU PAID THREE MILLION ENER FOR IT!!

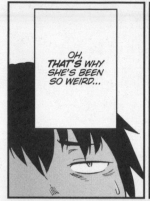

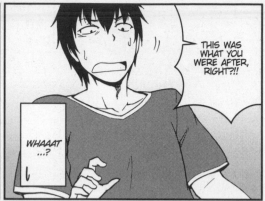

THIS WAS WHAT YOU WERE AFTER, RIGHT?!!
WHAAAT ...?
OH, THAT'S WHY SHE'S BEEN SO WEIRD...
LISTEN...
A MISUNDER-STANDING ...?
SHIVER
B-BUT THAT MEANS I...
SHIVER

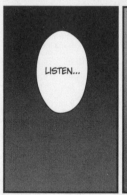

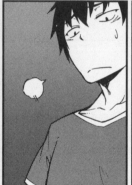

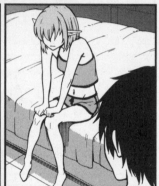

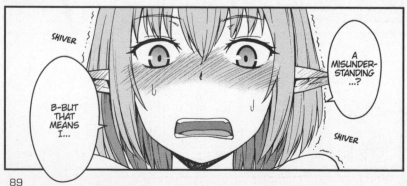

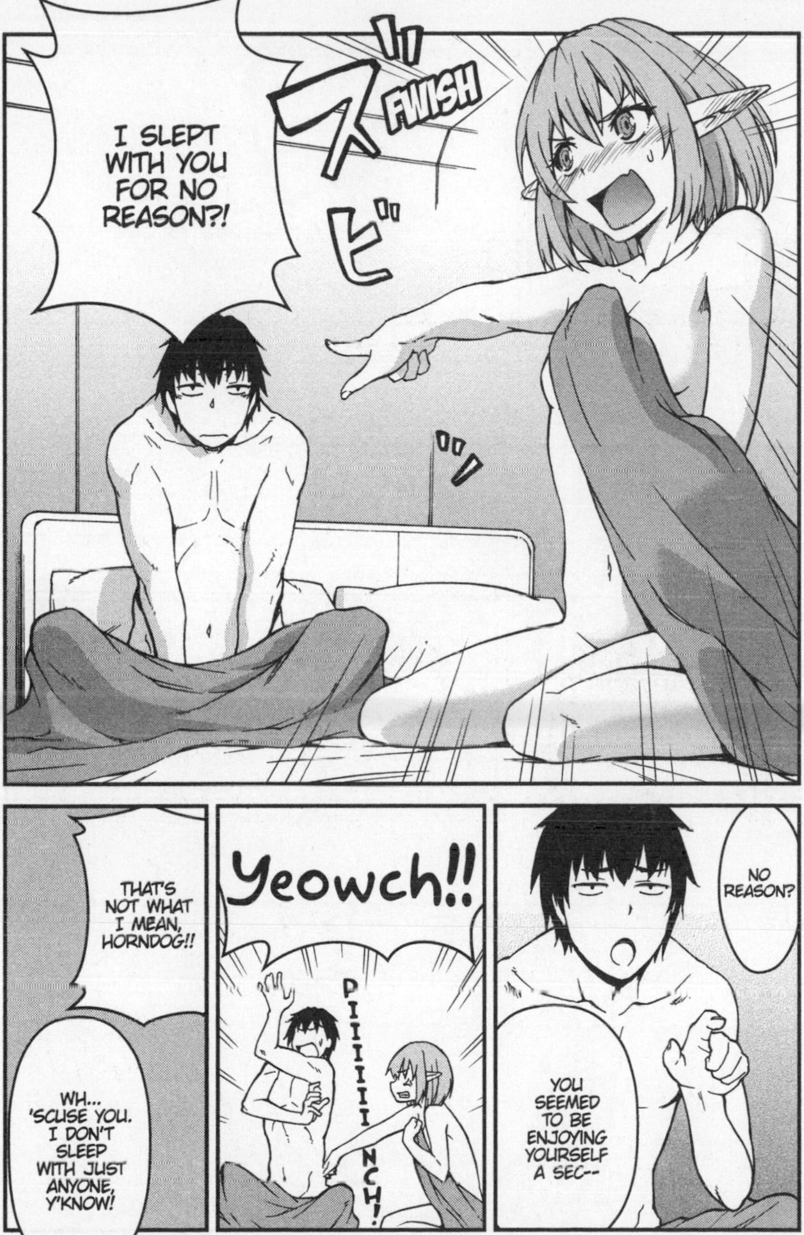
FWISH
I SLEPT WITH YOU FOR NO REASON?!
NO REASON?
YOU SEEMED TO BE ENJOYING YOURSELF A SEC--
Yeowch!!
PIIIIIIINCH!
THAT'S NOT WHAT I MEAN, HORNDOG!!
WH... 'SCUSE YOU. I DON'T SLEEP WITH JUST ANYONE, Y'KNOW!

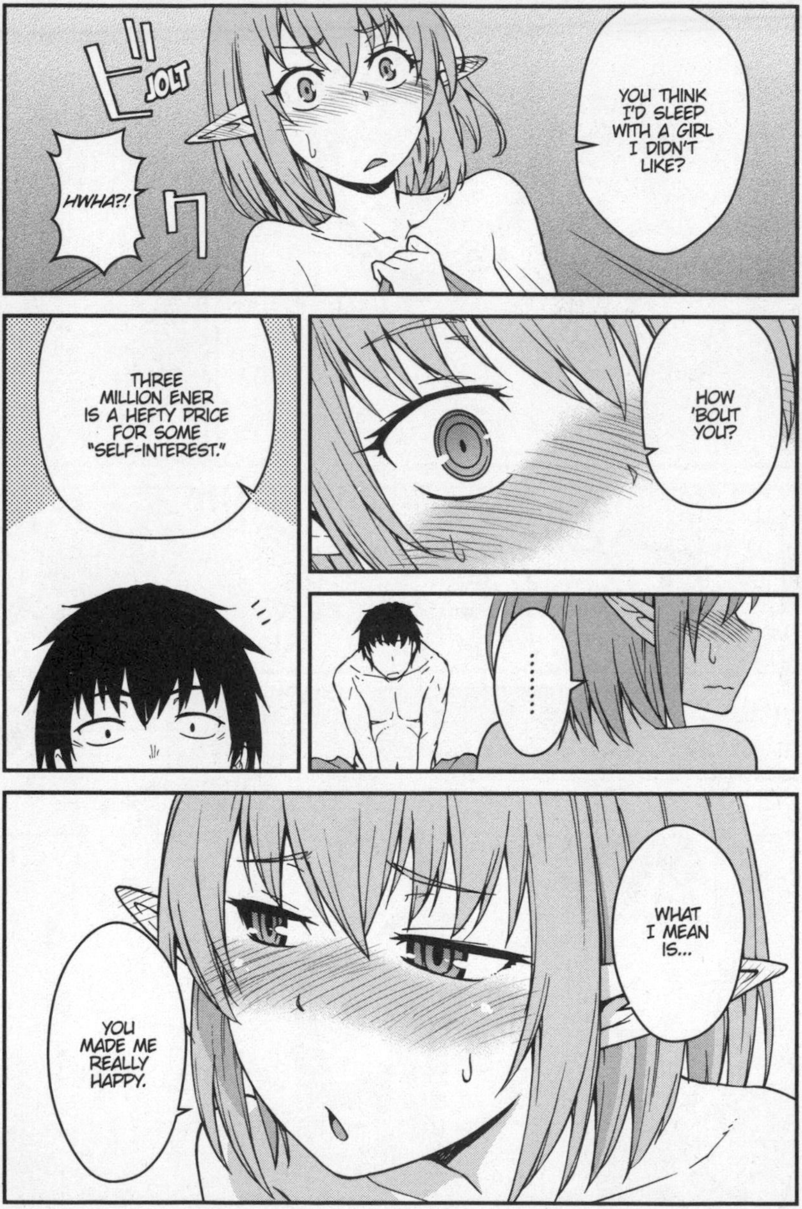
YOU THINK I'D SLEEP WITH A GIRL I DIDN'T LIKE?
JOLT
HWHA?!
HOW 'BOUT YOU?
THREE MILLION ENER IS A HEFTY PRICE FOR SOME "SELF-INTEREST."
......
WHAT I MEAN IS...
YOU MADE ME REALLY HAPPY.

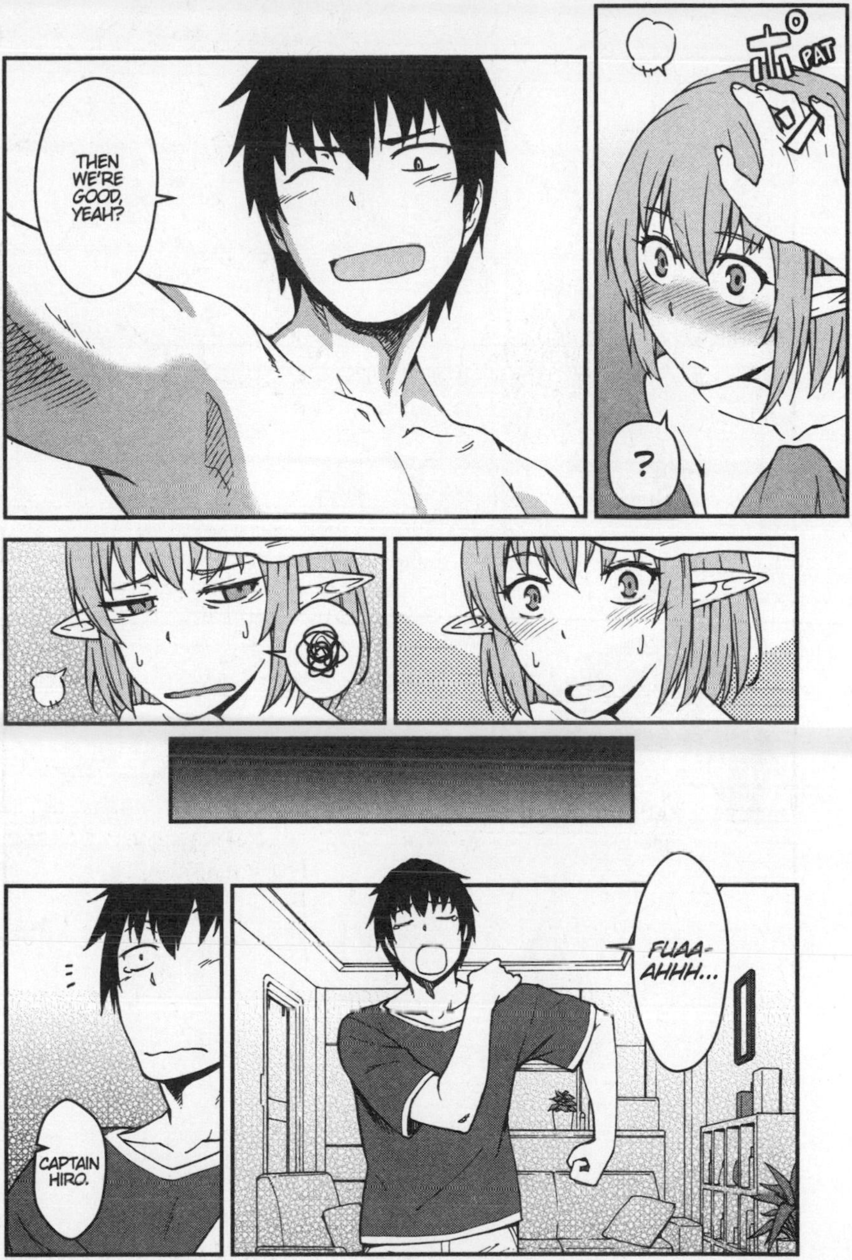
PAT
?
THEN WE'RE GOOD, YEAH?
FUAA-AHHH...
CAPTAIN HIRO.

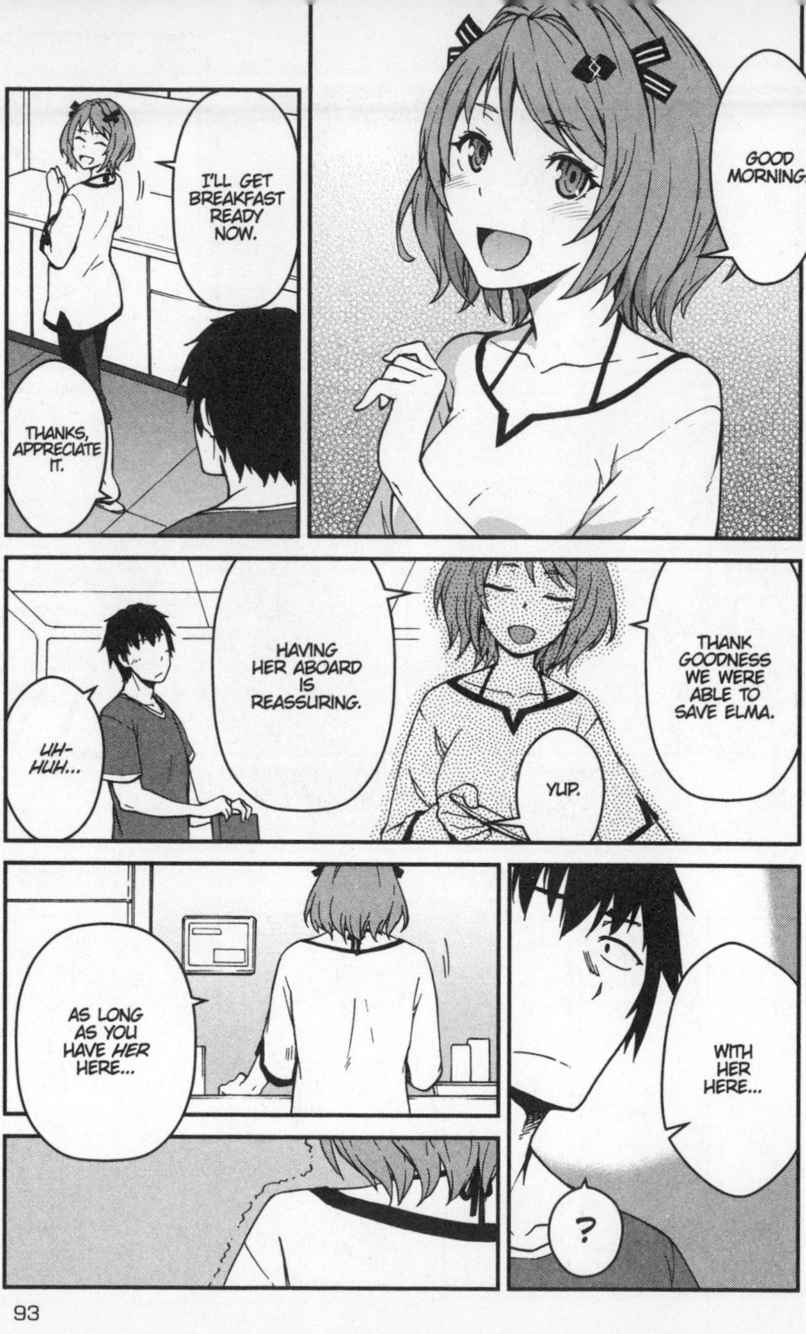
GOOD MORNING!
I'LL GET BREAKFAST READY NOW.
THANKS, APPRECIATE IT.
THANK GOODNESS WE WERE ABLE TO SAVE ELMA.
YUP.
HAVING HER ABOARD IS REASSURING.
UH-HUH...
WITH HER HERE...
?
AS LONG AS YOU HAVE *HER* HERE...

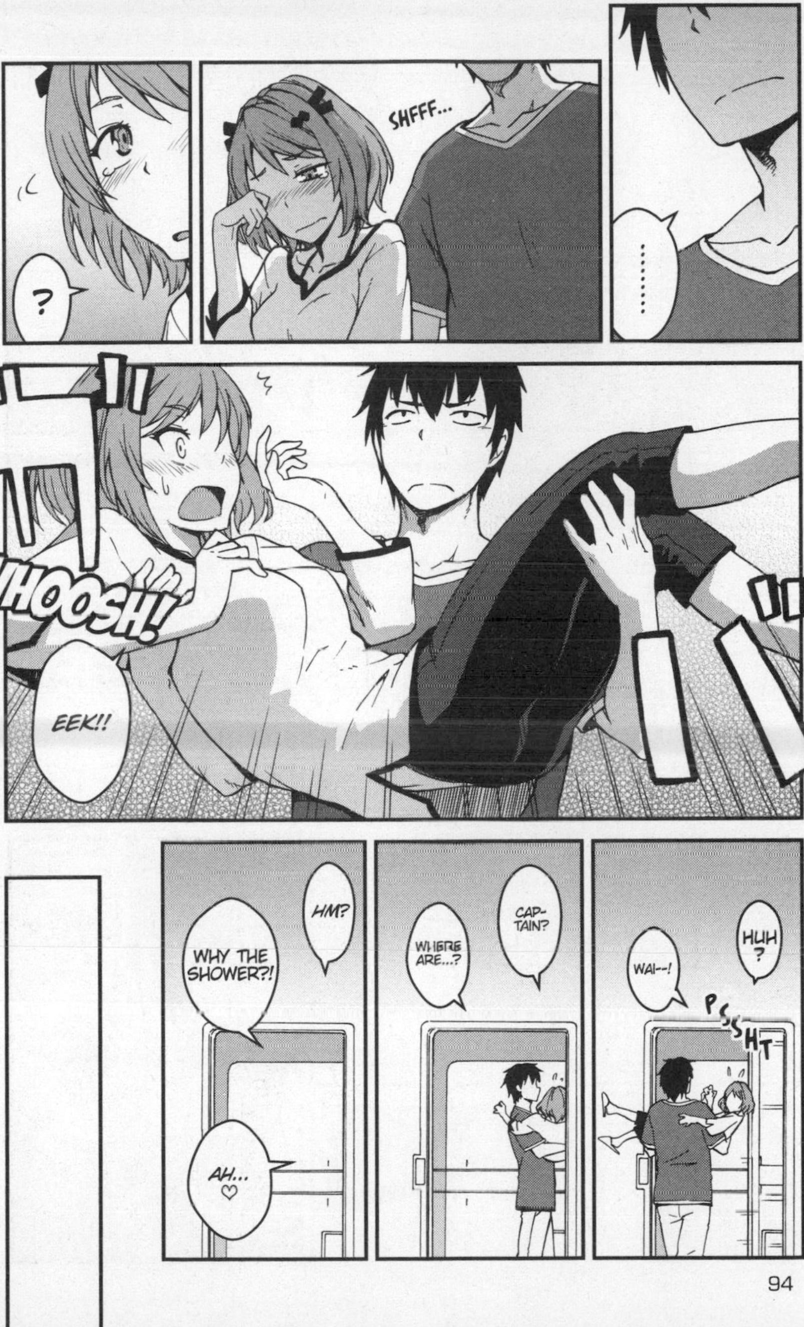
......
SHFFF...
?
WHOOSH!
EEK!!
HUH?
WAI--!
PSSHT
CAP-TAIN?
WHERE ARE...?
HM?
WHY THE SHOWER?!
AH... ♡

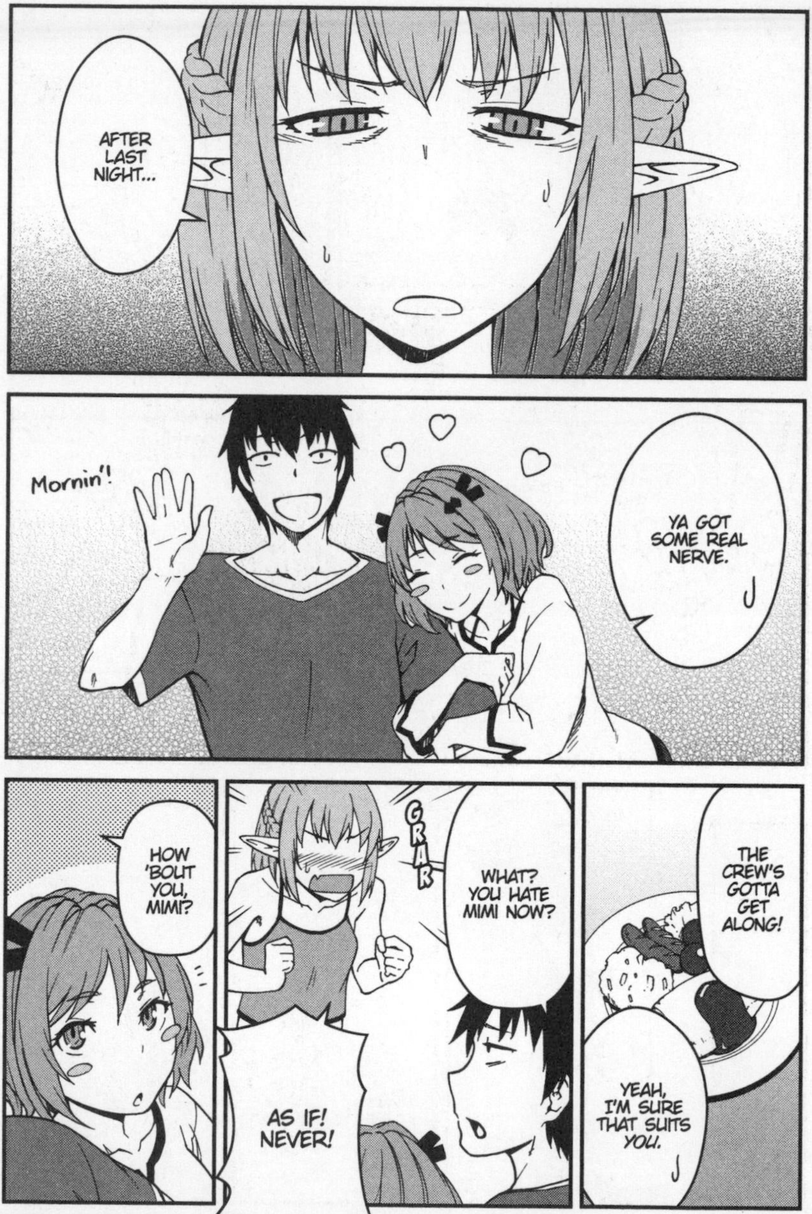
AFTER LAST NIGHT...
YA GOT SOME REAL NERVE.
Mornin'!
THE CREW'S GOTTA GET ALONG!
YEAH, I'M SURE THAT SUITS YOU.
WHAT? YOU HATE MIMI NOW?
GRAR
AS IF! NEVER!
HOW 'BOUT YOU, MIMI?

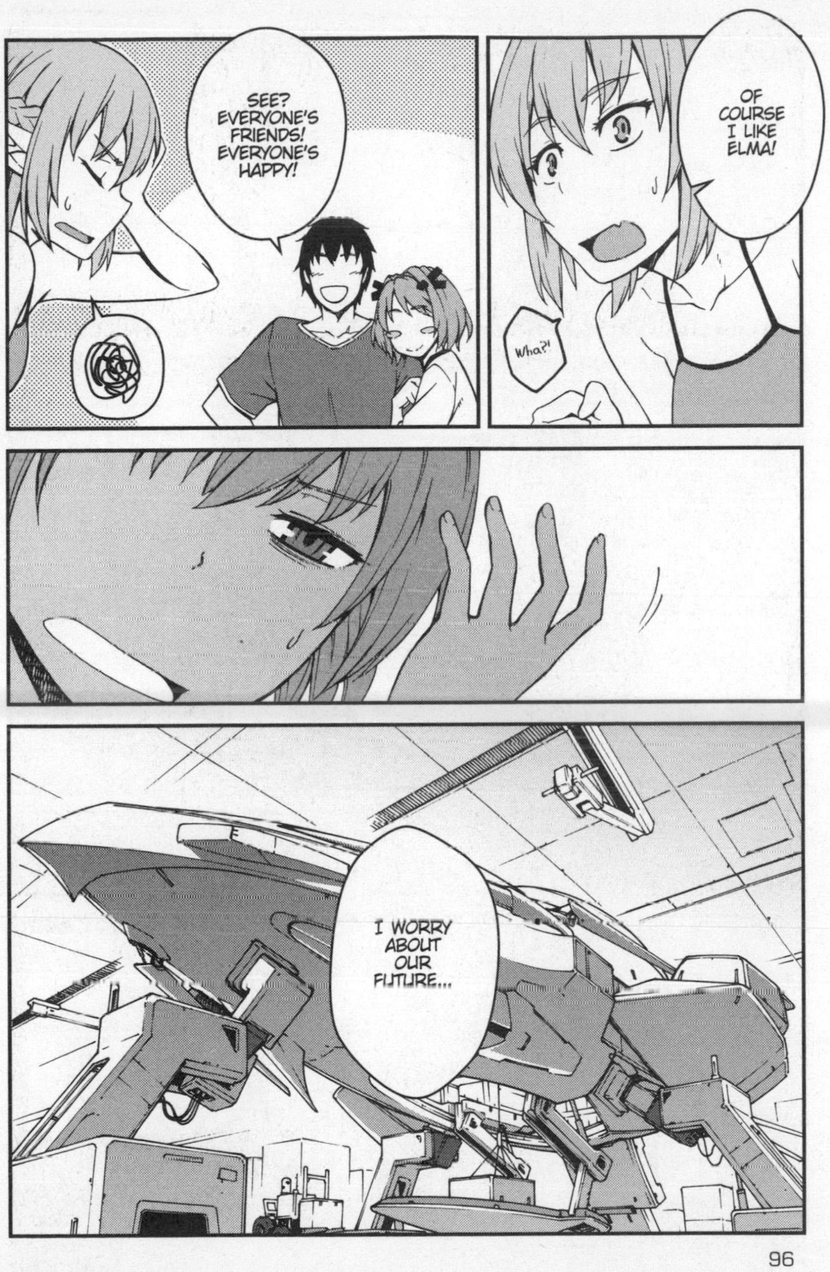
OF COURSE I LIKE ELMA!
Wha?!
SEE? EVERYONE'S FRIENDS! EVERYONE'S HAPPY!
I WORRY ABOUT OUR FUTURE...

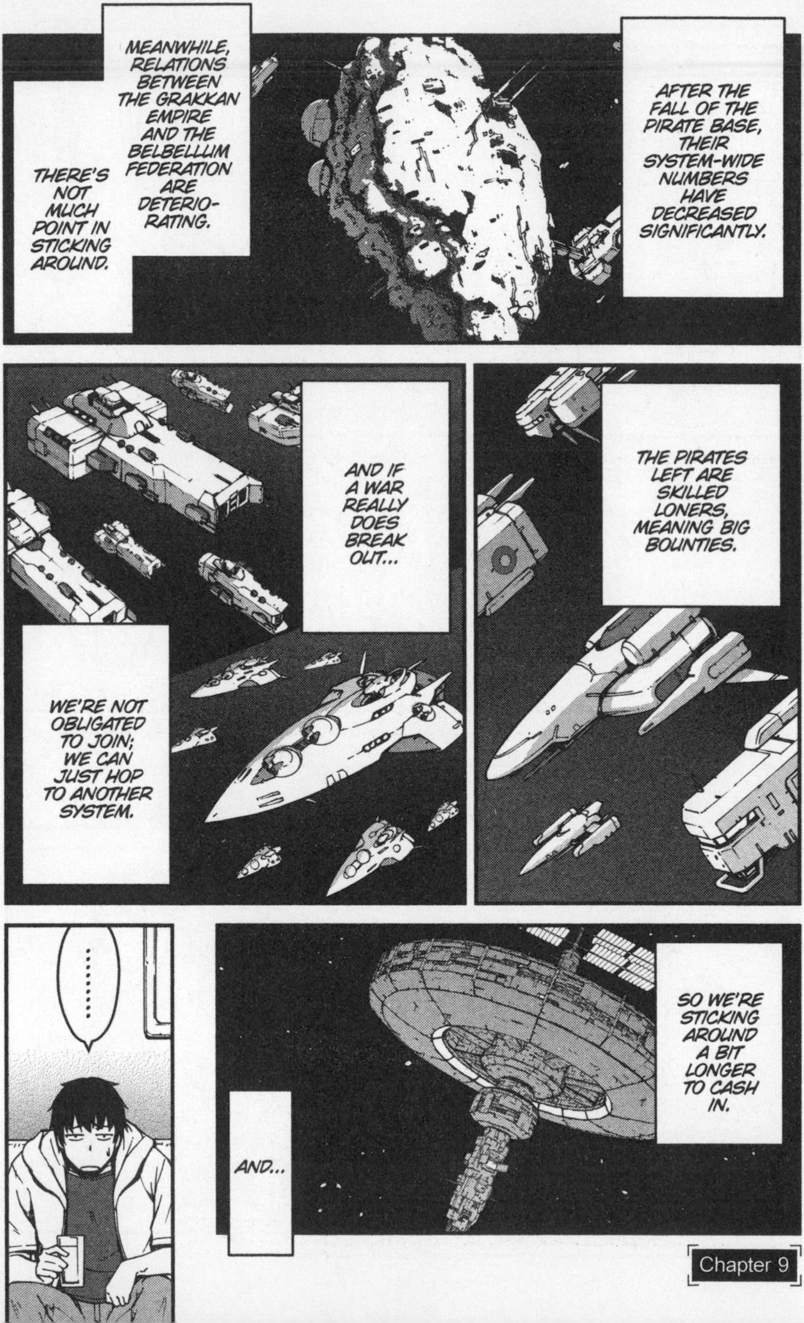
AFTER THE FALL OF THE PIRATE BASE, THEIR SYSTEM-WIDE NUMBERS HAVE DECREASED SIGNIFICANTLY.
MEANWHILE, RELATIONS BETWEEN THE GRAKKAN EMPIRE AND THE BELBELLUM FEDERATION ARE DETERIO-RATING.
THERE'S NOT MUCH POINT IN STICKING AROUND.
THE PIRATES LEFT ARE SKILLED LONERS, MEANING BIG BOUNTIES.
AND IF A WAR REALLY DOES BREAK OUT...
WE'RE NOT OBLIGATED TO JOIN; WE CAN JUST HOP TO ANOTHER SYSTEM.
SO WE'RE STICKING AROUND A BIT LONGER TO CASH IN.
AND...
……
Chapter 9

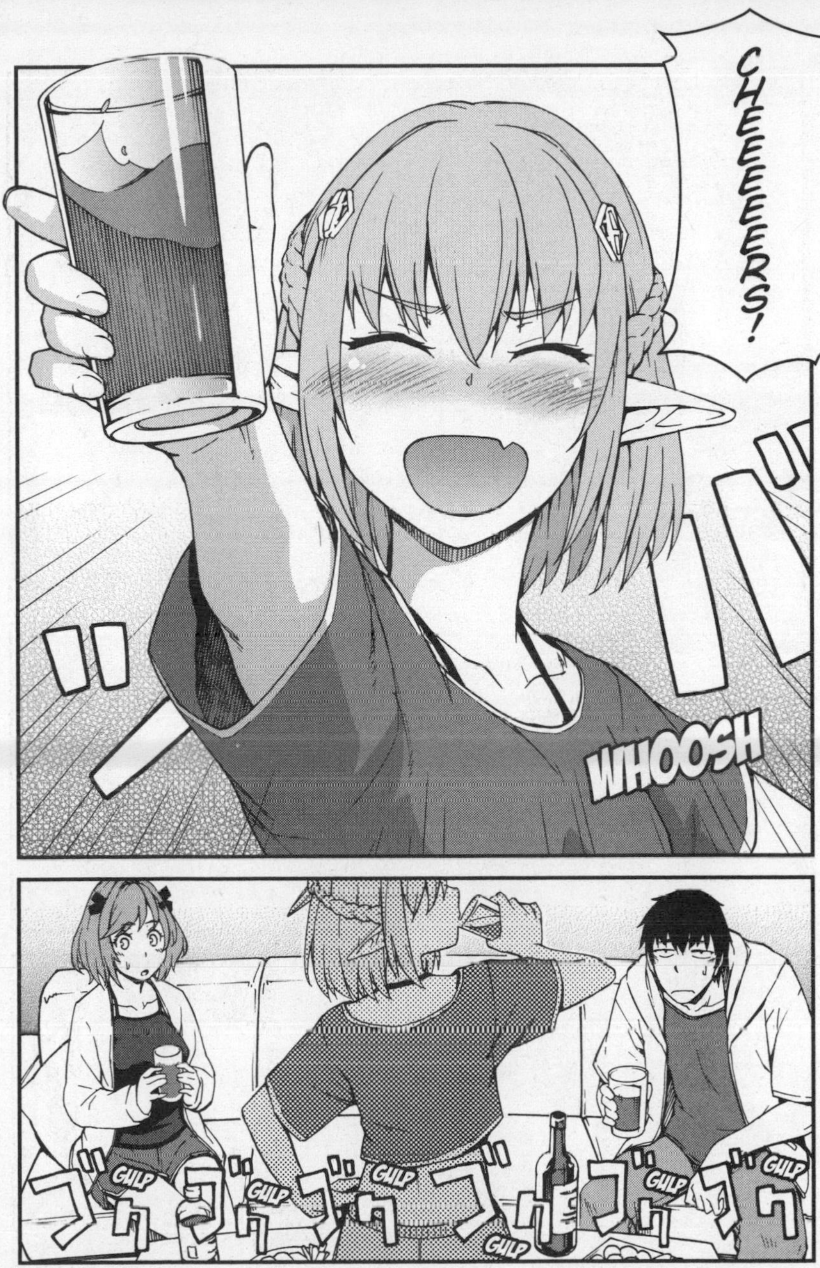
CHEEEEERS!
WHOOSH
GULP
GULP
GULP
GULP
GULP
GULP

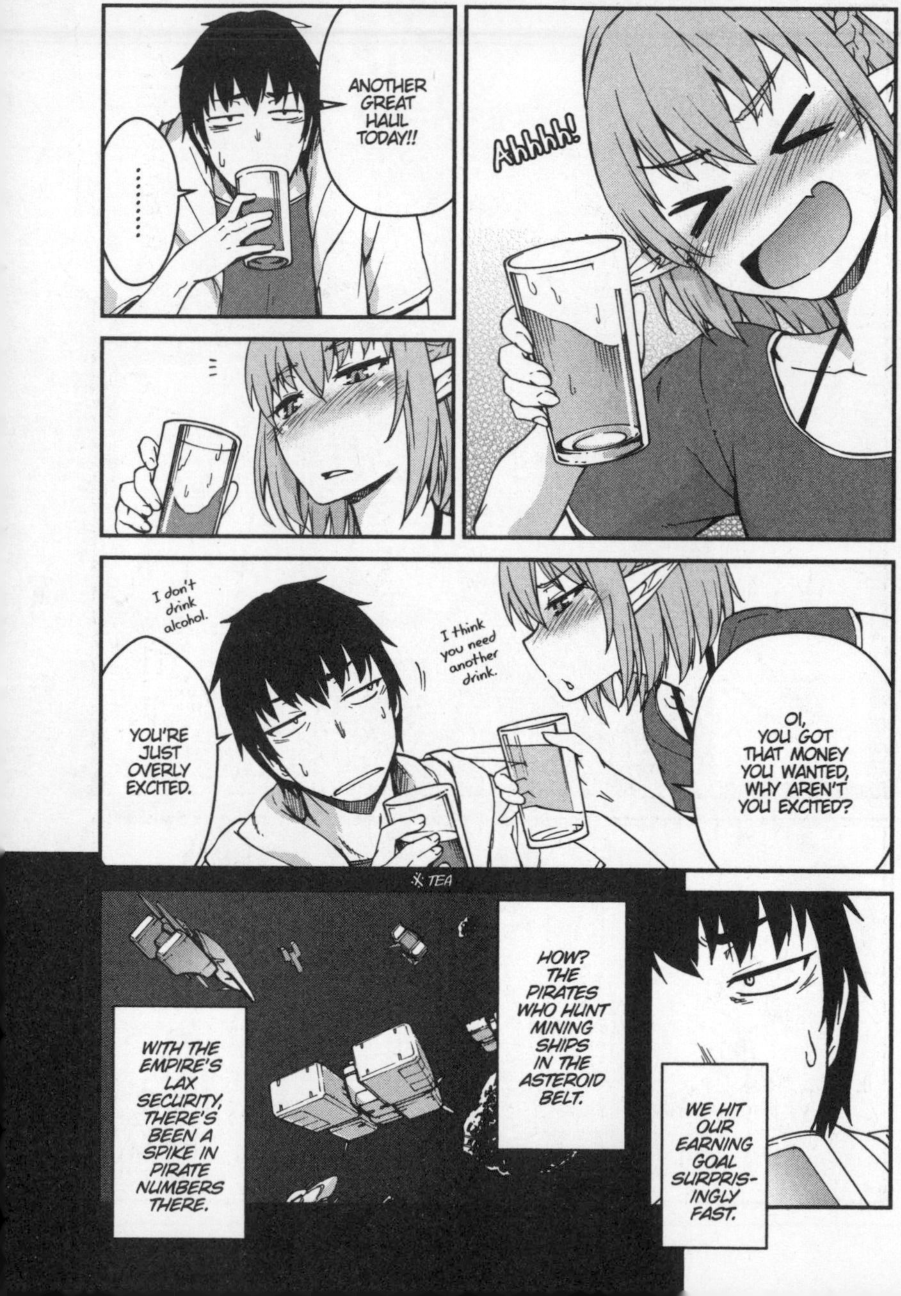

Ahhhh!
ANOTHER GREAT HAUL TODAY!!
......
OI, YOU GOT THAT MONEY YOU WANTED, WHY AREN'T YOU EXCITED?
I think you need another drink.
YOU'RE JUST OVERLY EXCITED.
I don't drink alcohol.
※TEA
WE HIT OUR EARNING GOAL SURPRISINGLY FAST.
HOW? THE PIRATES WHO HUNT MINING SHIPS IN THE ASTEROID BELT.
WITH THE EMPIRE'S LAX SECURITY, THERE'S BEEN A SPIKE IN PIRATE NUMBERS THERE.

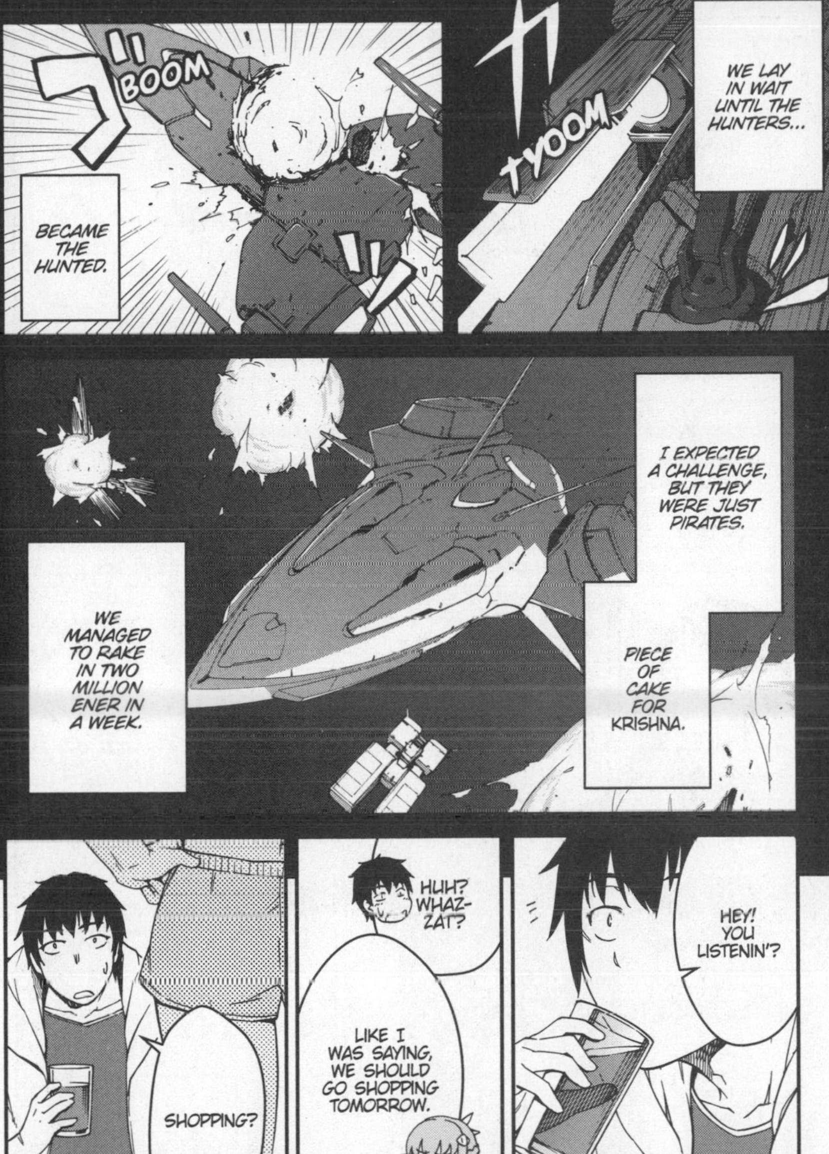
WE LAY IN WAIT UNTIL THE HUNTERS...
TYOOM
BOOM
BECAME THE HUNTED.
I EXPECTED A CHALLENGE, BUT THEY WERE JUST PIRATES.
PIECE OF CAKE FOR KRISHNA.
WE MANAGED TO RAKE IN TWO MILLION ENER IN A WEEK.
HEY! YOU LISTENIN'?
HUH? WHAZ-ZAT?
LIKE I WAS SAYING, WE SHOULD GO SHOPPING TOMORROW.
SHOPPING?

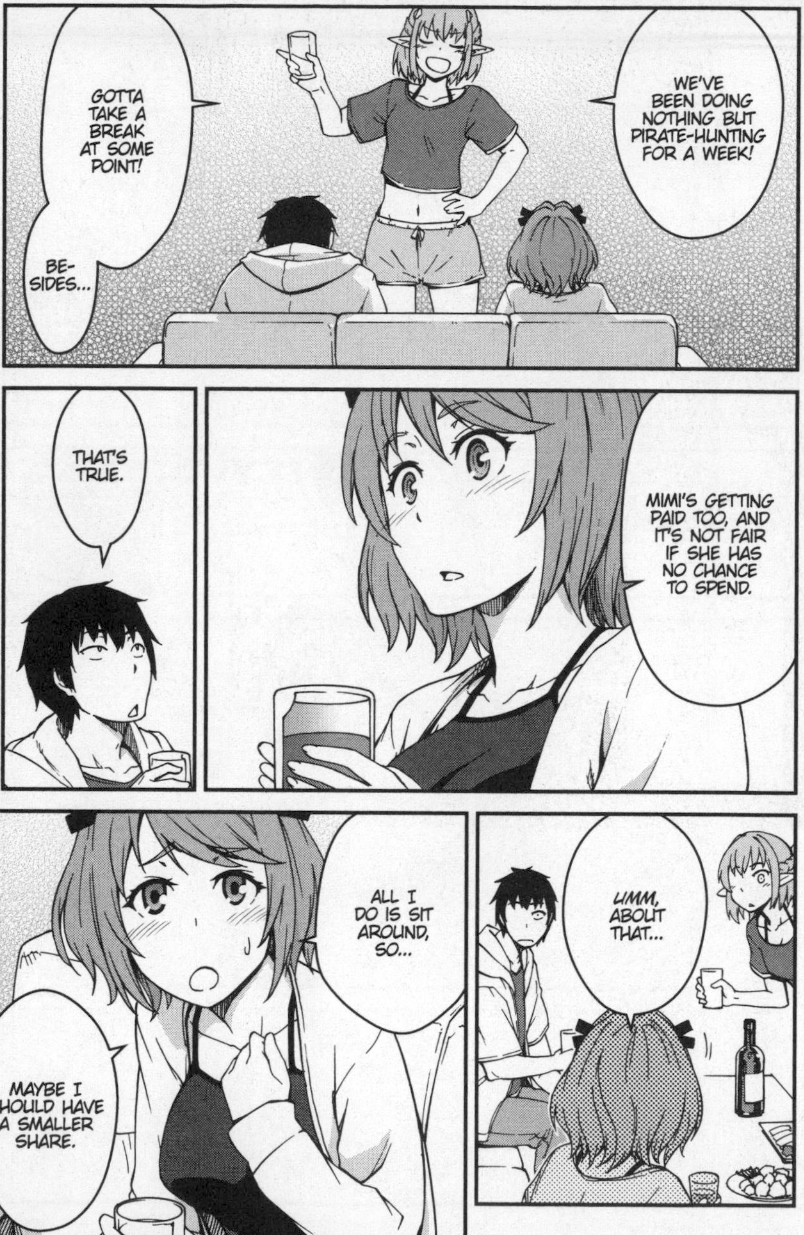
WE'VE BEEN DOING NOTHING BUT PIRATE-HUNTING FOR A WEEK!
GOTTA TAKE A BREAK AT SOME POINT!
BE-SIDES...
MIMI'S GETTING PAID TOO, AND IT'S NOT FAIR IF SHE HAS NO CHANCE TO SPEND.
THAT'S TRUE.
UMM, ABOUT THAT...
ALL I DO IS SIT AROUND, SO...
MAYBE I SHOULD HAVE A SMALLER SHARE.

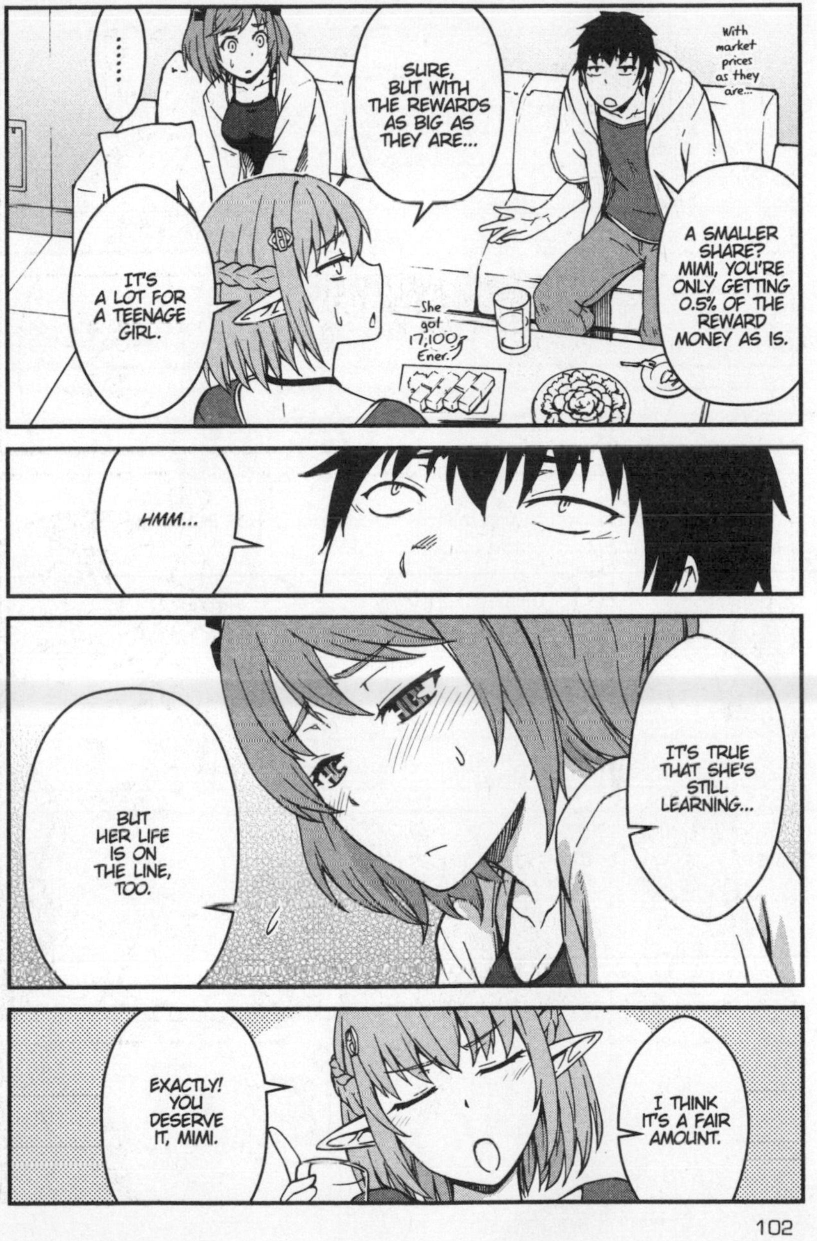
With market prices as they are...
SURE, BUT WITH THE REWARDS AS BIG AS THEY ARE...
......
A SMALLER SHARE? MIMI, YOU'RE ONLY GETTING 0.5% OF THE REWARD MONEY AS IS.
She got 17,100 Ener.
IT'S A LOT FOR A TEENAGE GIRL.
HMM...
IT'S TRUE THAT SHE'S STILL LEARNING...
BUT HER LIFE IS ON THE LINE, TOO.
I THINK IT'S A FAIR AMOUNT.
EXACTLY! YOU DESERVE IT, MIMI.

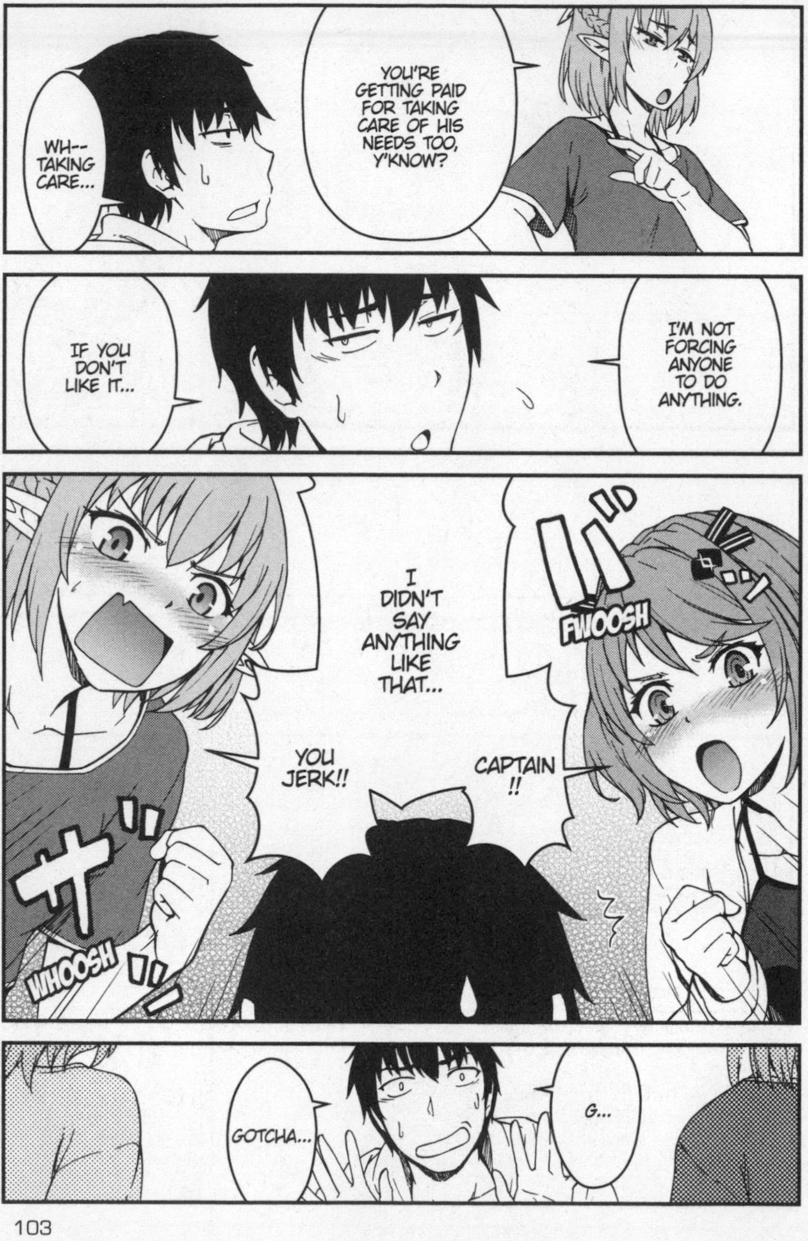
YOU'RE GETTING PAID FOR TAKING CARE OF HIS NEEDS TOO, Y'KNOW?
WH-- TAKING CARE...
I'M NOT FORCING ANYONE TO DO ANYTHING.
IF YOU DON'T LIKE IT...
FWOOSH
I DIDN'T SAY ANYTHING LIKE THAT...
CAPTAIN !!
YOU JERK!!
WHOOSH
G...
GOTCHA...

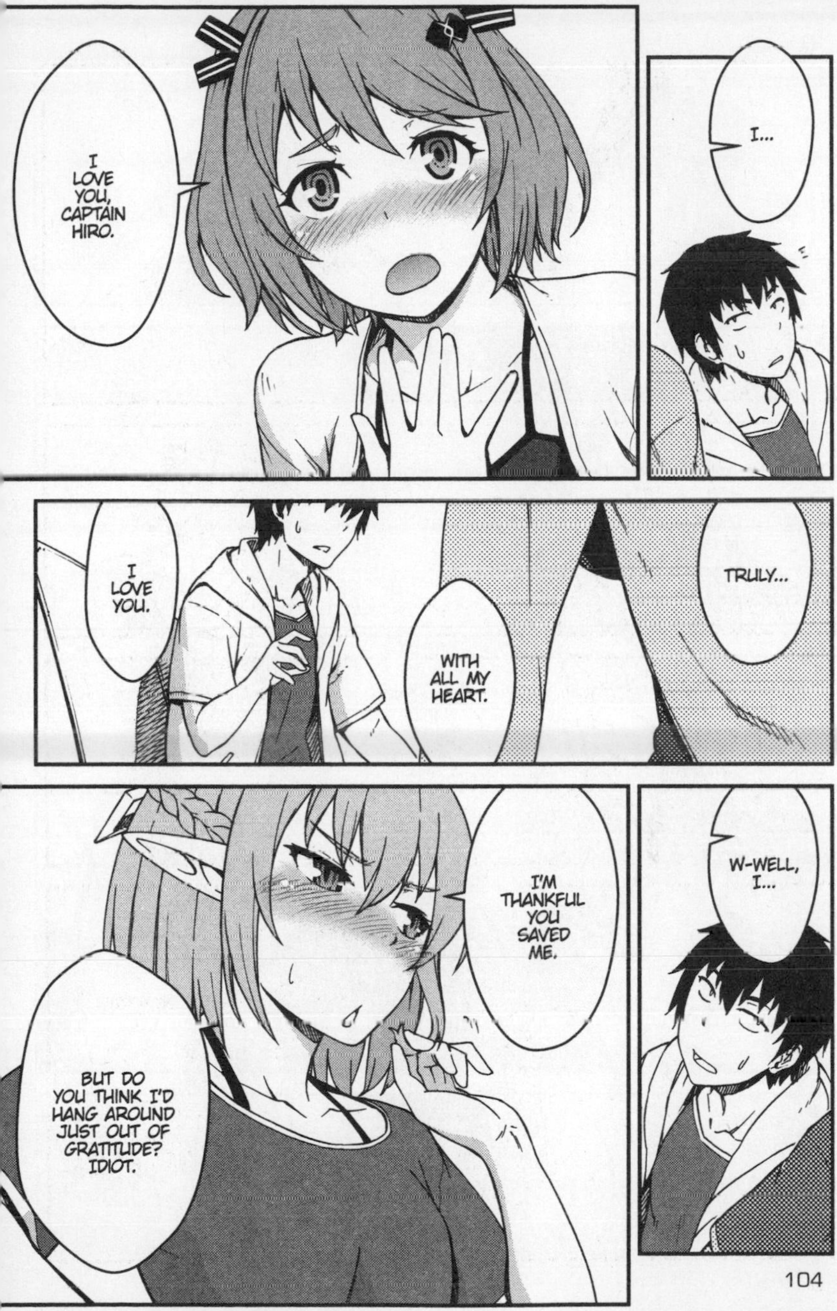
I...
I LOVE YOU, CAPTAIN HIRO.
TRULY...
WITH ALL MY HEART.
I LOVE YOU.
W-WELL, I...
I'M THANKFUL YOU SAVED ME.
BUT DO YOU THINK I'D HANG AROUND JUST OUT OF GRATITUDE? IDIOT.

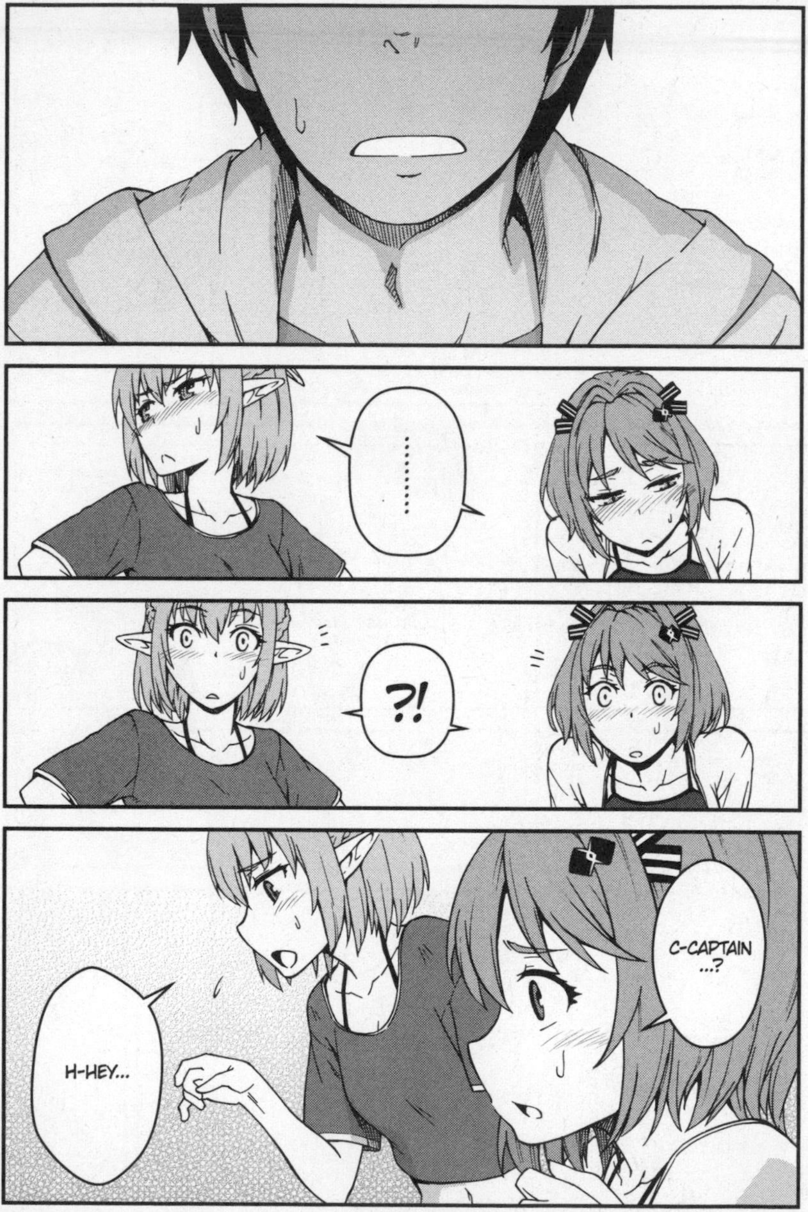
……
?!
C-CAPTAIN ...?
H-HEY...

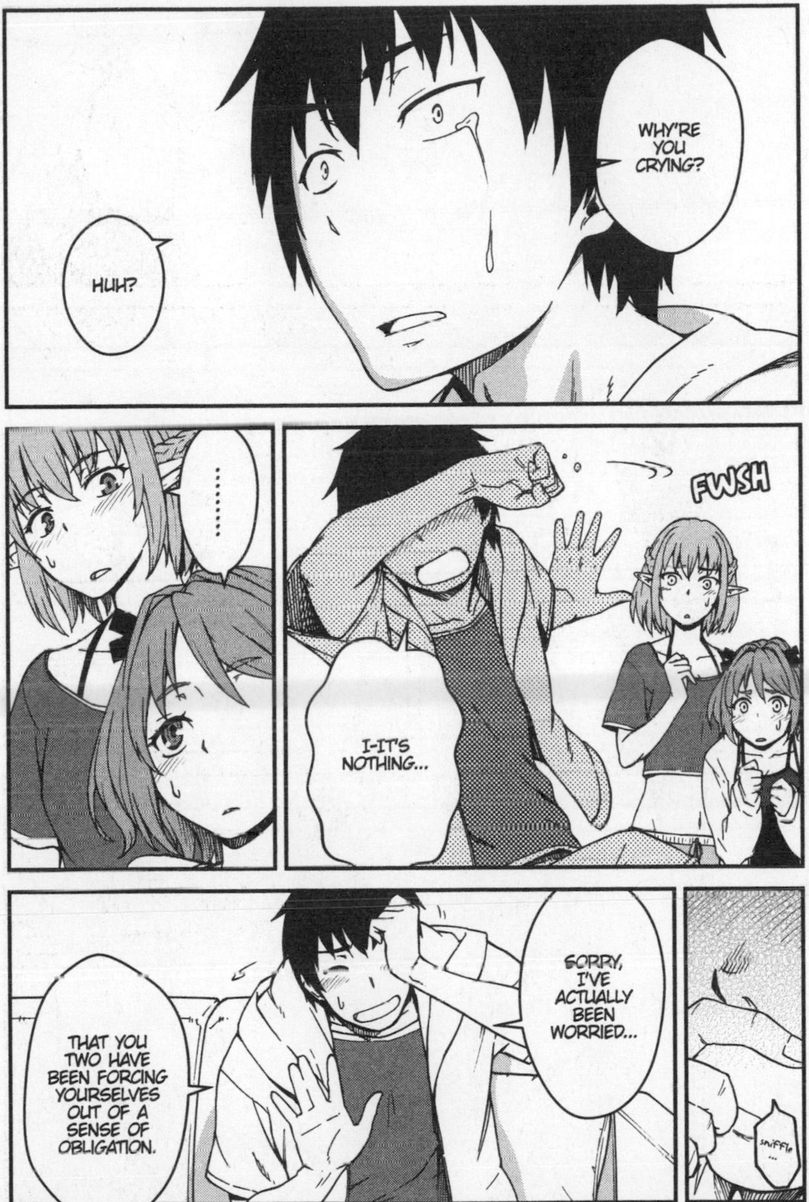
WHY'RE YOU CRYING?
HUH?
FWSH
I-IT'S NOTHING...
......
sniffle ...
SORRY, I'VE ACTUALLY BEEN WORRIED...
THAT YOU TWO HAVE BEEN FORCING YOURSELVES OUT OF A SENSE OF OBLIGATION.

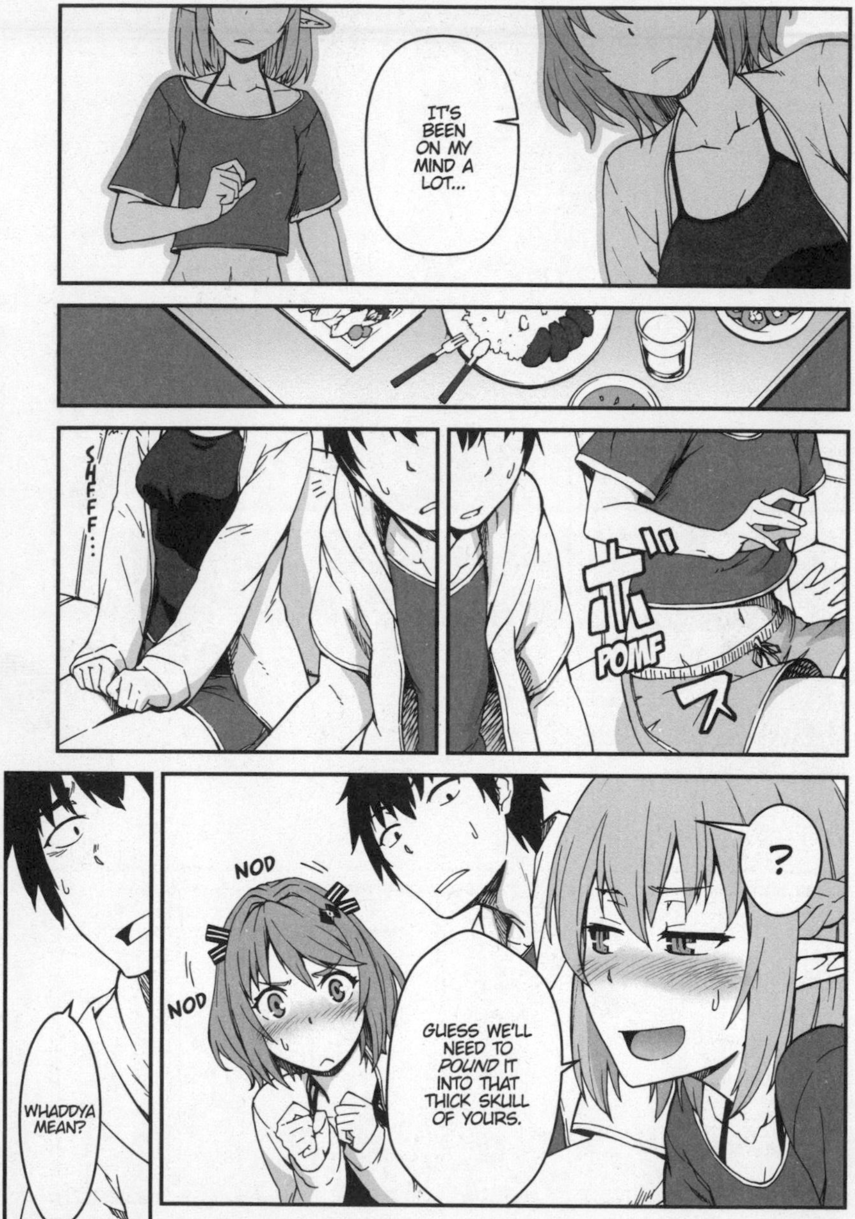
IT'S BEEN ON MY MIND A LOT...
ボス
POMF
SHFFF...
?
NOD
GUESS WE'LL NEED TO *POUND* IT INTO THAT THICK SKULL OF YOURS.
NOD
WHADDYA MEAN?

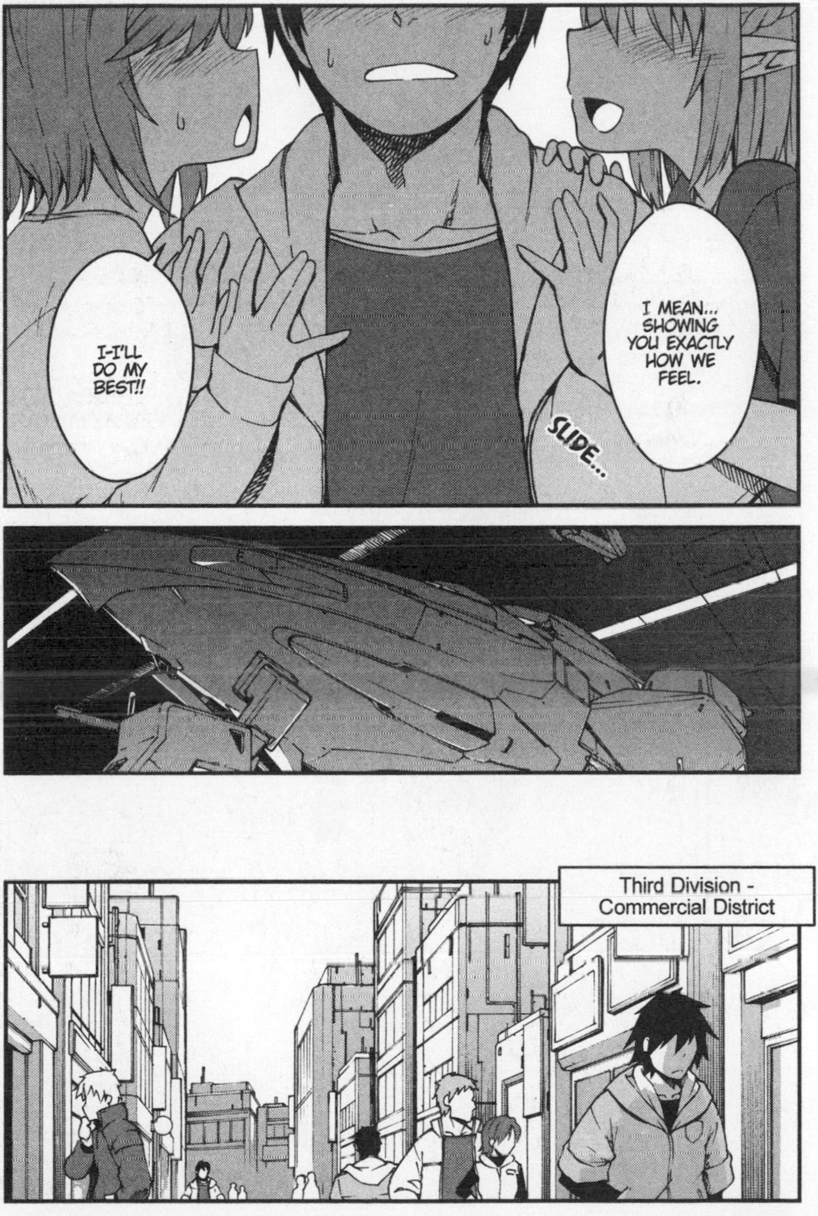
I MEAN... SHOWING YOU EXACTLY HOW WE FEEL.
SLIDE...
I-I'LL DO MY BEST!!
Third Division - Commercial District

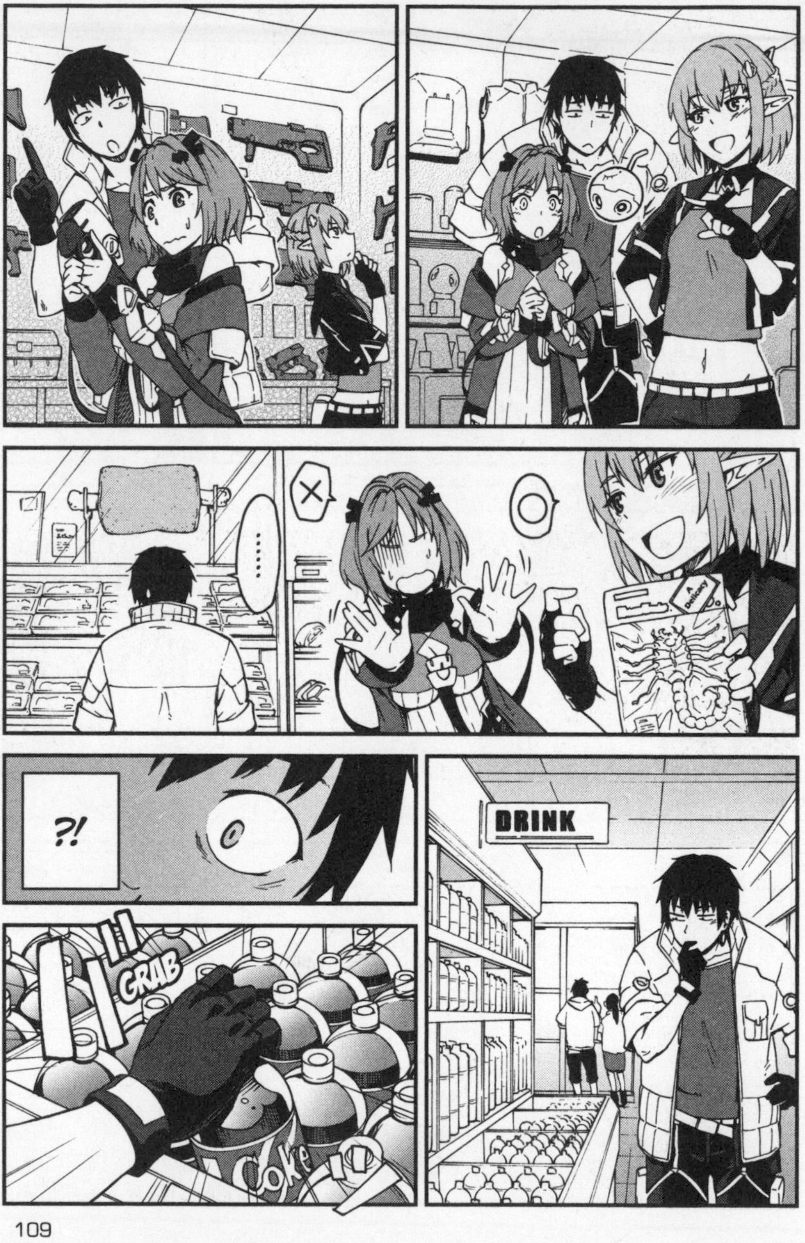
○
A Delicacy
×
......
DRINK
?!
GRAB
Coke

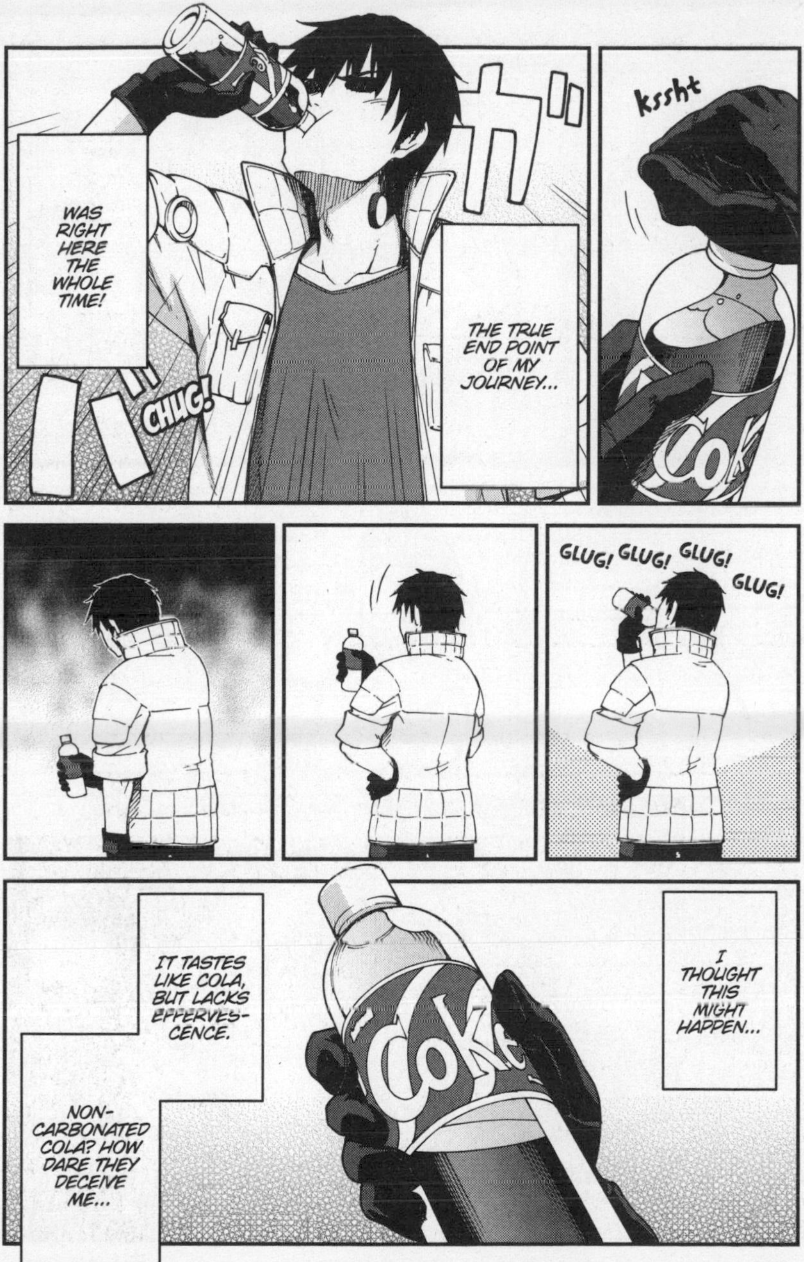
ksssht
Coke
THE TRUE END POINT OF MY JOURNEY...
WAS RIGHT HERE THE WHOLE TIME!
CHUG!
GLUG! GLUG! GLUG! GLUG!
I THOUGHT THIS MIGHT HAPPEN...
Coke
IT TASTES LIKE COLA, BUT LACKS EFFERVES-CENCE.
NON-CARBONATED COLA? HOW DARE THEY DECEIVE ME...

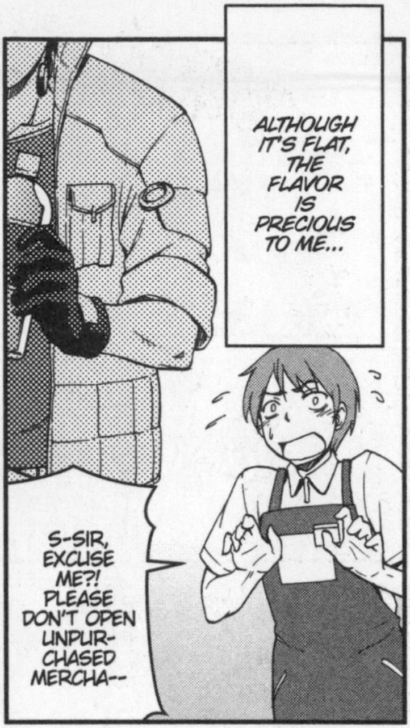
ALTHOUGH IT'S FLAT, THE FLAVOR IS PRECIOUS TO ME...
S-SIR, EXCUSE ME?! PLEASE DON'T OPEN UNPUR-CHASED MERCHA--

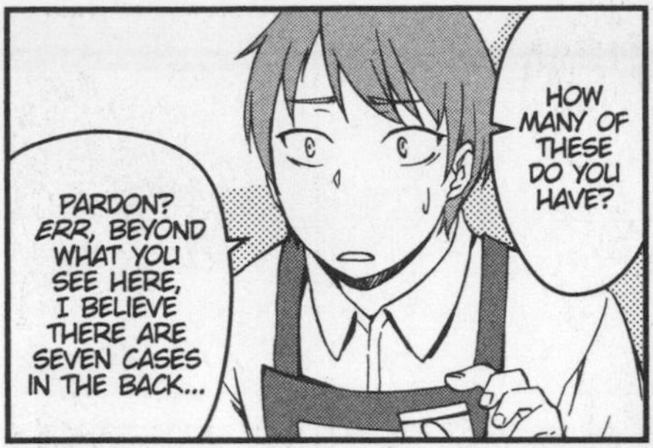
HOW MANY OF THESE DO YOU HAVE?
PARDON? *ERR*, BEYOND WHAT YOU SEE HERE, I BELIEVE THERE ARE SEVEN CASES IN THE BACK...

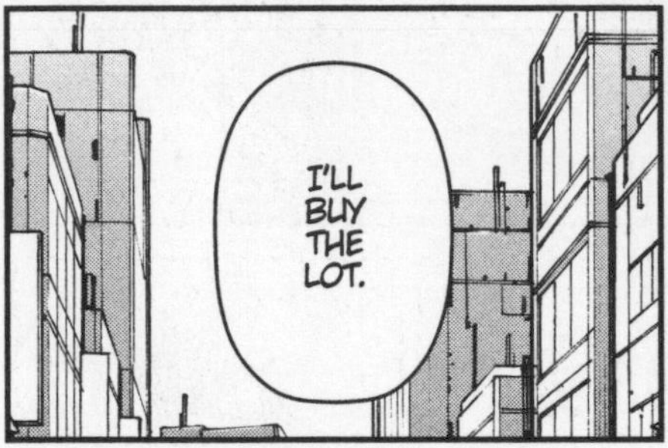
I'LL BUY THE LOT.

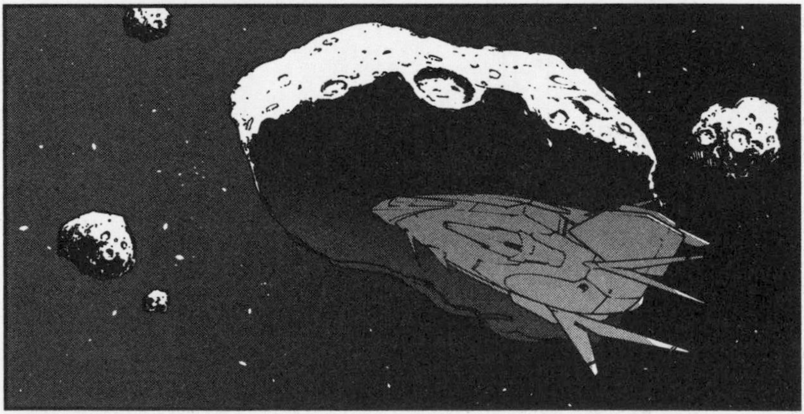

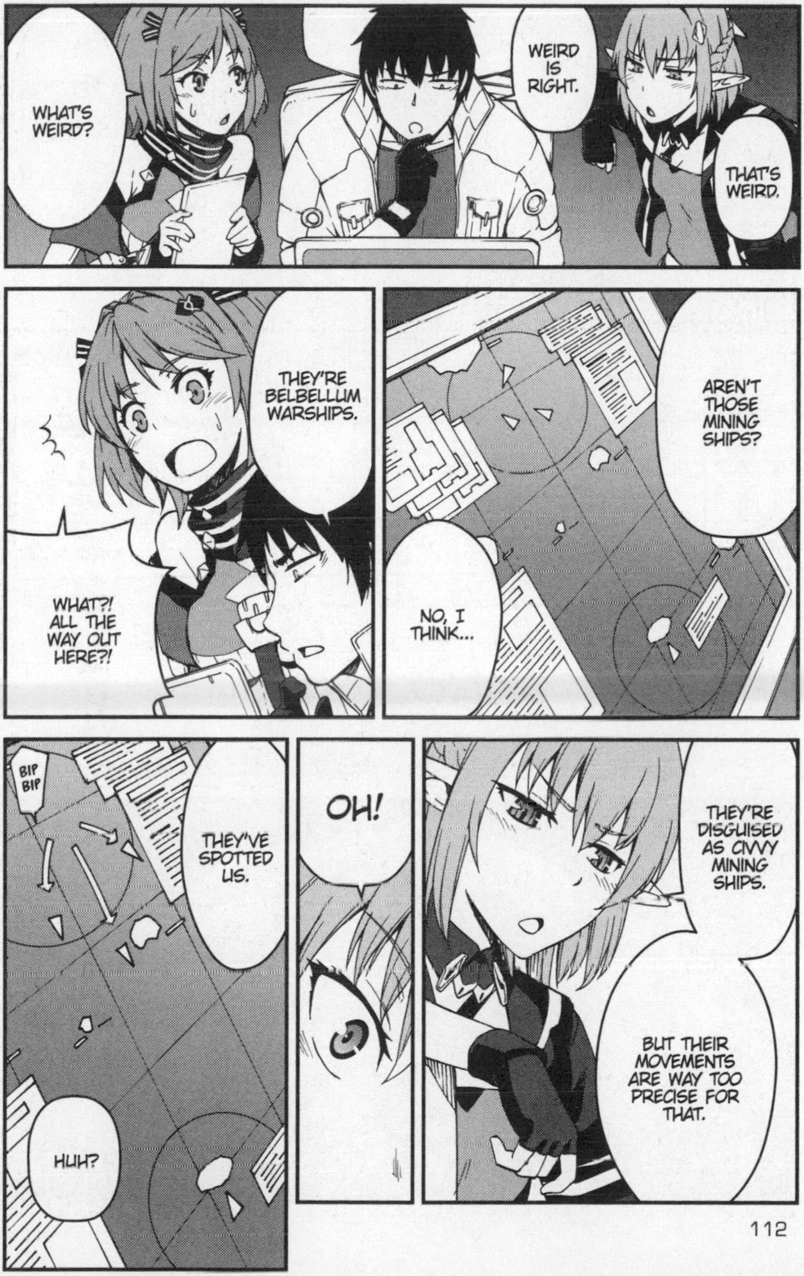
THAT'S WEIRD.
WEIRD IS RIGHT.
WHAT'S WEIRD?
AREN'T THOSE MINING SHIPS?
NO, I THINK...
THEY'RE BELBELLUM WARSHIPS.
WHAT?! ALL THE WAY OUT HERE?!
THEY'RE DISGUISED AS CIVVY MINING SHIPS.
BUT THEIR MOVEMENTS ARE WAY TOO PRECISE FOR THAT.
OH!
BIP BIP
THEY'VE SPOTTED US.
HUH?

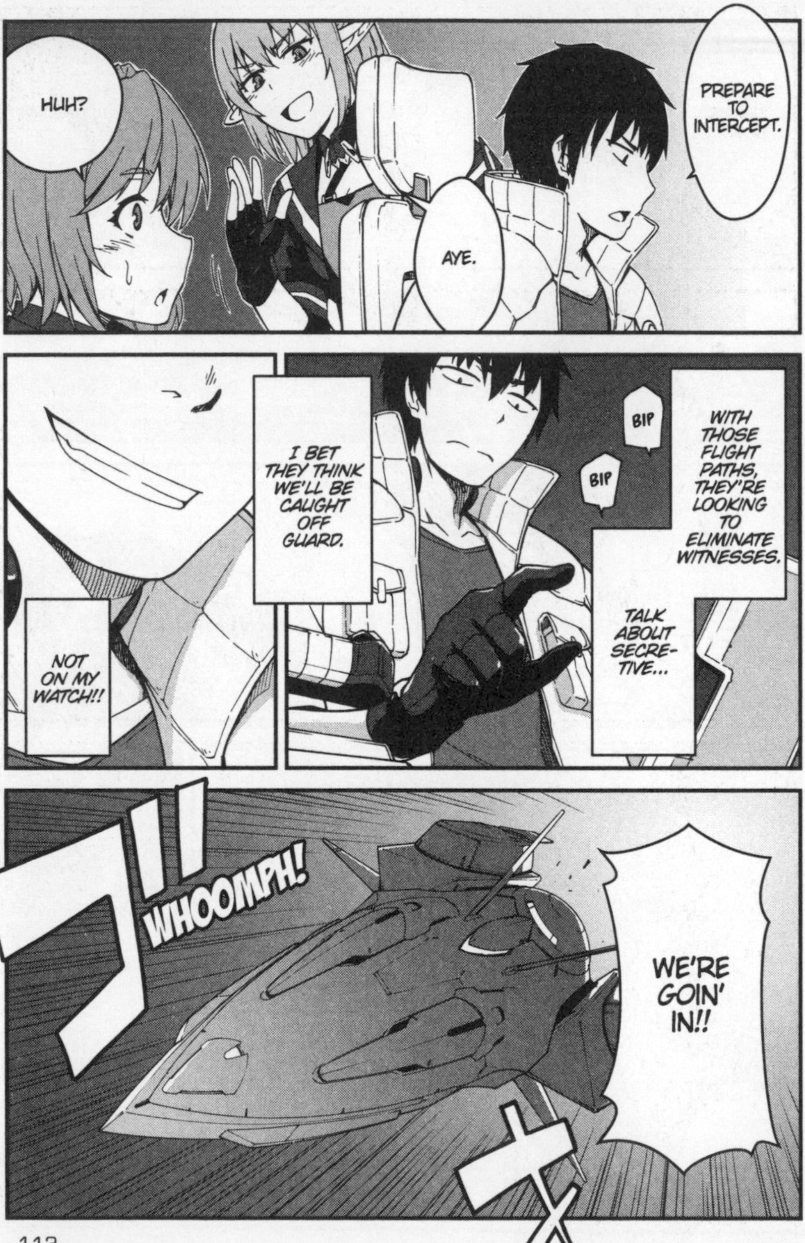
PREPARE TO INTERCEPT.
AYE.
HUH?
WITH THOSE FLIGHT PATHS, THEY'RE LOOKING TO ELIMINATE WITNESSES.
BIP
BIP
TALK ABOUT SECRETIVE...
I BET THEY THINK WE'LL BE CAUGHT OFF GUARD.
NOT ON MY WATCH!!
WE'RE GOIN' IN!!
WHOOMPH!

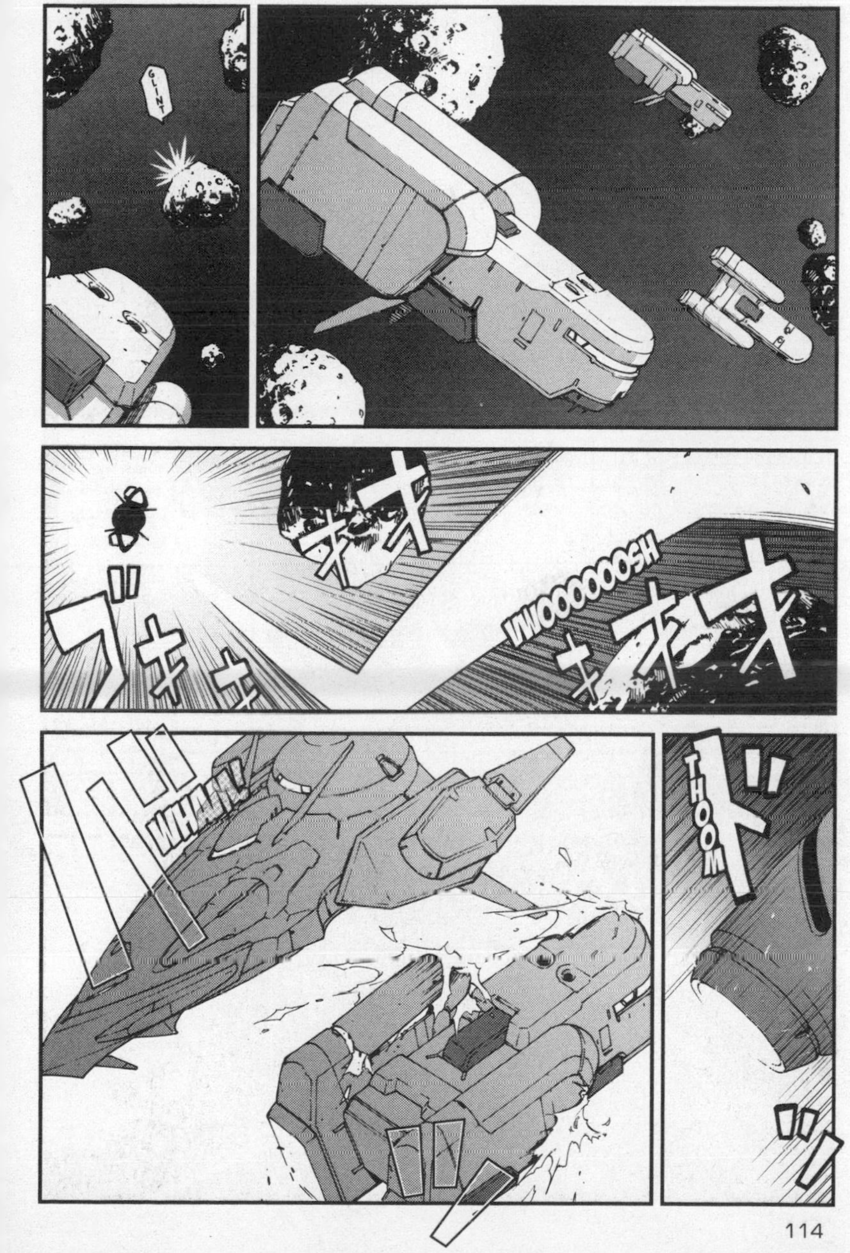
GLINT
WOOOOOOOSH
THOOM
WHAM!

GA-CHUNK
TYOOM
GRAK
BSHEWN!!
CRAK
GA-CHUNK
GA-THUNK
TYOOM
PTSWEN
TSEW

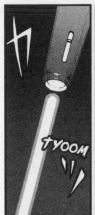

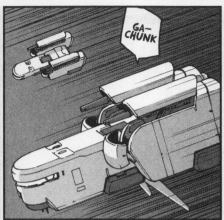

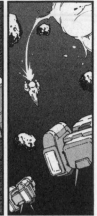

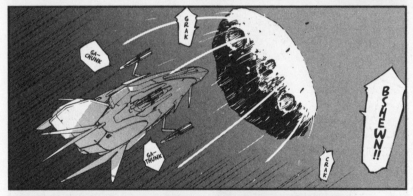

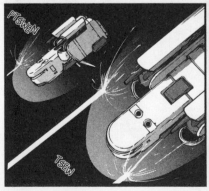

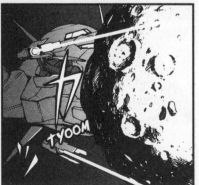

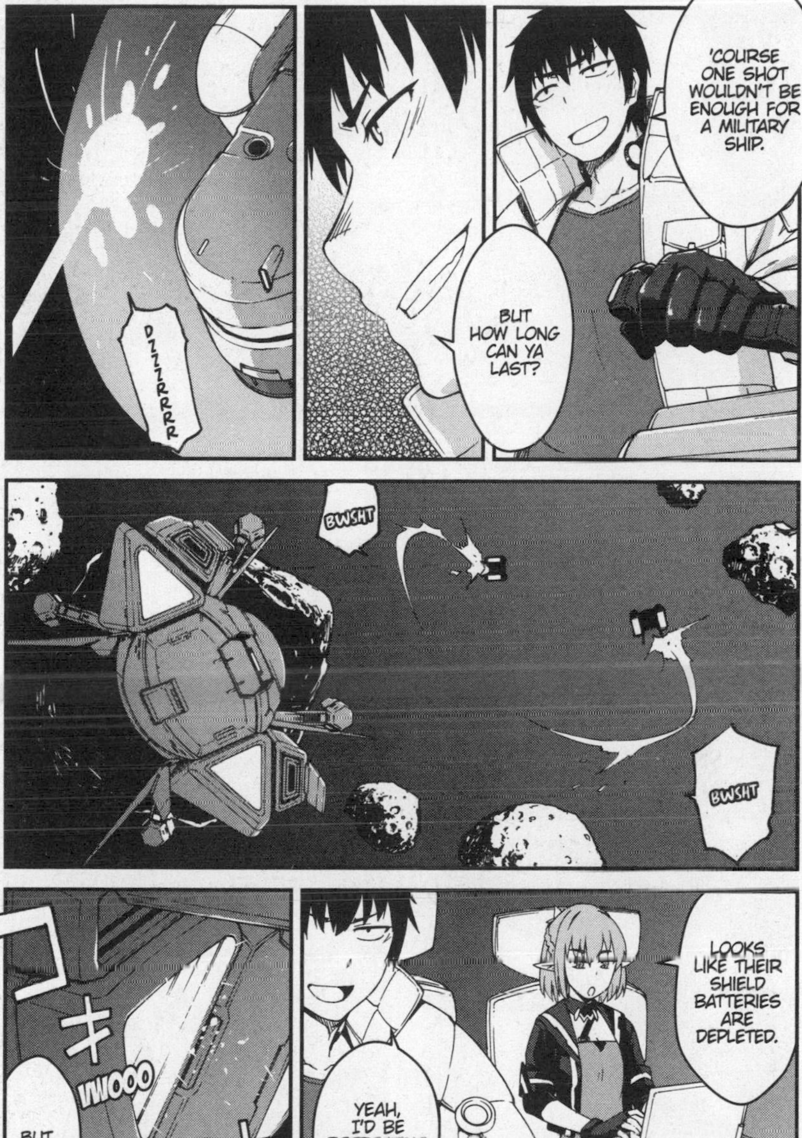
'COURSE ONE SHOT WOULDN'T BE ENOUGH FOR A MILITARY SHIP.
BUT HOW LONG CAN YA LAST?
DZZZRRRR
BWSHT
BWSHT
LOOKS LIKE THEIR SHIELD BATTERIES ARE DEPLETED.
YEAH, I'D BE RETREATING AS WELL.
VWOOO
BUT...

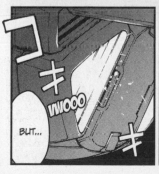

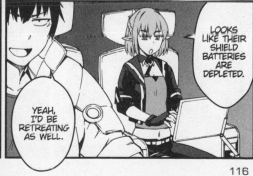

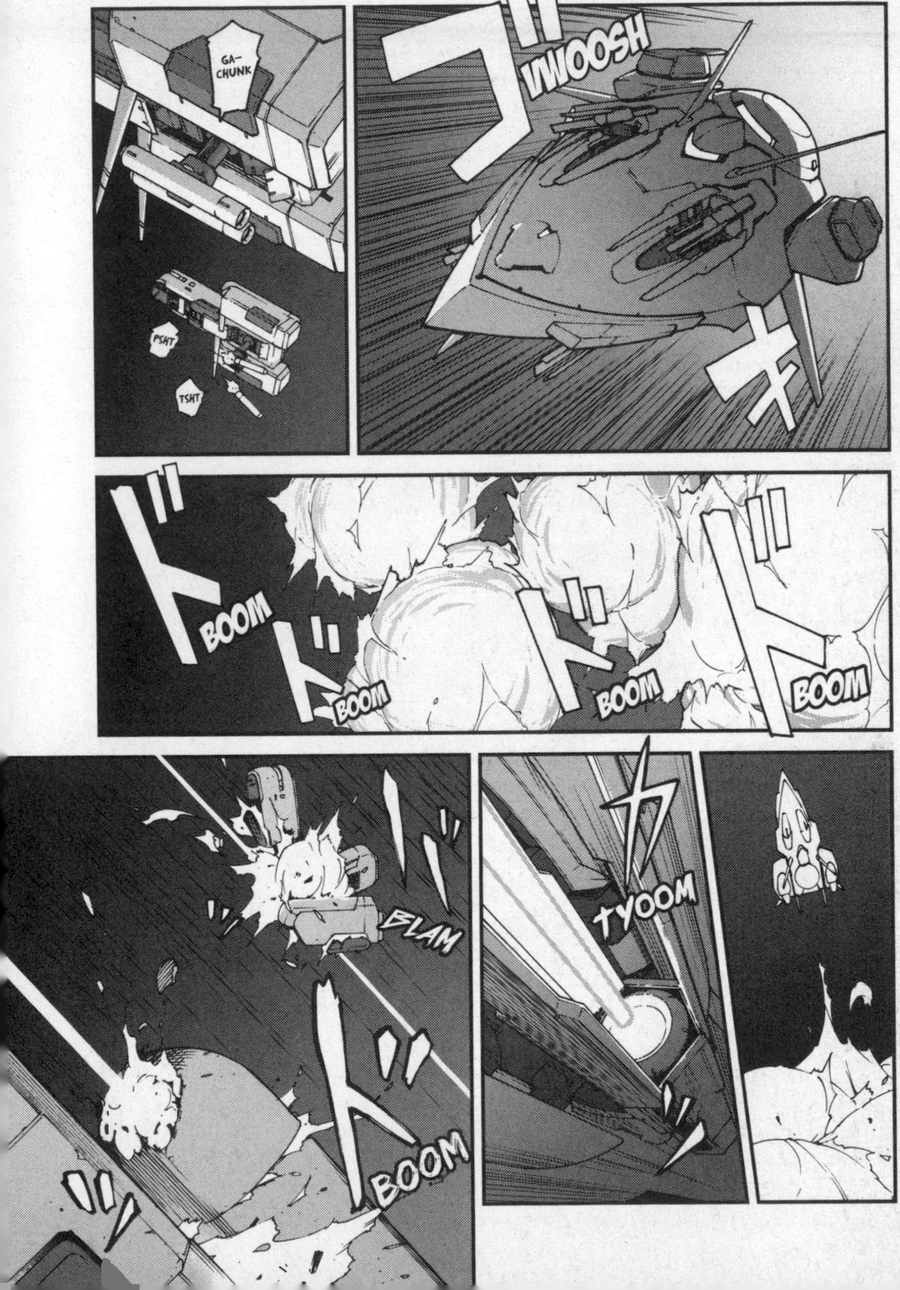

ゴ
VWOOSH
オ
GA-CHUNK
PSHT
TSHT
ド
BOOM
ド
BOOM
ド
BOOM
ド
BOOM
カ
TYOOM
BLAM
ド
BOOM

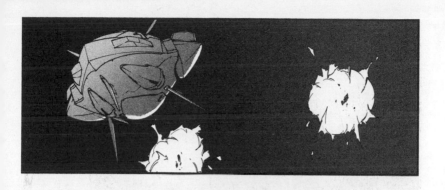

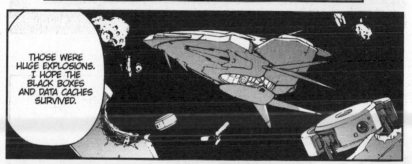

THOSE WERE HUGE EXPLOSIONS. I HOPE THE BLACK BOXES AND DATA CACHES SURVIVED.
IS THAT DATA IMPORTANT?
THE IMPERIAL FLEET WILL PAY BIG TIME FOR MILITARY DATA!
AND BE-SIDES...
I'VE GOT A CONNECTION IN THE FLEET.

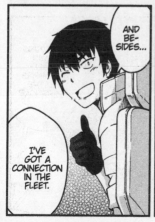

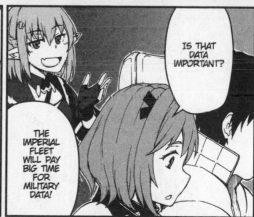

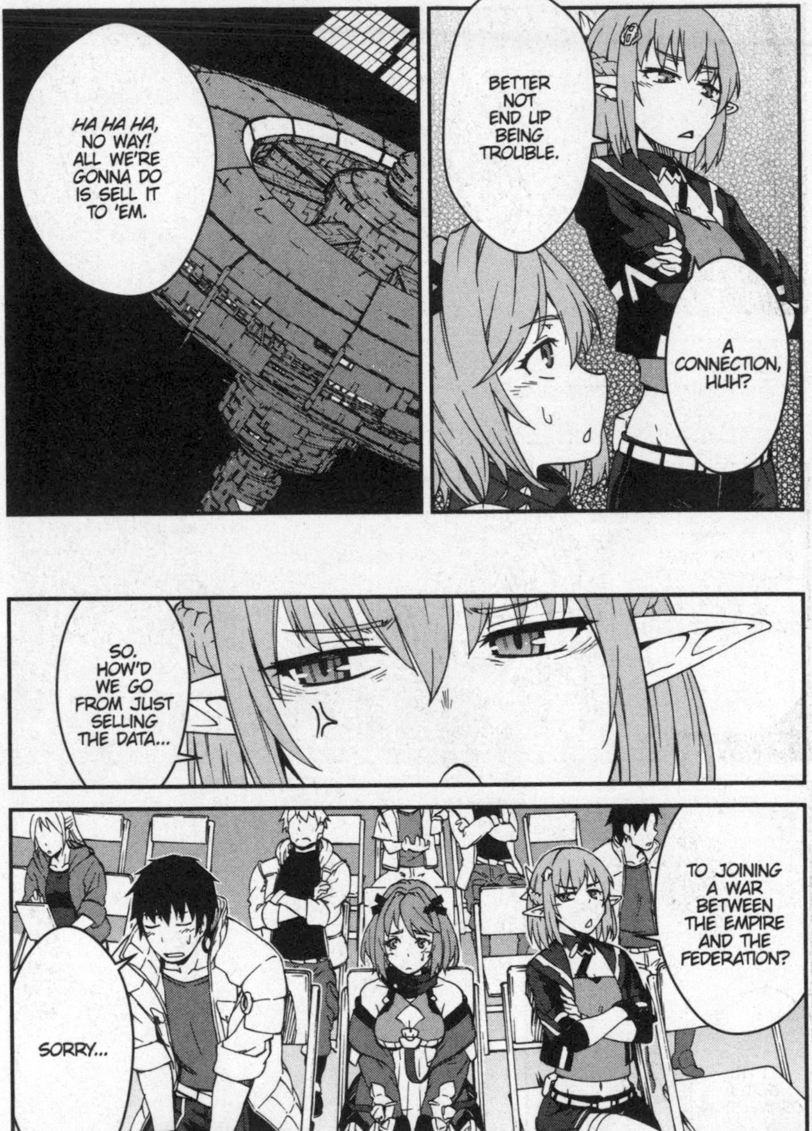
A CONNECTION, HUH?
BETTER NOT END UP BEING TROUBLE.
HA HA HA, NO WAY! ALL WE'RE GONNA DO IS SELL IT TO 'EM.
SO. HOW'D WE GO FROM JUST SELLING THE DATA...
TO JOINING A WAR BETWEEN THE EMPIRE AND THE FEDERATION?
SORRY...

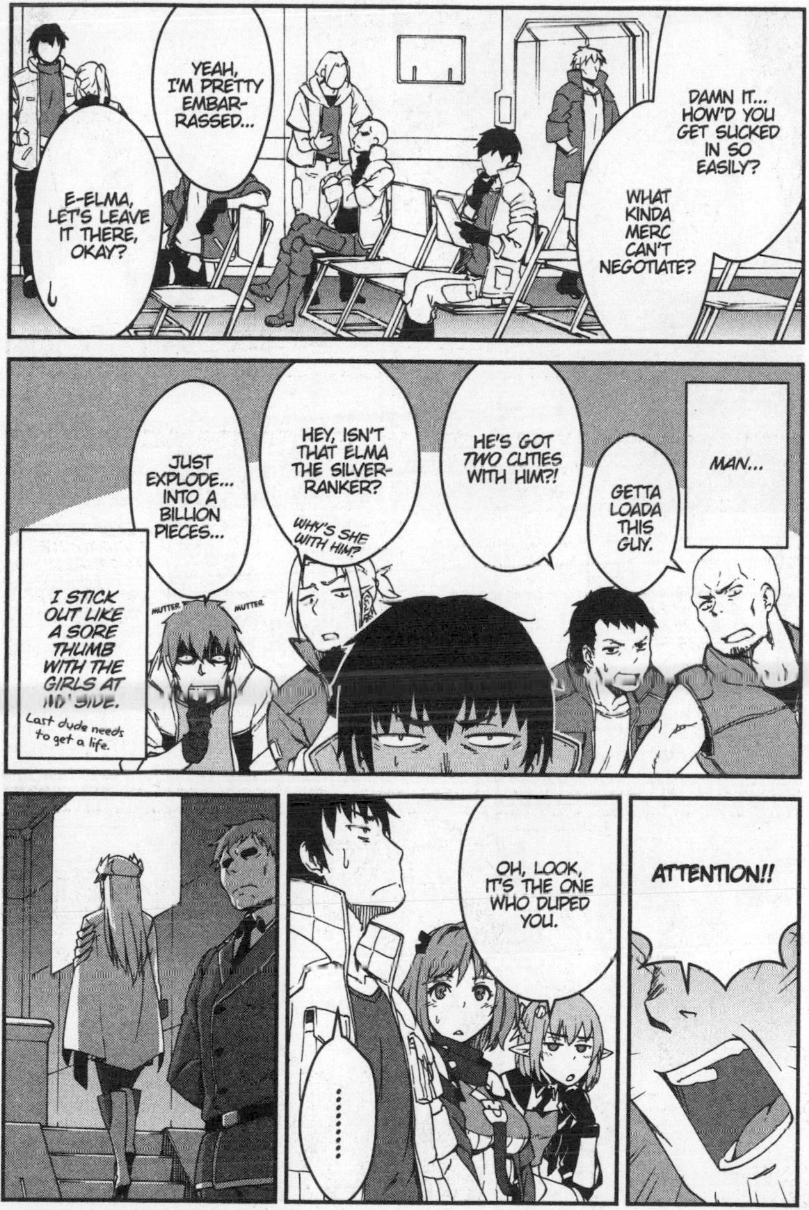
DAMN IT... HOW'D YOU GET SUCKED IN SO EASILY?
WHAT KINDA MERC CAN'T NEGOTIATE?
YEAH, I'M PRETTY EMBARRASSED...
E-ELMA, LET'S LEAVE IT THERE, OKAY?
MAN...
GETTA LOADA THIS GUY.
HE'S GOT TWO CUTIES WITH HIM?!
HEY, ISN'T THAT ELMA THE SILVER-RANKER?
WHY'S SHE WITH HIM?
JUST EXPLODE... INTO A BILLION PIECES...
MUTTER MUTTER
I STICK OUT LIKE A SORE THUMB WITH THE GIRLS AT MY SIDE.
Last dude needs to get a life.
ATTENTION!!
OH, LOOK, IT'S THE ONE WHO DUPED YOU.
......

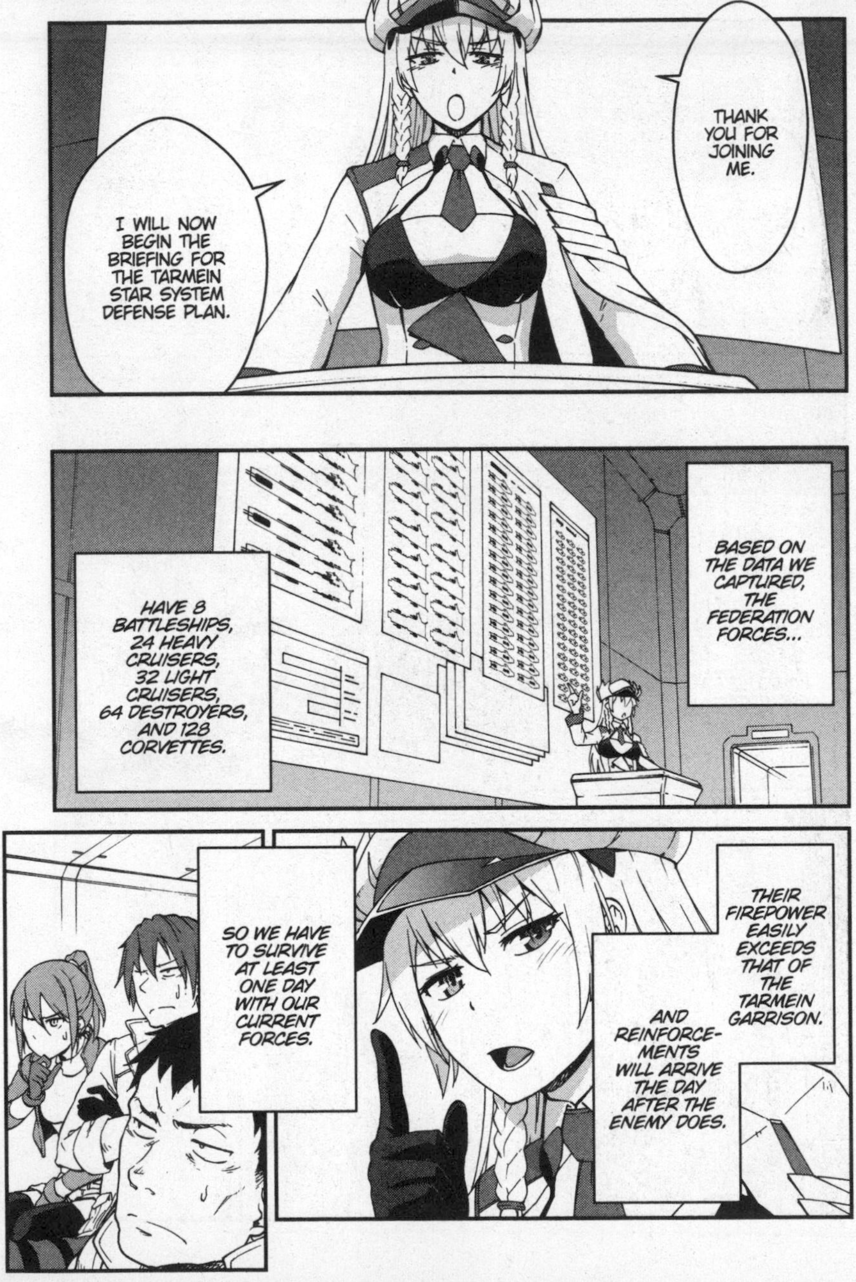
THANK YOU FOR JOINING ME.
I WILL NOW BEGIN THE BRIEFING FOR THE TARMEIN STAR SYSTEM DEFENSE PLAN.
BASED ON THE DATA WE CAPTURED, THE FEDERATION FORCES...
HAVE 8 BATTLESHIPS, 24 HEAVY CRUISERS, 32 LIGHT CRUISERS, 64 DESTROYERS, AND 128 CORVETTES.
THEIR FIREPOWER EASILY EXCEEDS THAT OF THE TARMEIN GARRISON.
AND REINFORCE-MENTS WILL ARRIVE THE DAY AFTER THE ENEMY DOES.
SO WE HAVE TO SURVIVE AT LEAST ONE DAY WITH OUR CURRENT FORCES.

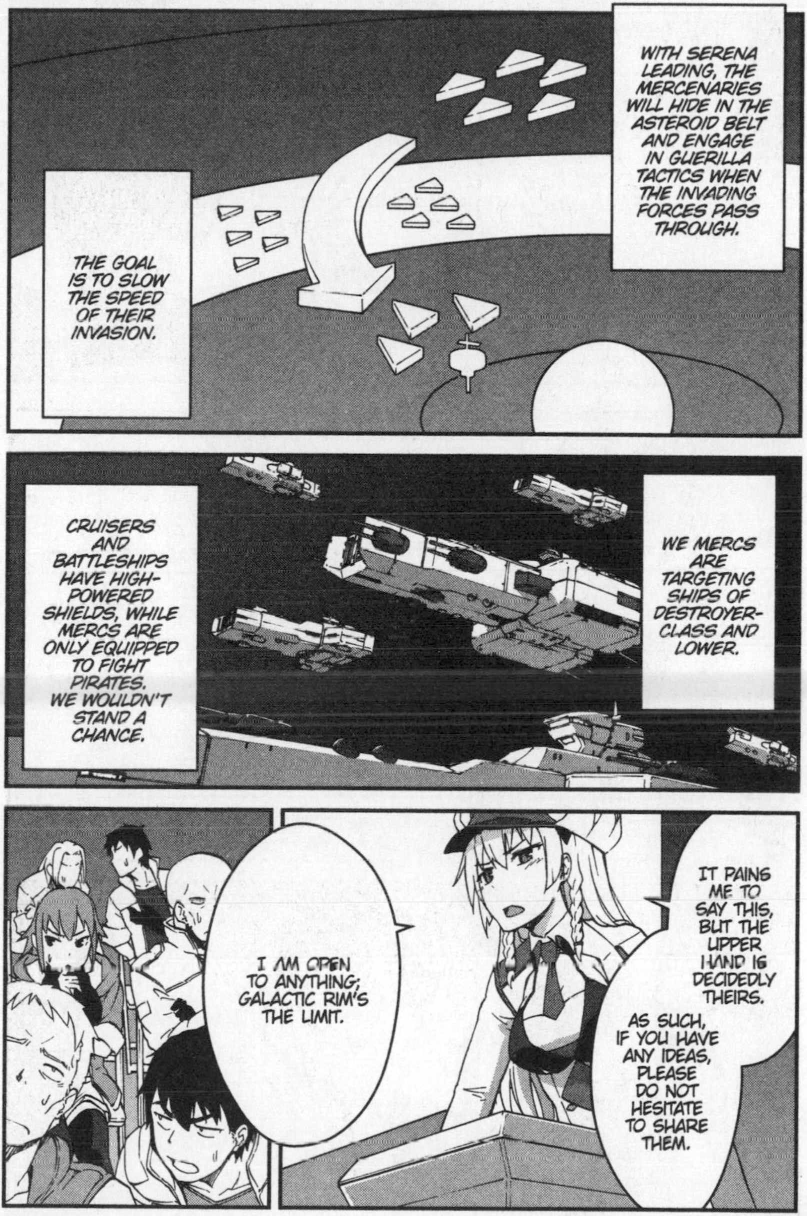
WITH SERENA LEADING, THE MERCENARIES WILL HIDE IN THE ASTEROID BELT AND ENGAGE IN GUERILLA TACTICS WHEN THE INVADING FORCES PASS THROUGH.
THE GOAL IS TO SLOW THE SPEED OF THEIR INVASION.
WE MERCS ARE TARGETING SHIPS OF DESTROYER-CLASS AND LOWER.
CRUISERS AND BATTLESHIPS HAVE HIGH-POWERED SHIELDS, WHILE MERCS ARE ONLY EQUIPPED TO FIGHT PIRATES. WE WOULDN'T STAND A CHANCE.
IT PAINS ME TO SAY THIS, BUT THE UPPER HAND IS DECIDEDLY THEIRS.
AS SUCH, IF YOU HAVE ANY IDEAS, PLEASE DO NOT HESITATE TO SHARE THEM.
I AM OPEN TO ANYTHING; GALACTIC RIM'S THE LIMIT.

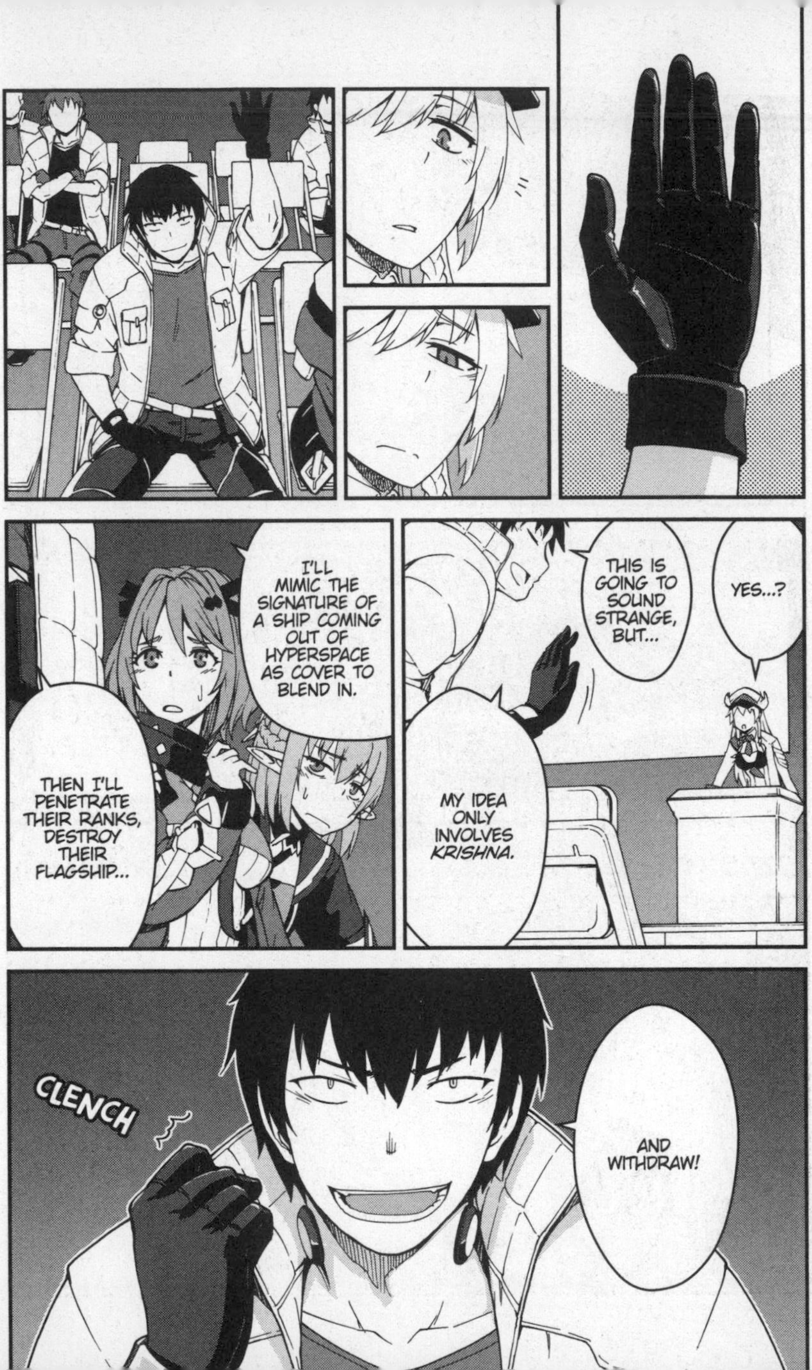
YES...?
THIS IS GOING TO SOUND STRANGE, BUT...
MY IDEA ONLY INVOLVES *KRISHNA.*
I'LL MIMIC THE SIGNATURE OF A SHIP COMING OUT OF HYPERSPACE AS COVER TO BLEND IN.
THEN I'LL PENETRATE THEIR RANKS, DESTROY THEIR FLAGSHIP...
AND WITHDRAW!
CLENCH

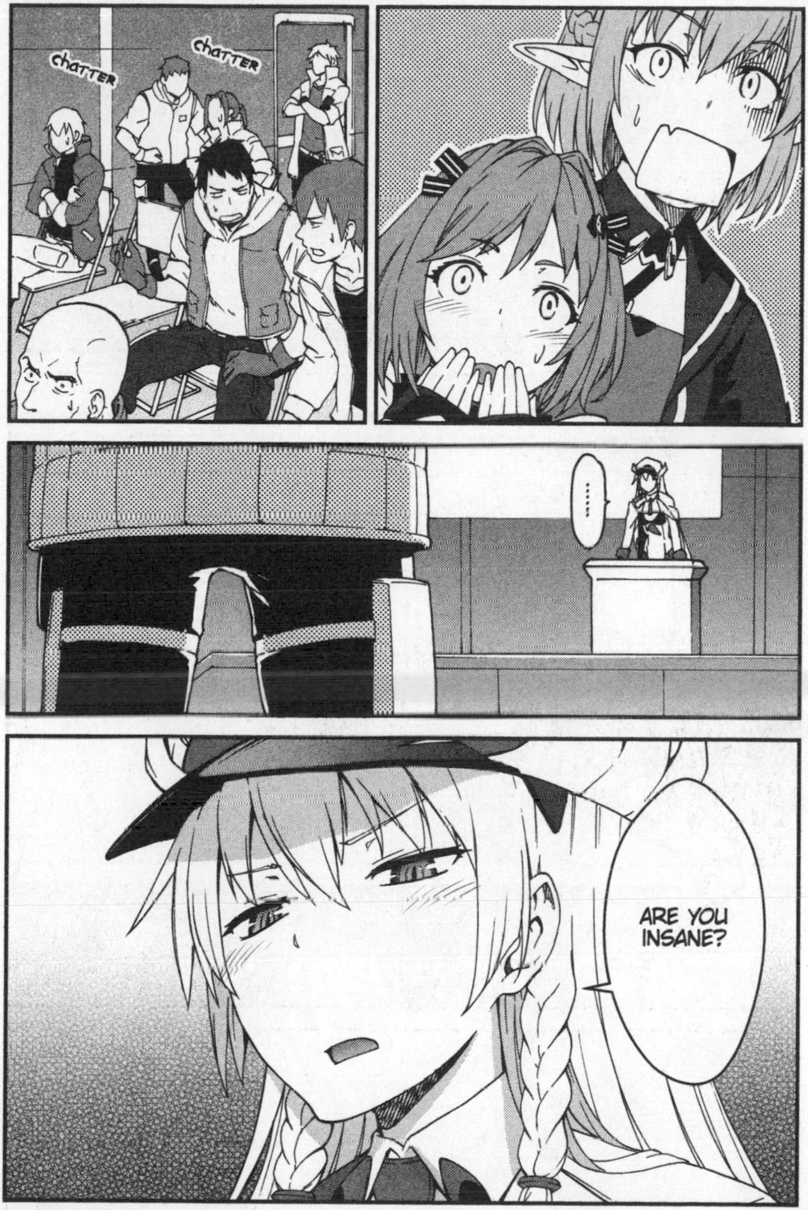
CHATTER
CHATTER
......
ARE YOU INSANE?

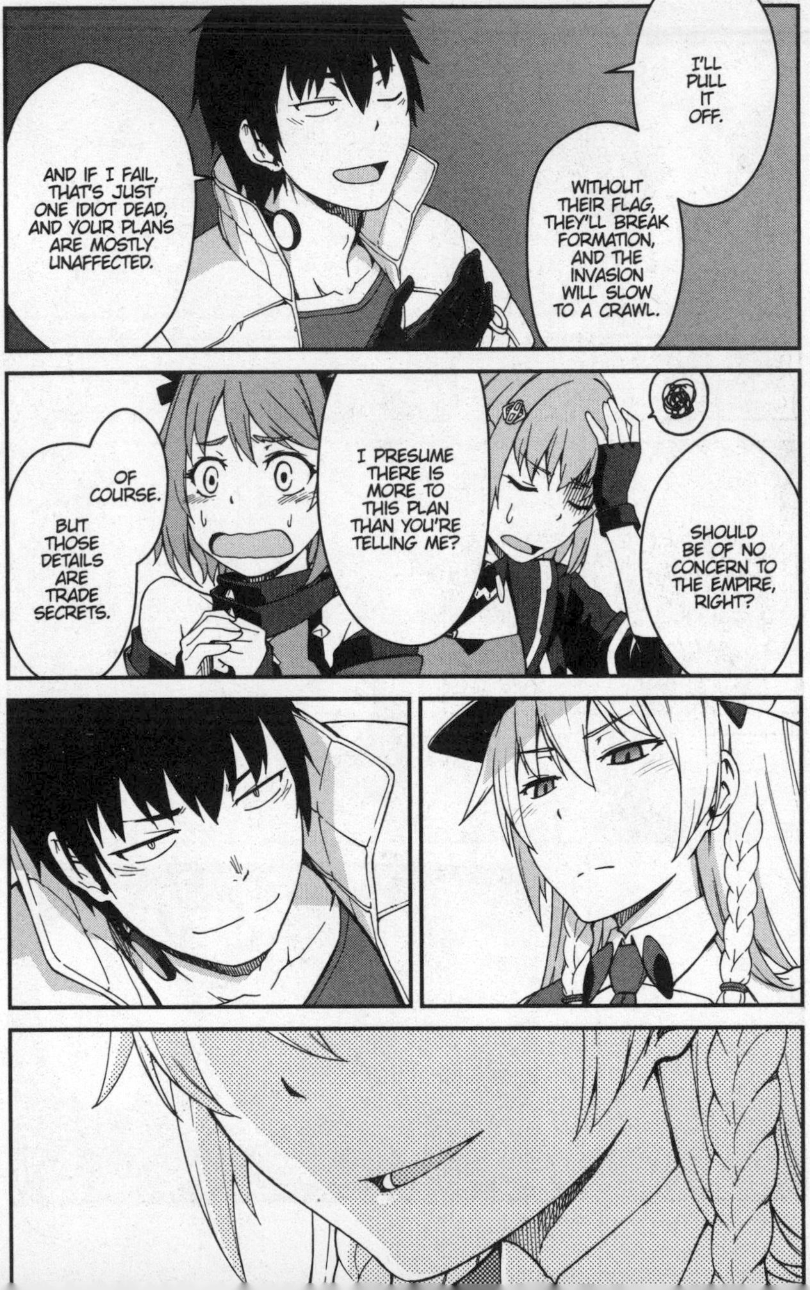
I'LL PULL IT OFF.
WITHOUT THEIR FLAG, THEY'LL BREAK FORMATION, AND THE INVASION WILL SLOW TO A CRAWL.
AND IF I FAIL, THAT'S JUST ONE IDIOT DEAD, AND YOUR PLANS ARE MOSTLY UNAFFECTED.
SHOULD BE OF NO CONCERN TO THE EMPIRE, RIGHT?
I PRESUME THERE IS MORE TO THIS PLAN THAN YOU'RE TELLING ME?
OF COURSE.
BUT THOSE DETAILS ARE TRADE SECRETS.

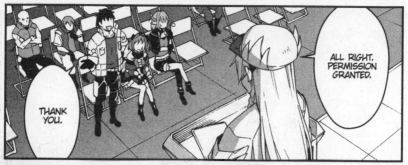

ALL RIGHT. PERMISSION GRANTED.

THANK YOU.

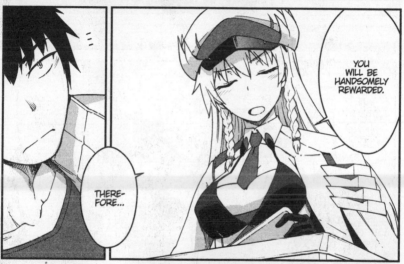

YOU WILL BE HANDSOMELY REWARDED.

THERE- FORE...

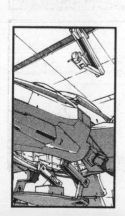

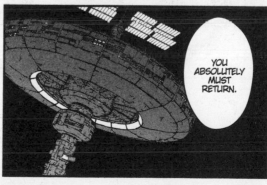

YOU ABSOLUTELY MUST RETURN.

126

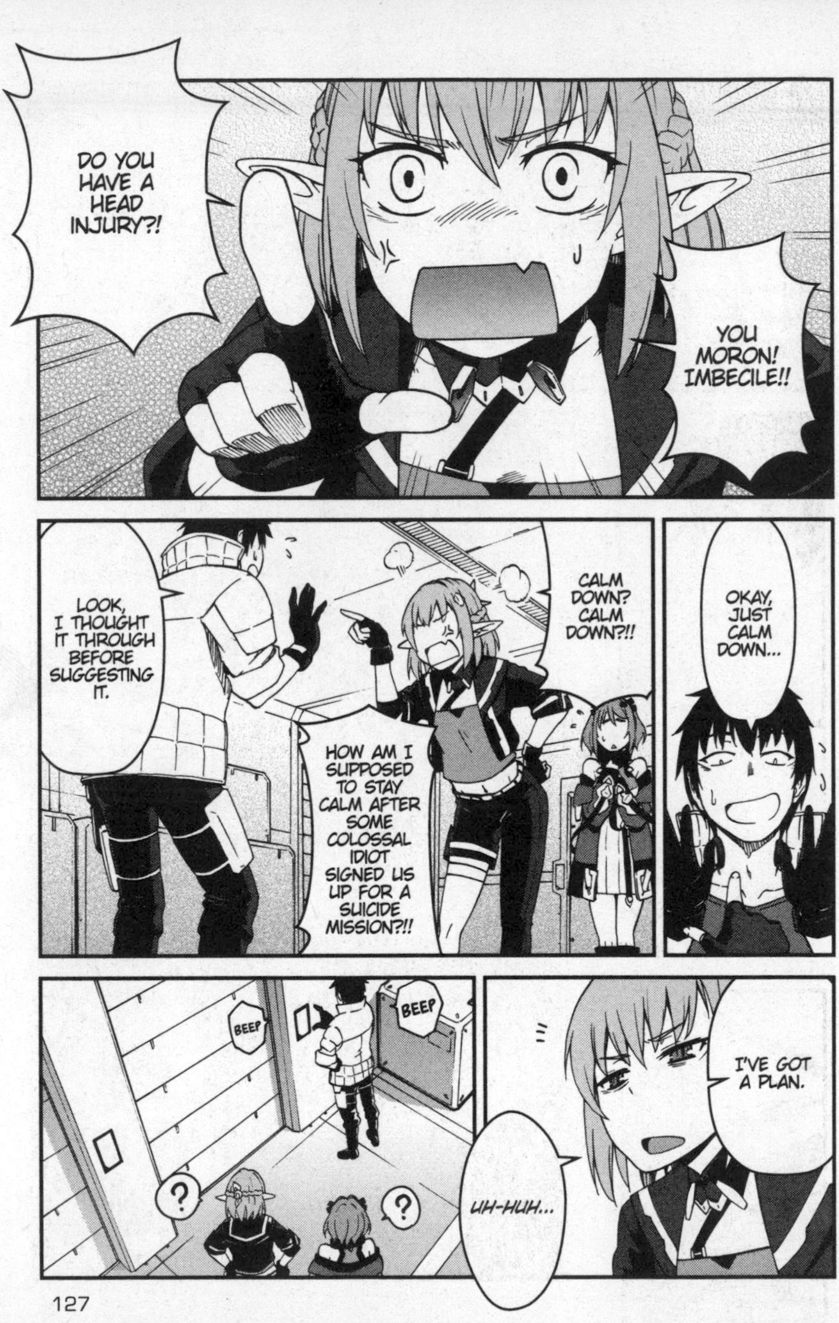
DO YOU HAVE A HEAD INJURY?!
YOU MORON! IMBECILE!!
OKAY, JUST CALM DOWN...
CALM DOWN? CALM DOWN?!!
HOW AM I SUPPOSED TO STAY CALM AFTER SOME COLOSSAL IDIOT SIGNED US UP FOR A SUICIDE MISSION?!!
LOOK, I THOUGHT IT THROUGH BEFORE SUGGESTING IT.
I'VE GOT A PLAN.
UH-HUH...
BEEP
BEEP
?
?

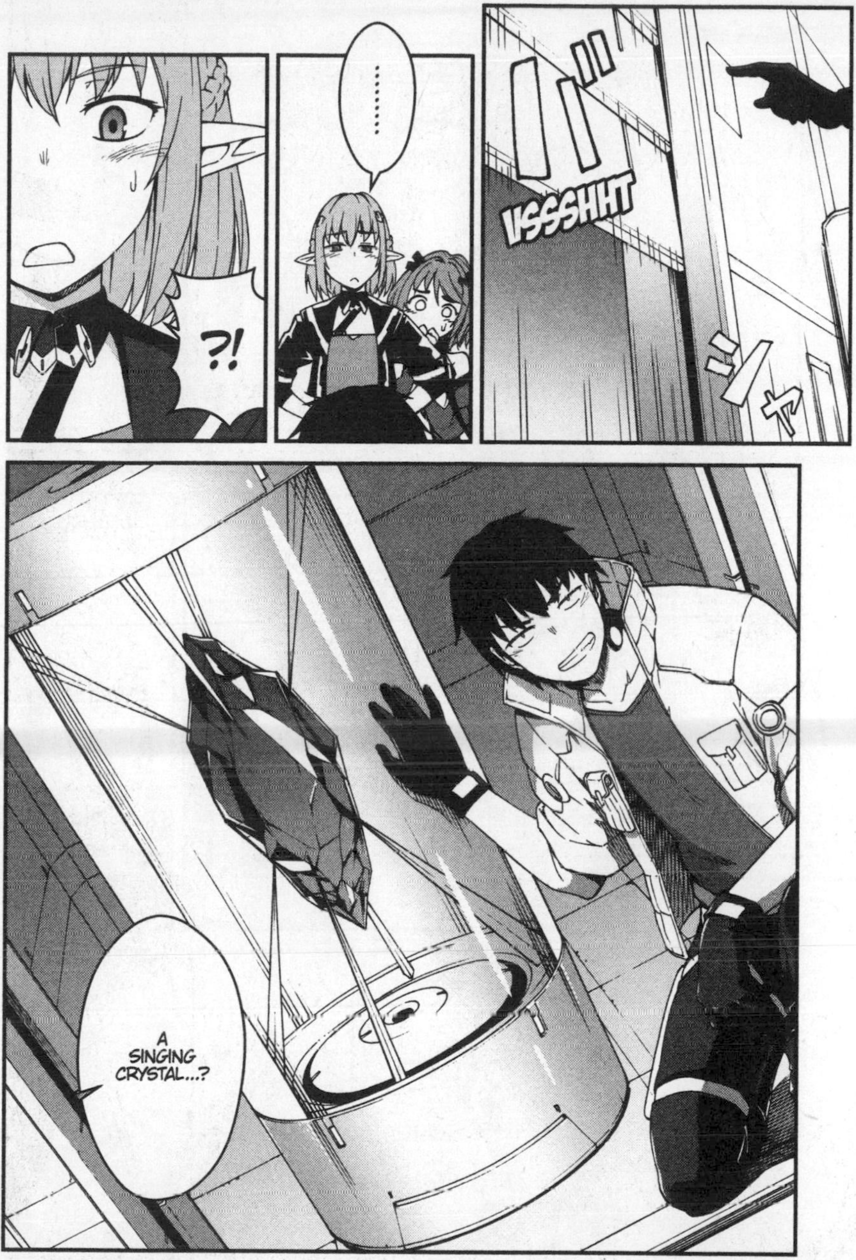

VSSSHHT
シャ
......
?!
A SINGING CRYSTAL...?

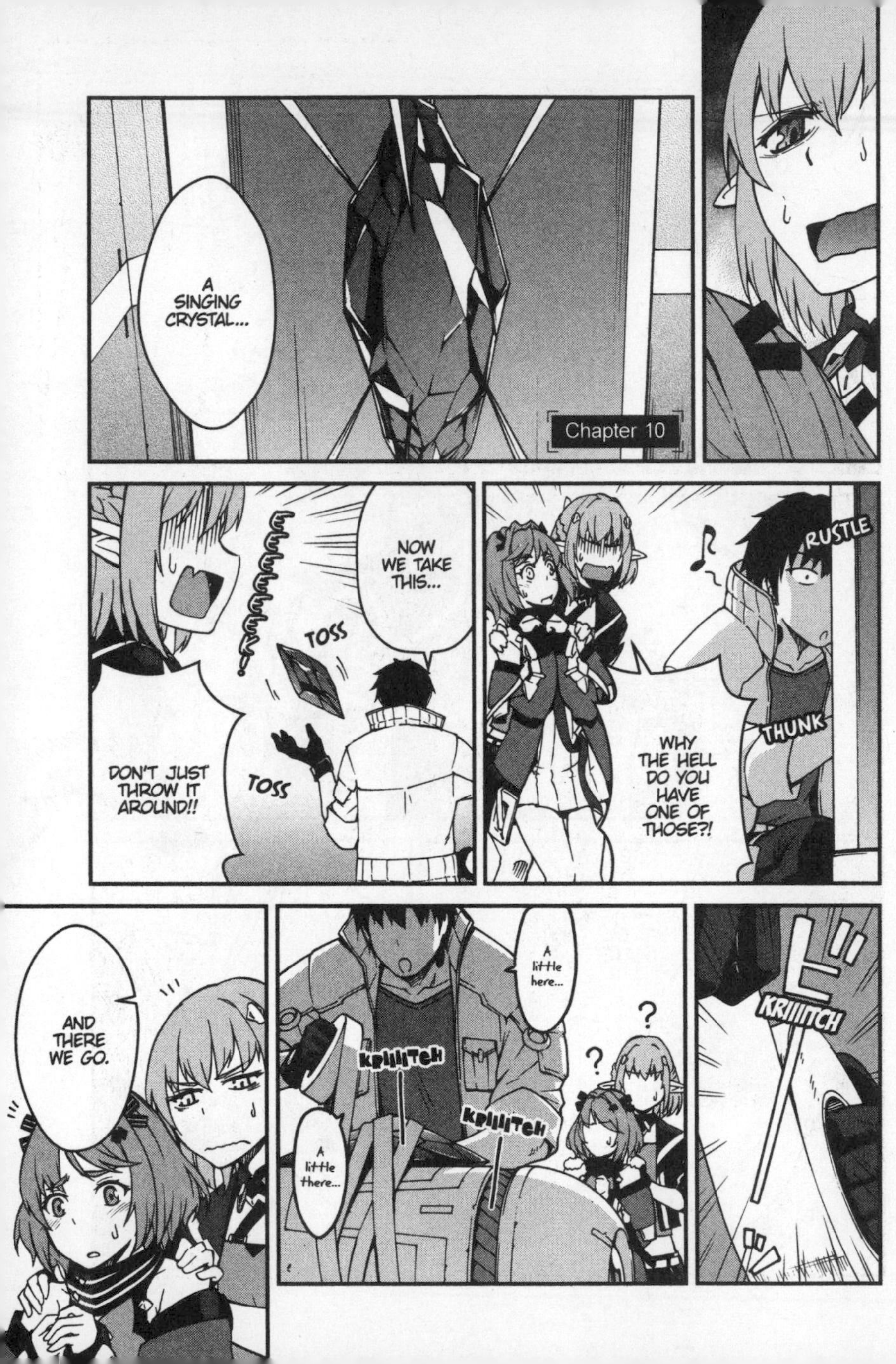
A SINGING CRYSTAL...
Chapter 10
RUSTLE
THUNK
WHY THE HELL DO YOU HAVE ONE OF THOSE?!
NOW WE TAKE THIS...
TOSS
TOSS
DON'T JUST THROW IT AROUND!!
KRIIIITCH
A little here...
KRIIIITCH
KRIIIITCH
A little there...
?
?
AND THERE WE GO.

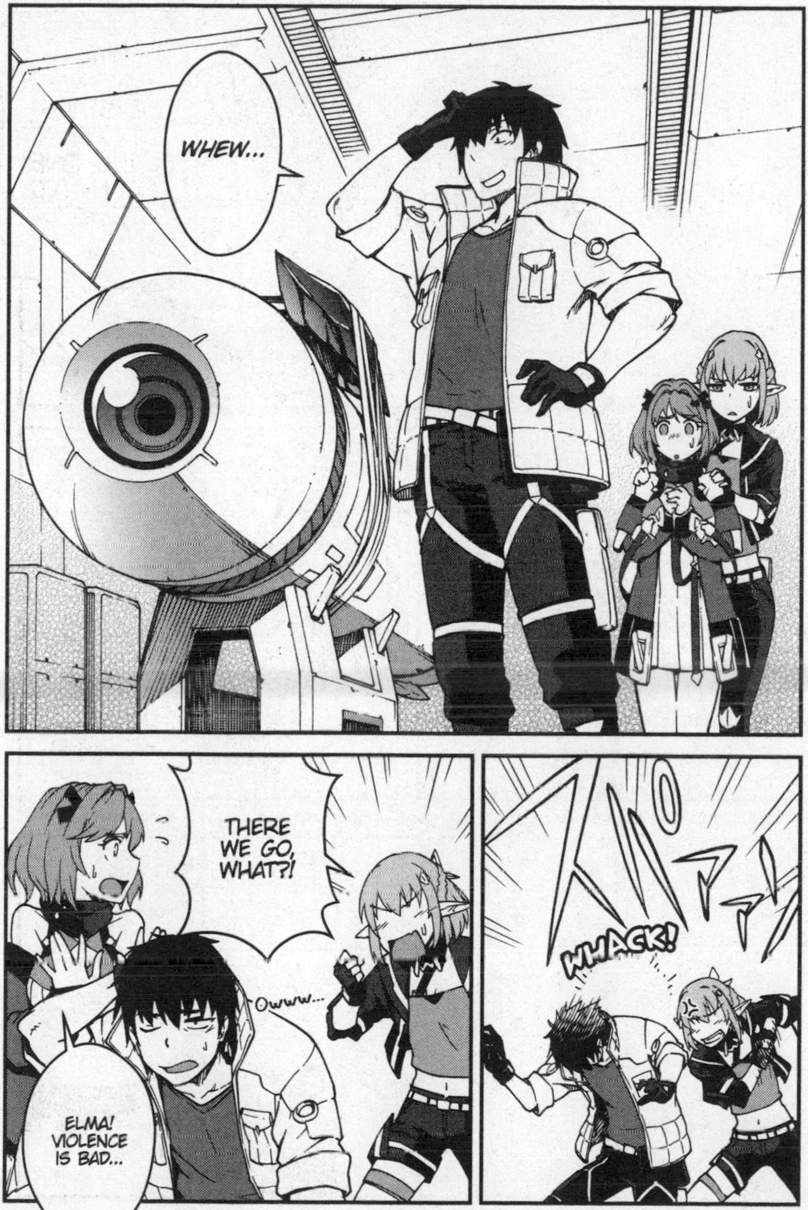
WHEW...
WHACK!
THERE WE GO, WHAT?!
OWWW...
ELMA! VIOLENCE IS BAD...

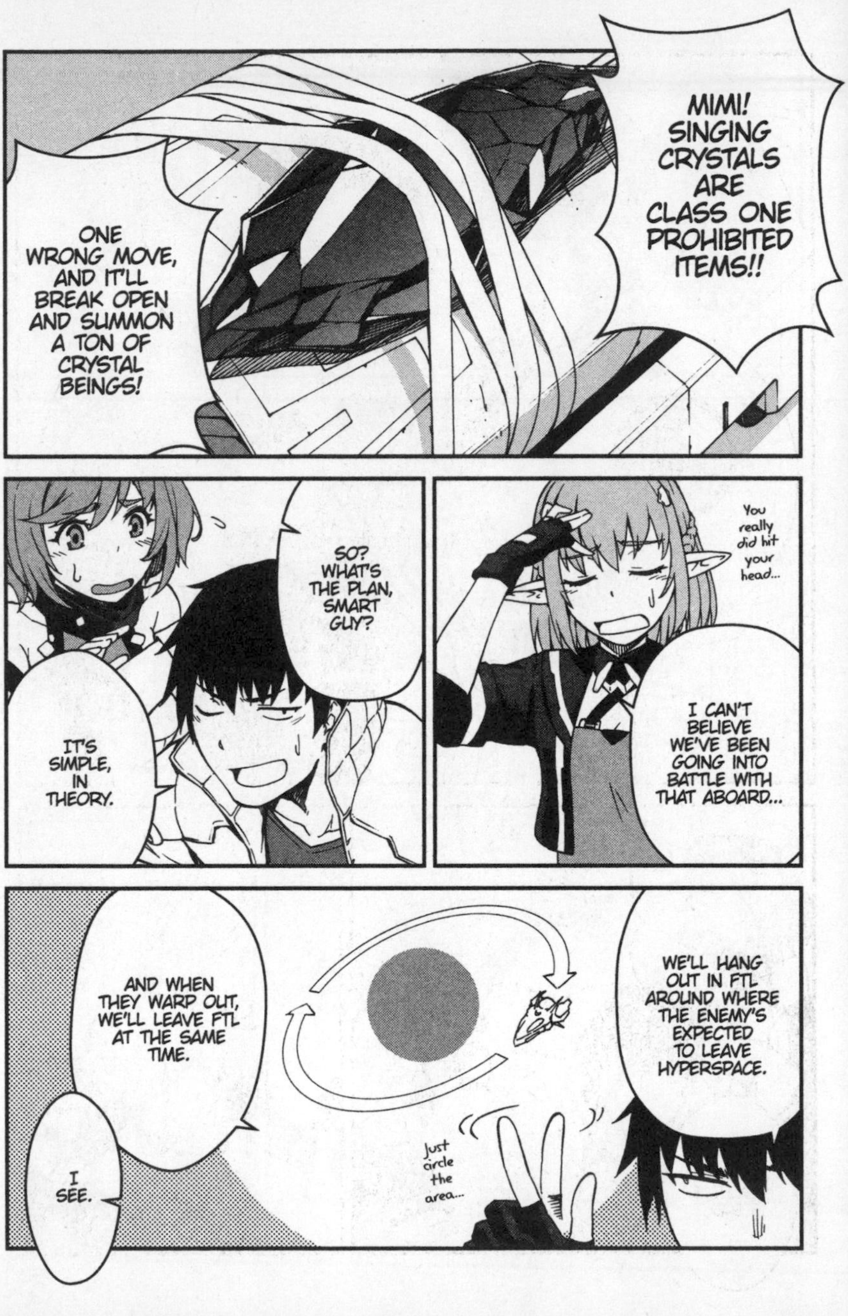
MIMI! SINGING CRYSTALS ARE CLASS ONE PROHIBITED ITEMS!!
ONE WRONG MOVE, AND IT'LL BREAK OPEN AND SUMMON A TON OF CRYSTAL BEINGS!
You really did hit your head...
I CAN'T BELIEVE WE'VE BEEN GOING INTO BATTLE WITH THAT ABOARD...
SO? WHAT'S THE PLAN, SMART GUY?
IT'S SIMPLE, IN THEORY.
WE'LL HANG OUT IN FTL AROUND WHERE THE ENEMY'S EXPECTED TO LEAVE HYPERSPACE.
Just circle the area...
AND WHEN THEY WARP OUT, WE'LL LEAVE FTL AT THE SAME TIME.
I SEE.

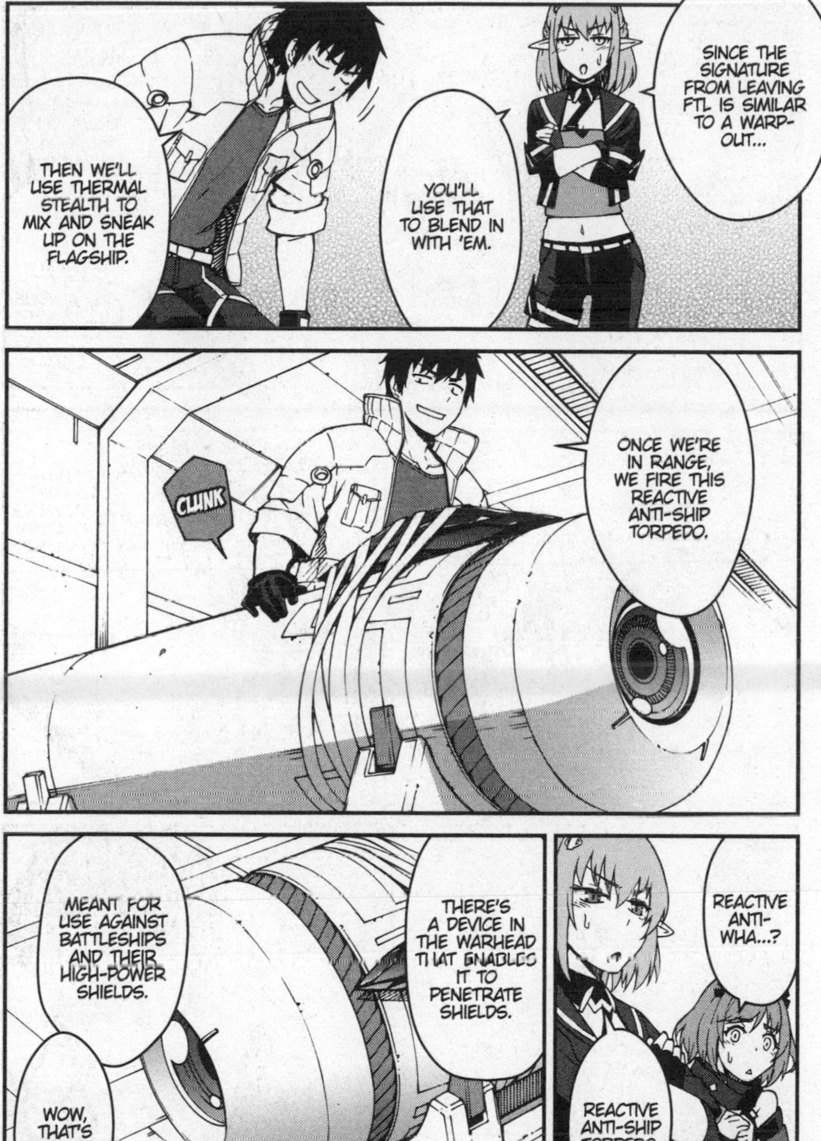
SINCE THE SIGNATURE FROM LEAVING FTL IS SIMILAR TO A WARP-OUT...
YOU'LL USE THAT TO BLEND IN WITH 'EM.
THEN WE'LL USE THERMAL STEALTH TO MIX AND SNEAK UP ON THE FLAGSHIP.
ONCE WE'RE IN RANGE, WE FIRE THIS REACTIVE ANTI-SHIP TORPEDO.
CLINK
REACTIVE ANTI-WHA...?
REACTIVE ANTI-SHIP TORPEDO.
THERE'S A DEVICE IN THE WARHEAD THAT ENABLES IT TO PENETRATE SHIELDS.
MEANT FOR USE AGAINST BATTLESHIPS AND THEIR HIGH-POWER SHIELDS.
WOW, THAT'S AMAZING...

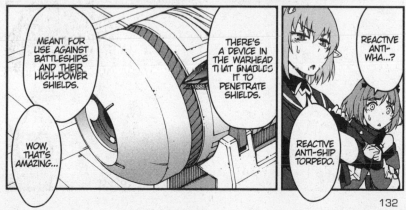

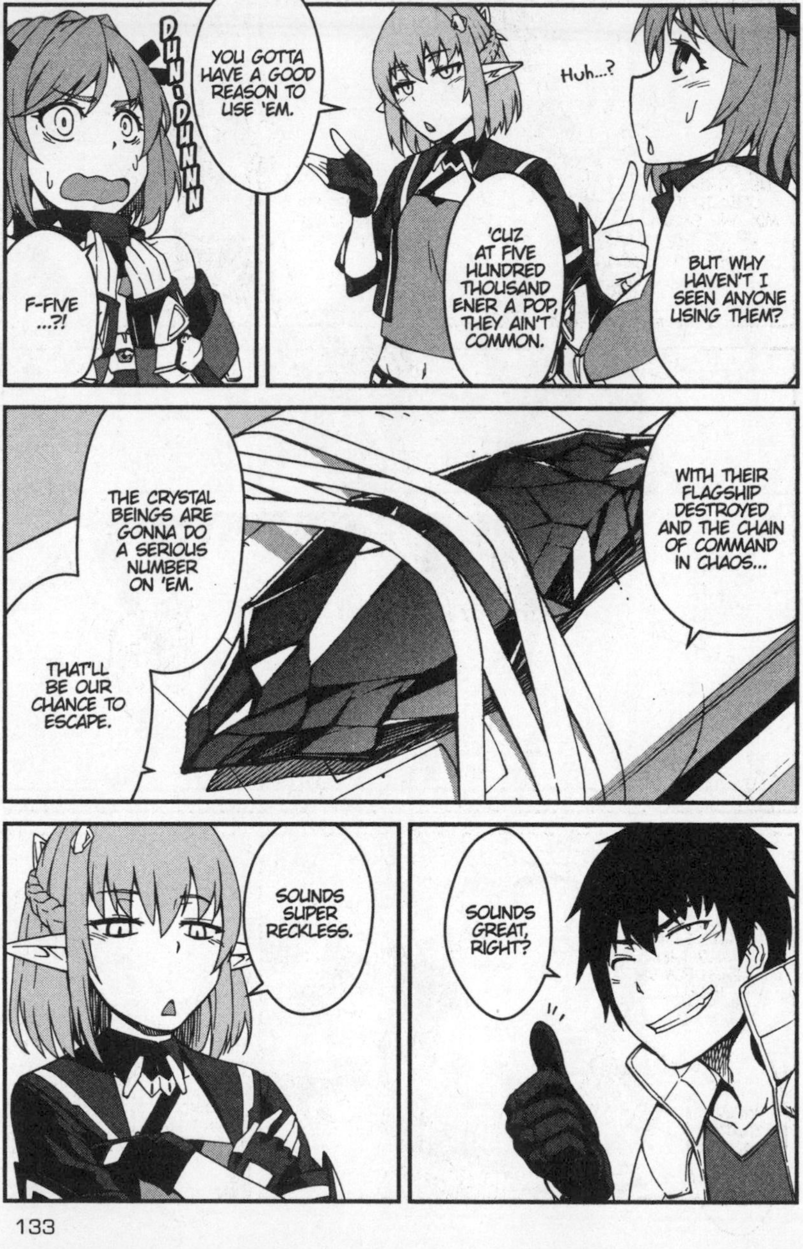
Huh...?
BUT WHY HAVEN'T I SEEN ANYONE USING THEM?
'CUZ AT FIVE HUNDRED THOUSAND ENER A POP, THEY AIN'T COMMON.
YOU GOTTA HAVE A GOOD REASON TO USE 'EM.
DUN-DUNNN
F-FIVE ...?!
WITH THEIR FLAGSHIP DESTROYED AND THE CHAIN OF COMMAND IN CHAOS...
THE CRYSTAL BEINGS ARE GONNA DO A SERIOUS NUMBER ON 'EM.
THAT'LL BE OUR CHANCE TO ESCAPE.
SOUNDS GREAT, RIGHT?
SOUNDS SUPER RECKLESS.

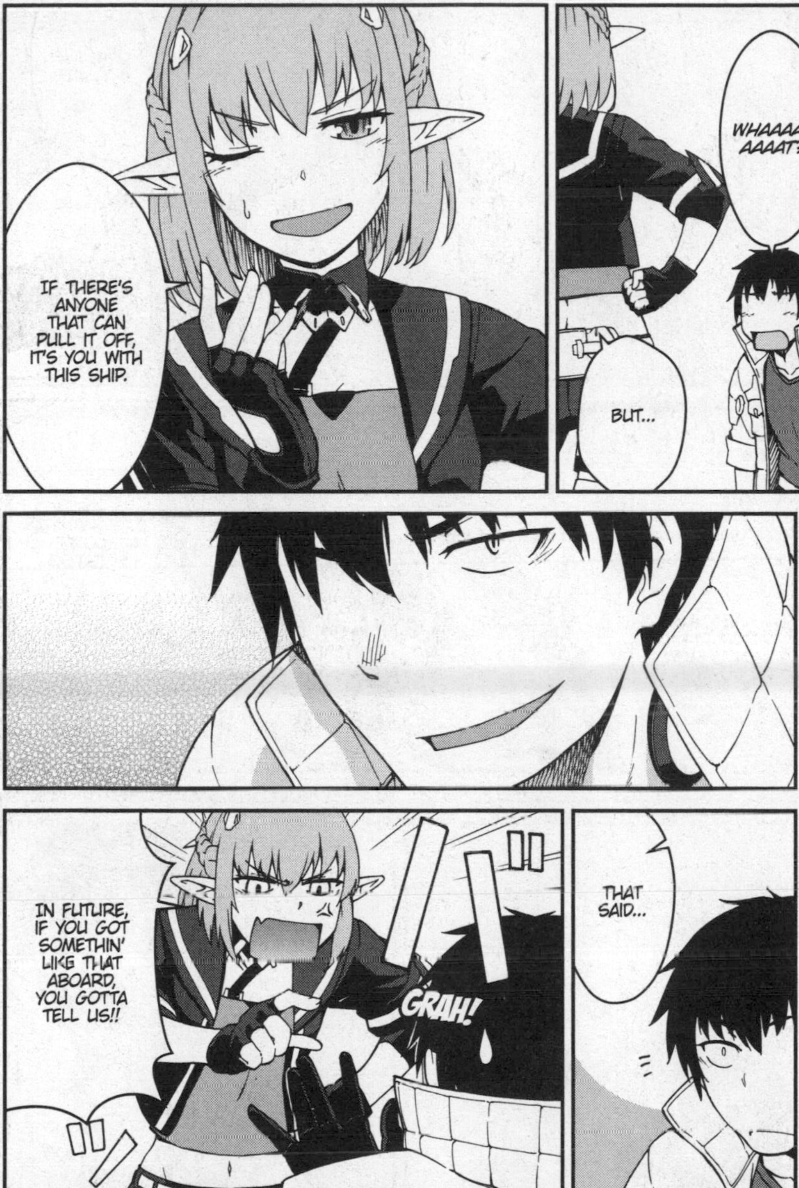
WHAAAA-AAAAT?
BUT...
IF THERE'S ANYONE THAT CAN PULL IT OFF, IT'S YOU WITH THIS SHIP.
THAT SAID...
IN FUTURE, IF YOU GOT SOMETHIN' LIKE THAT ABOARD, YOU GOTTA TELL US!!
GRAH!

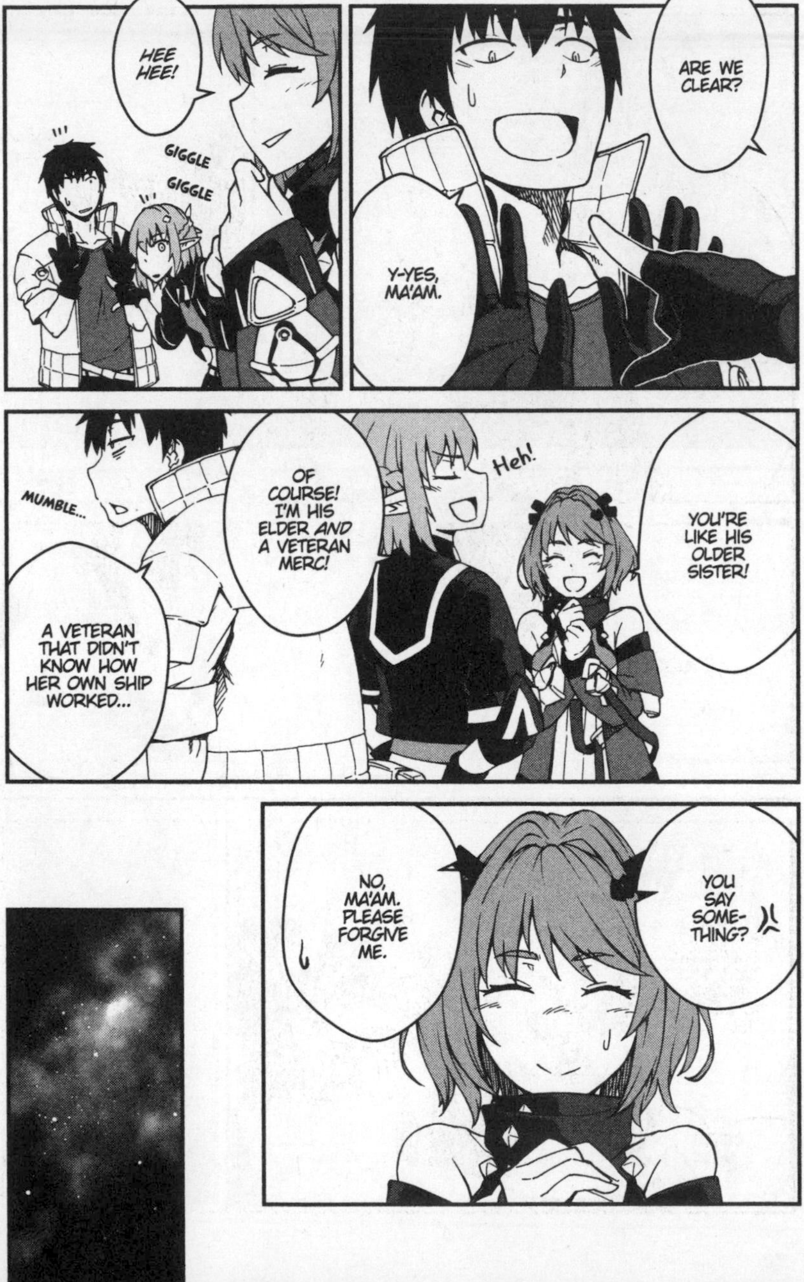
ARE WE CLEAR?
Y-YES, MA'AM.
HEE HEE!
GIGGLE
GIGGLE
YOU'RE LIKE HIS OLDER SISTER!
Heh!
OF COURSE! I'M HIS ELDER AND A VETERAN MERC!
MUMBLE...
A VETERAN THAT DIDN'T KNOW HOW HER OWN SHIP WORKED...
YOU SAY SOME-THING?
NO, MA'AM. PLEASE FORGIVE ME.

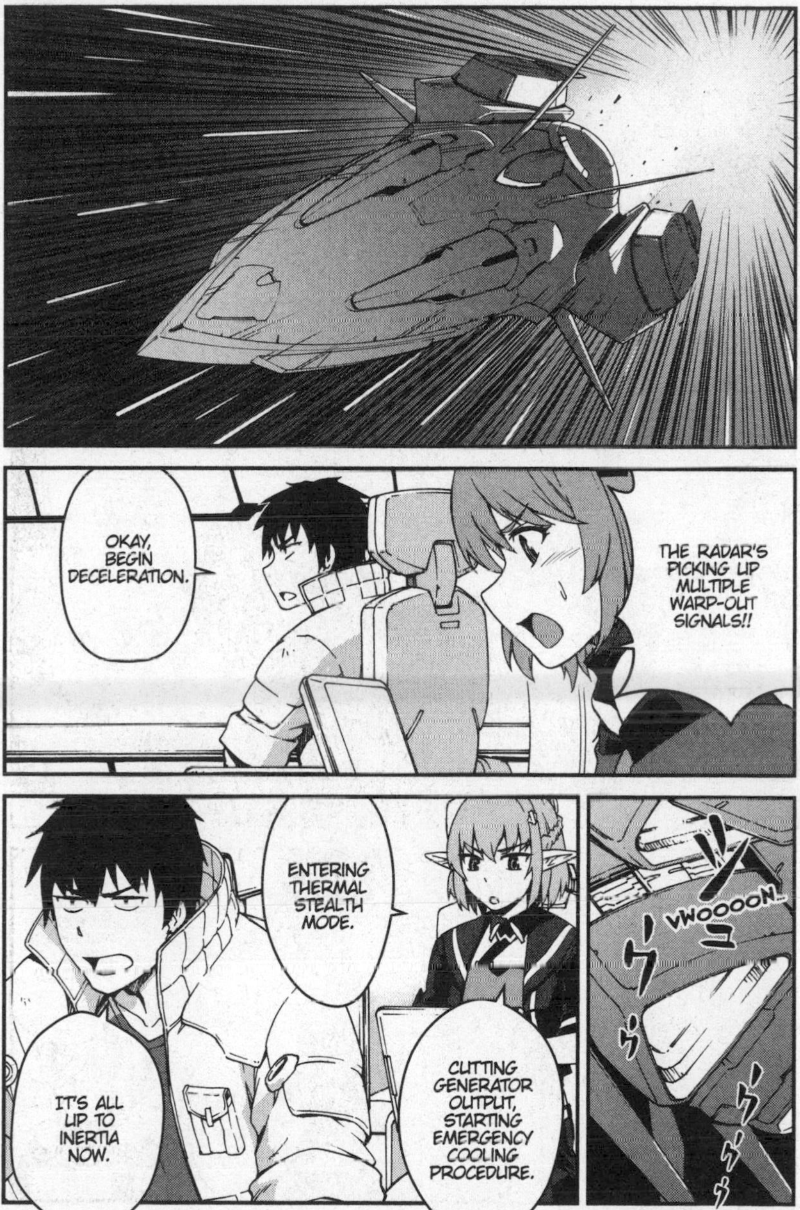
THE RADAR'S PICKING UP MULTIPLE WARP-OUT SIGNALS!!
OKAY, BEGIN DECELERATION.
VWOOOON...
ENTERING THERMAL STEALTH MODE.
CUTTING GENERATOR OUTPUT, STARTING EMERGENCY COOLING PROCEDURE.
IT'S ALL UP TO INERTIA NOW.

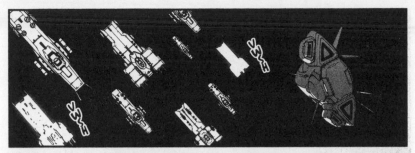

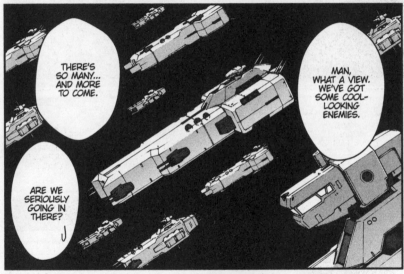

VWSH
VWSH
MAN, WHAT A VIEW. WE'VE GOT SOME COOL-LOOKING ENEMIES.
THERE'S SO MANY... AND MORE TO COME.
ARE WE SERIOUSLY GOING IN THERE?
NO ADDITIONAL WARP-OUT SIGNALS DETECTED.
THE FEDERATION FLEET IS NOW MOVING.
ALL RIGHT.
REBOOT THE COOLING EQUIPMENT.
SET GENERATOR OUTPUT TO MAX.
CLENCH

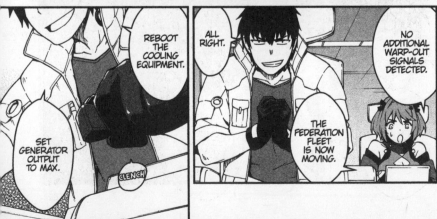

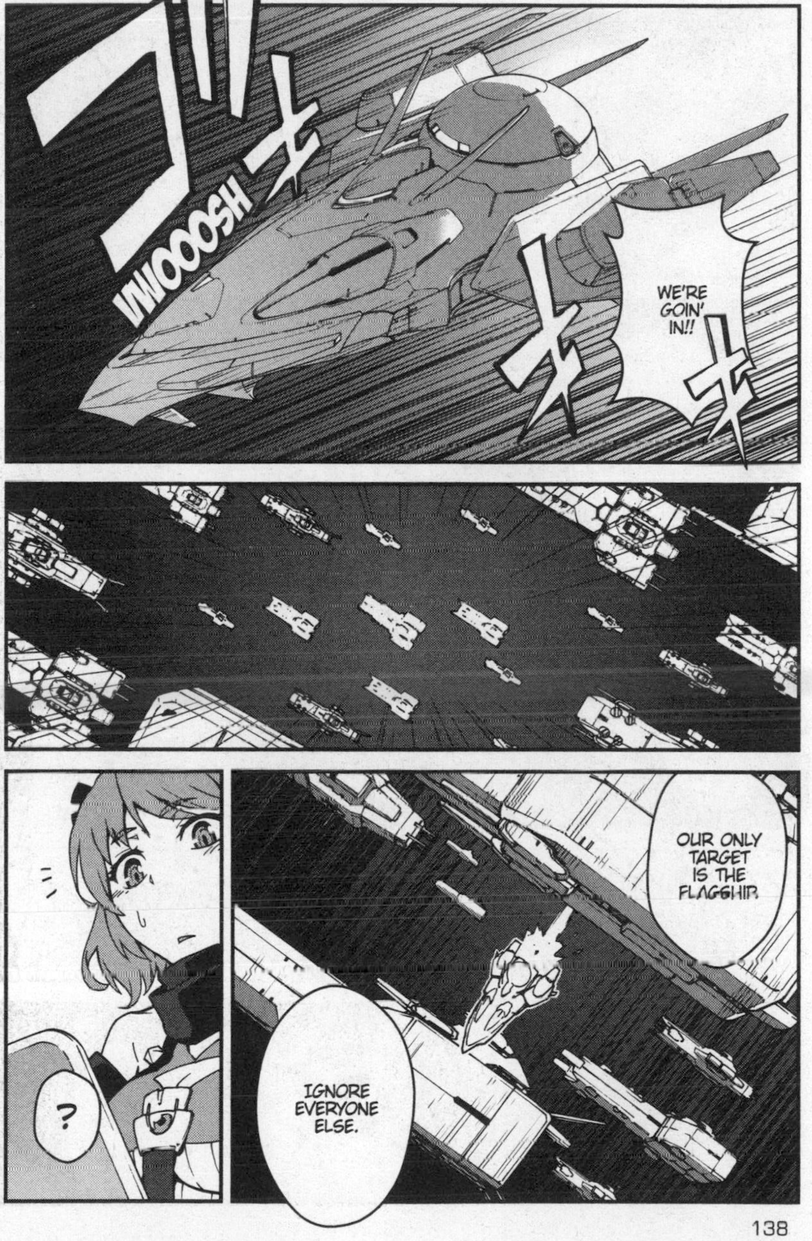
VWOOOSH
WE'RE GOIN' IN!!
OUR ONLY TARGET IS THE FLAGSHIP.
IGNORE EVERYONE ELSE.
?

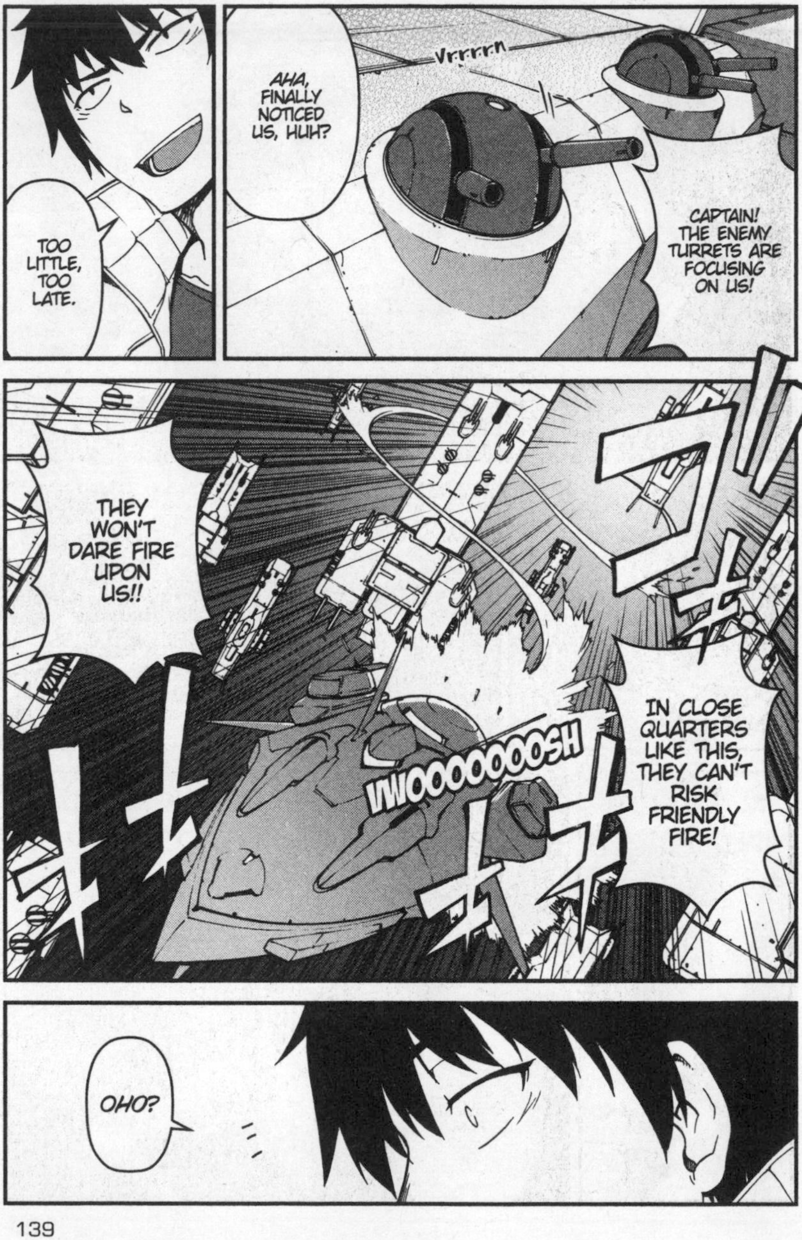
Vrrrrn
CAPTAIN! THE ENEMY TURRETS ARE FOCUSING ON US!
AHA, FINALLY NOTICED US, HUH?
TOO LITTLE, TOO LATE.
IN CLOSE QUARTERS LIKE THIS, THEY CAN'T RISK FRIENDLY FIRE!
VWOOOOOOOOSH
THEY WON'T DARE FIRE UPON US!!
OHO?

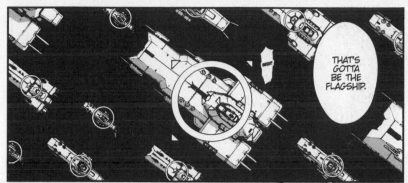

THAT'S GOTTA BE THE FLAGSHIP.

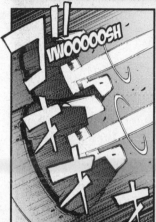

VWOOOOOOSH

GA-CLUNK

BWOOSH

EAT THIS!!

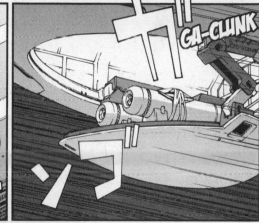

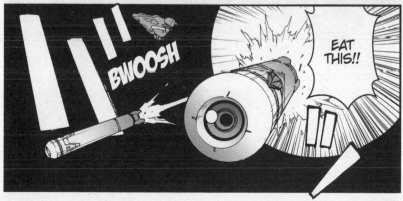

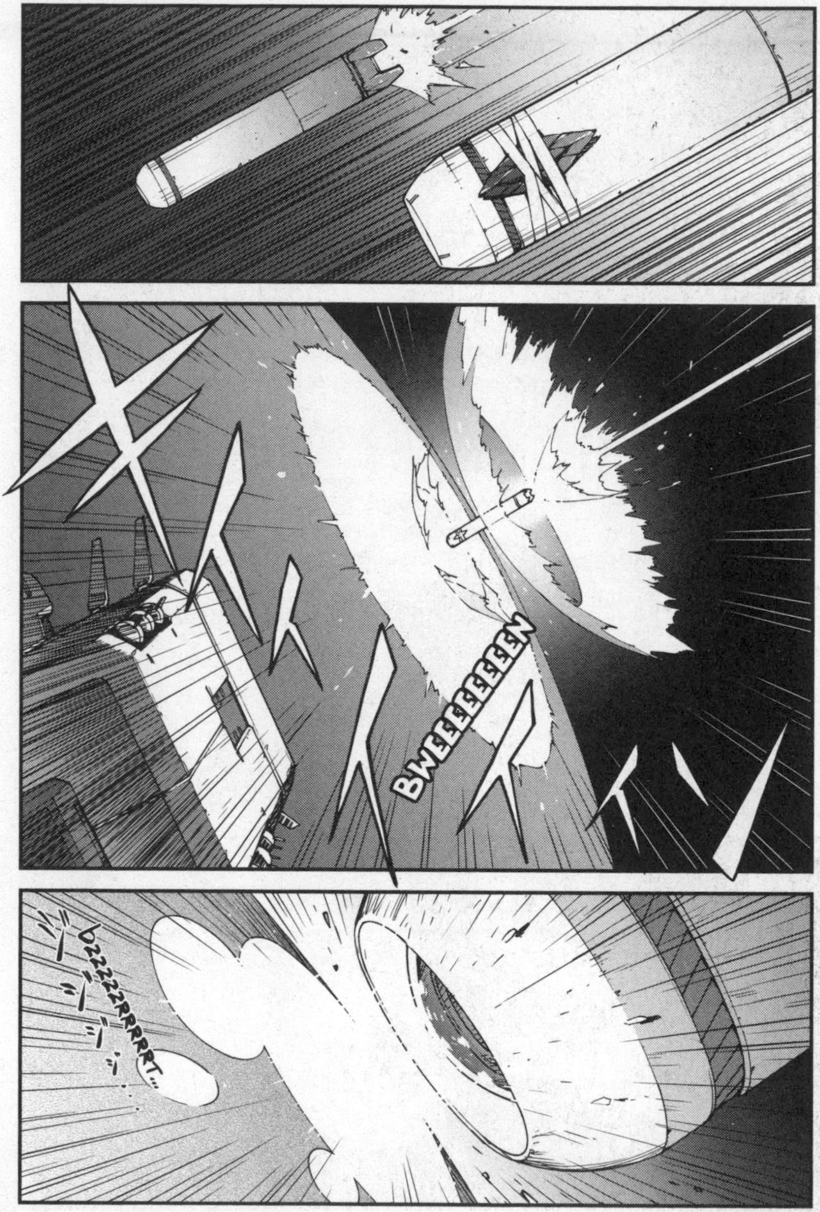
BWEEEEEEEEN
DZZZZZRRRRRT...

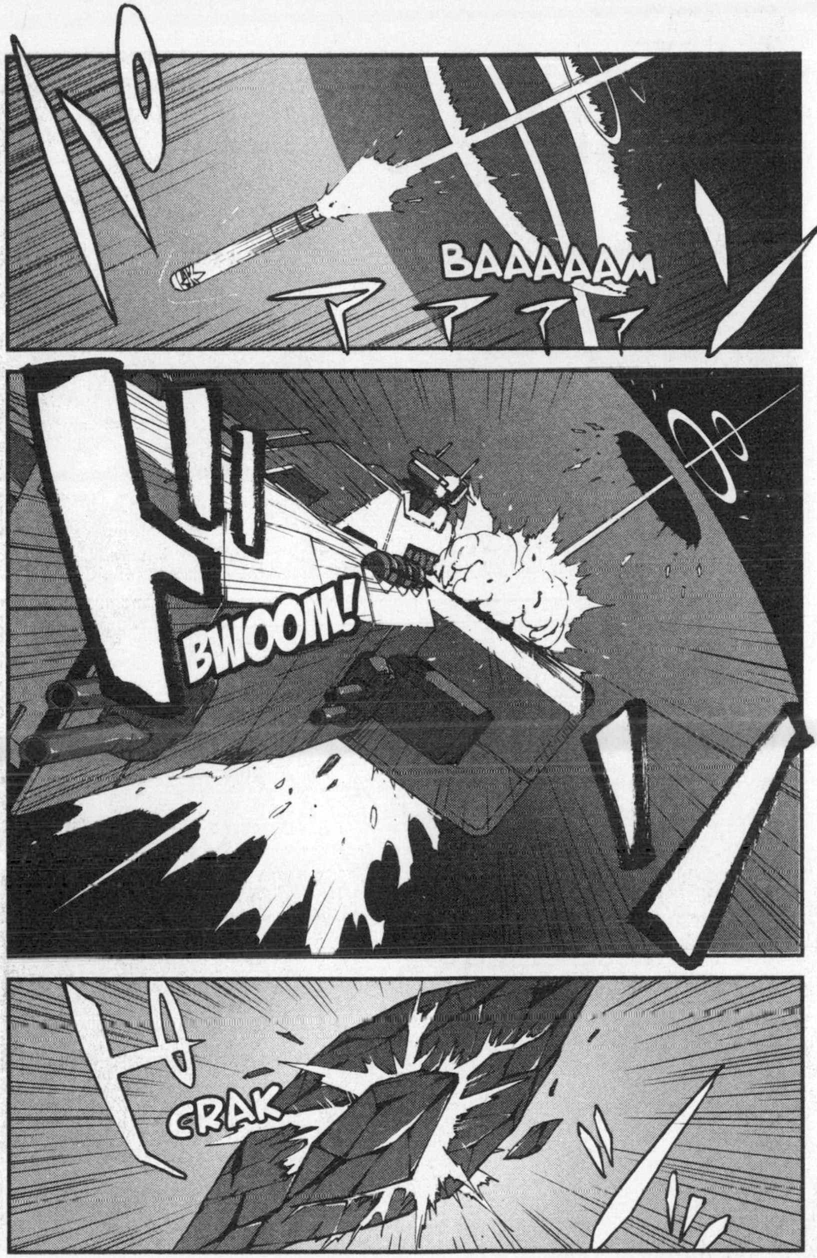
BAAAAAM
BWOOM!
CRAK

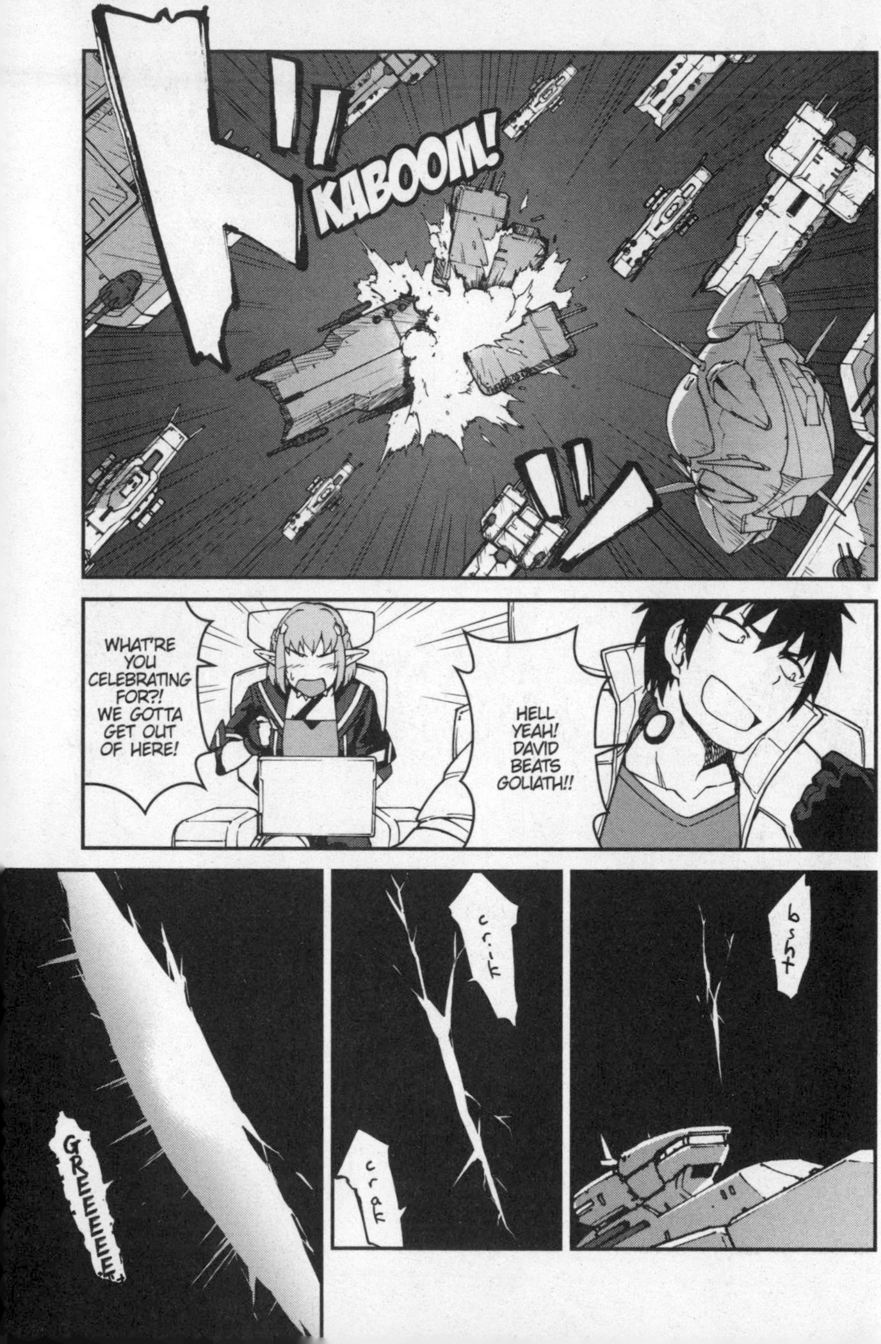
KABOOM!
HELL YEAH! DAVID BEATS GOLIATH!!
WHAT'RE YOU CELEBRATING FOR?! WE GOTTA GET OUT OF HERE!
bsht
crik
crak
GREEEEEET

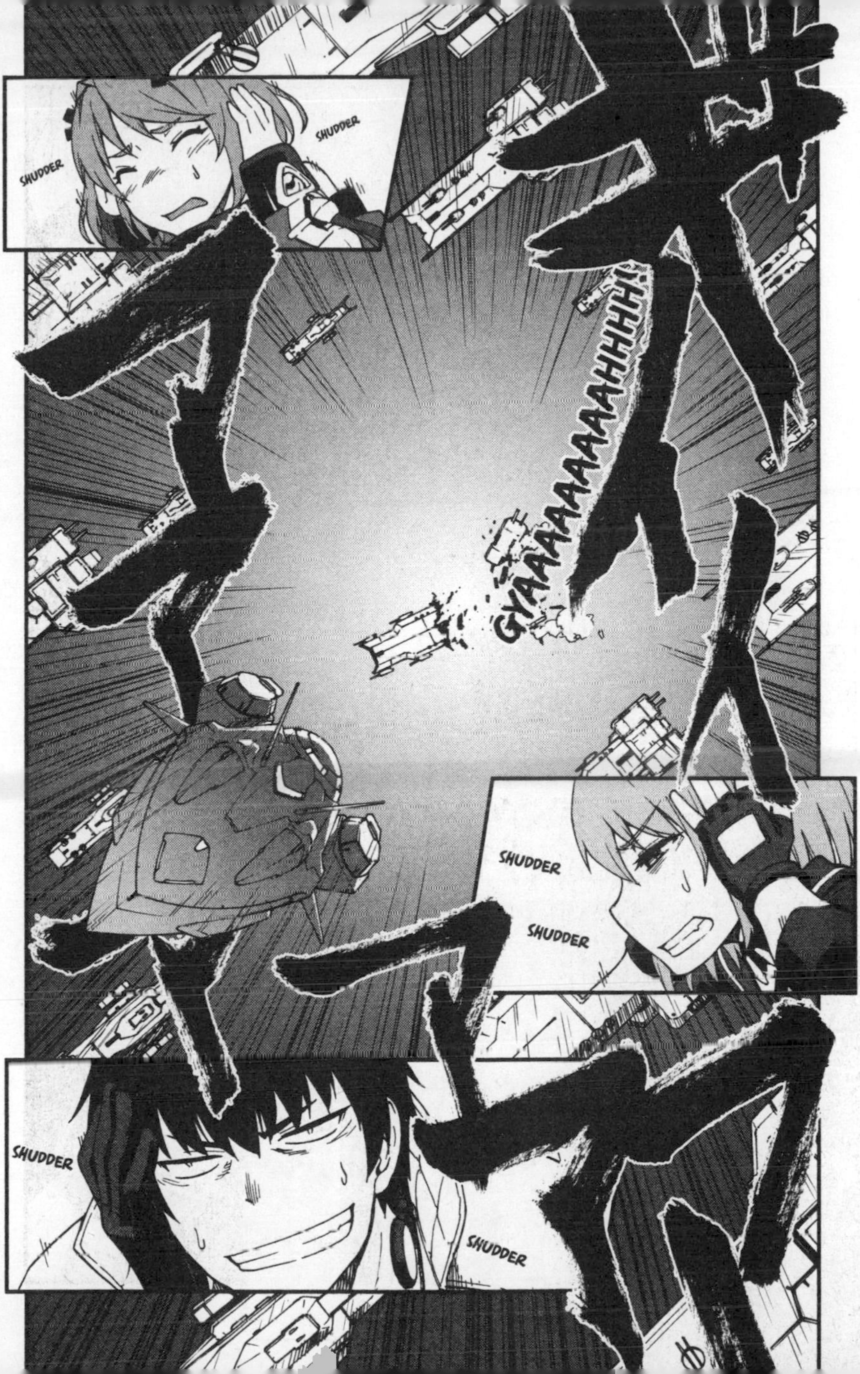
SHUDDER
SHUDDER
GYAAAAAAAAHHHH!!
SHUDDER
SHUDDER
SHUDDER
SHUDDER

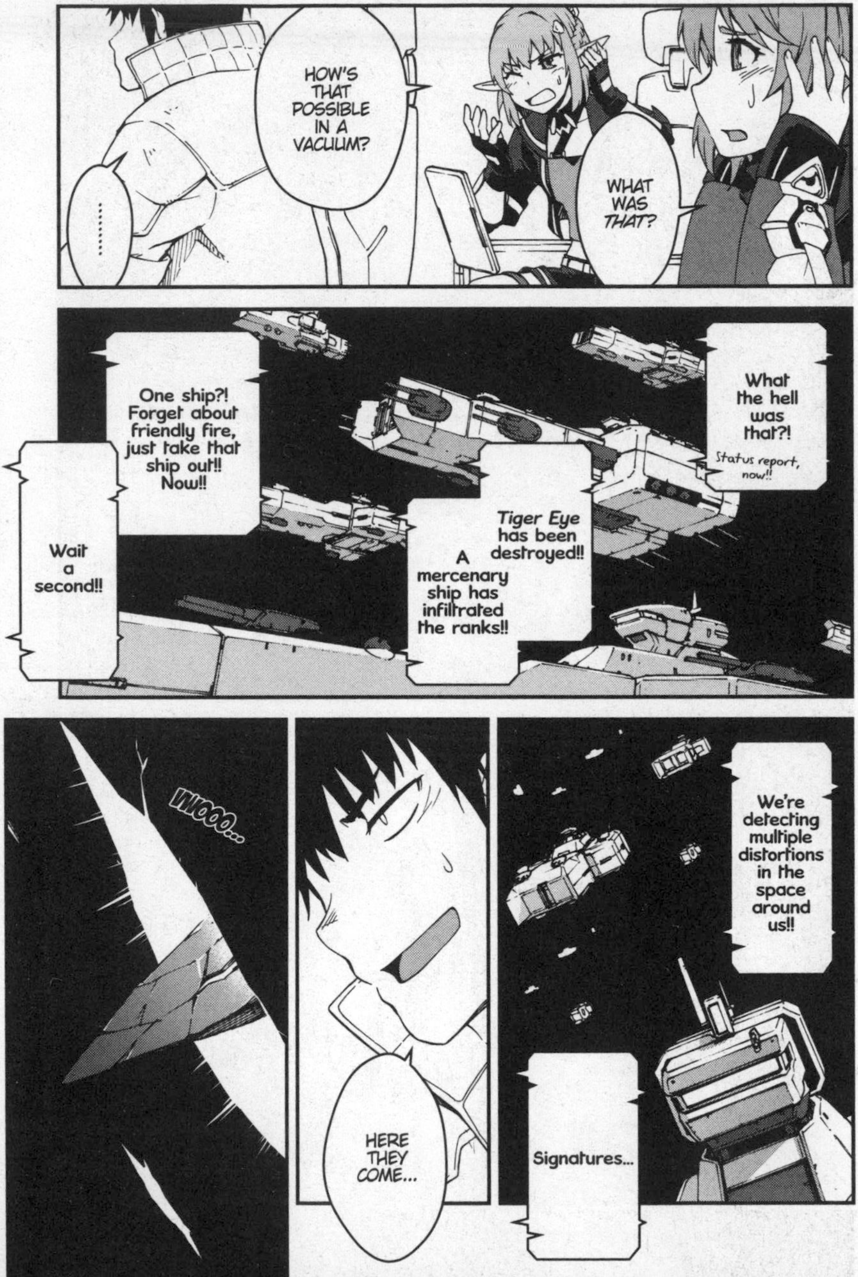
WHAT WAS *THAT?*
HOW'S THAT POSSIBLE IN A VACUUM?
......
What the hell was that?!
Status report, now!!
Tiger Eye has been destroyed!!
A mercenary ship has infiltrated the ranks!!
One ship?! Forget about friendly fire, just take that ship out!! Now!!
Wait a second!!
We're detecting multiple distortions in the space around us!!
Signatures...
HERE THEY COME...
VWOOO...

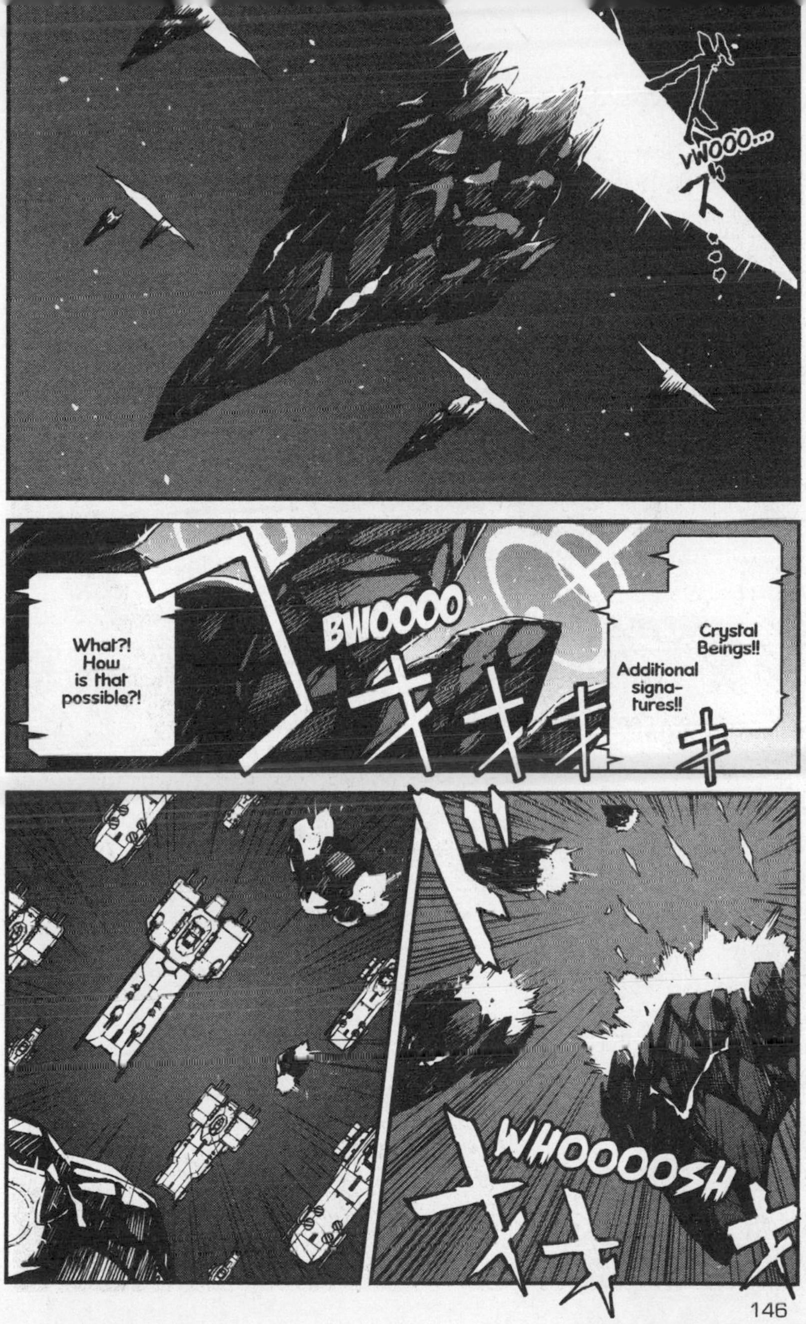
VWOOO...
Crystal Beings!!
Additional signatures!!
BWOOOO
What?! How is that possible?!
WHOOOOSH

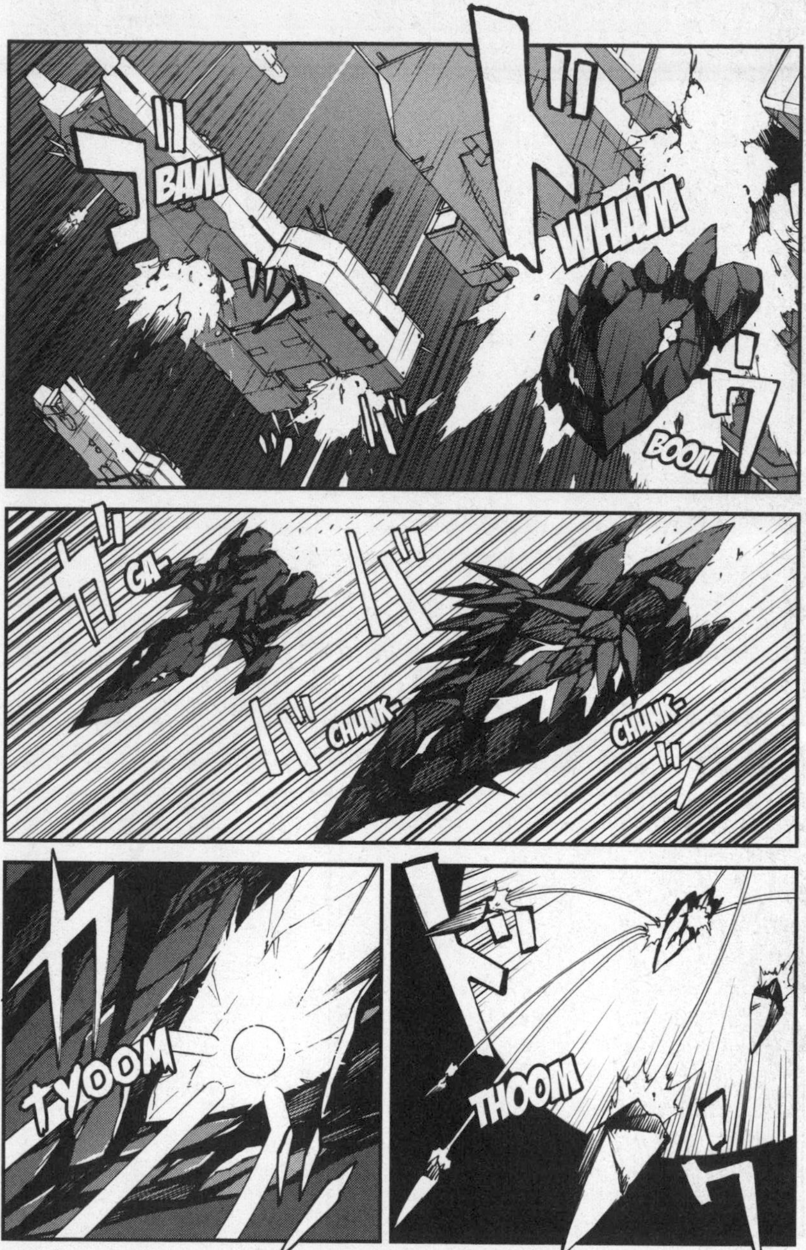
WHAM
BAM
BOOM
GA-
CHUNK-
CHUNK-
THOOM
TYOOM

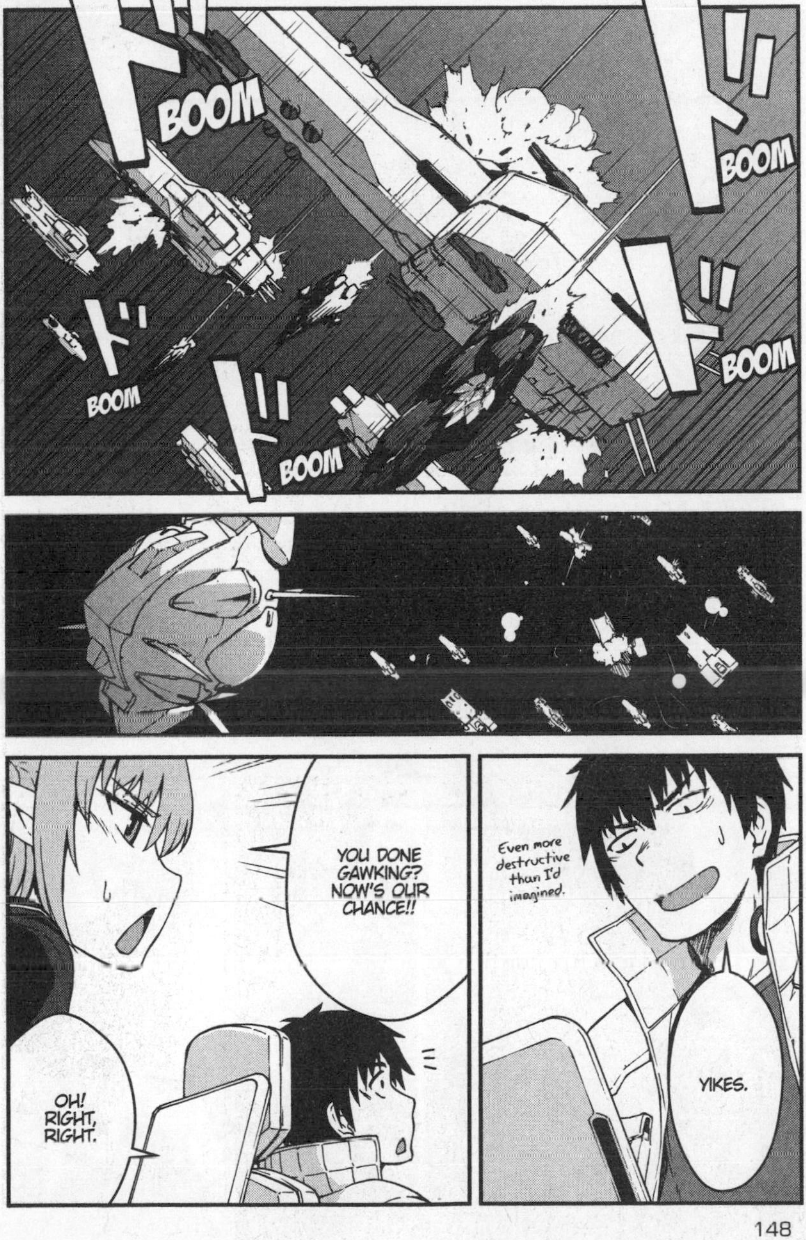
ド
BOOM
ド
BOOM
ド
BOOM
ド
BOOM
ド
BOOM
Even more destructive than I'd imagined.
YIKES.
YOU DONE GAWKING? NOW'S OUR CHANCE!!
OH! RIGHT, RIGHT.

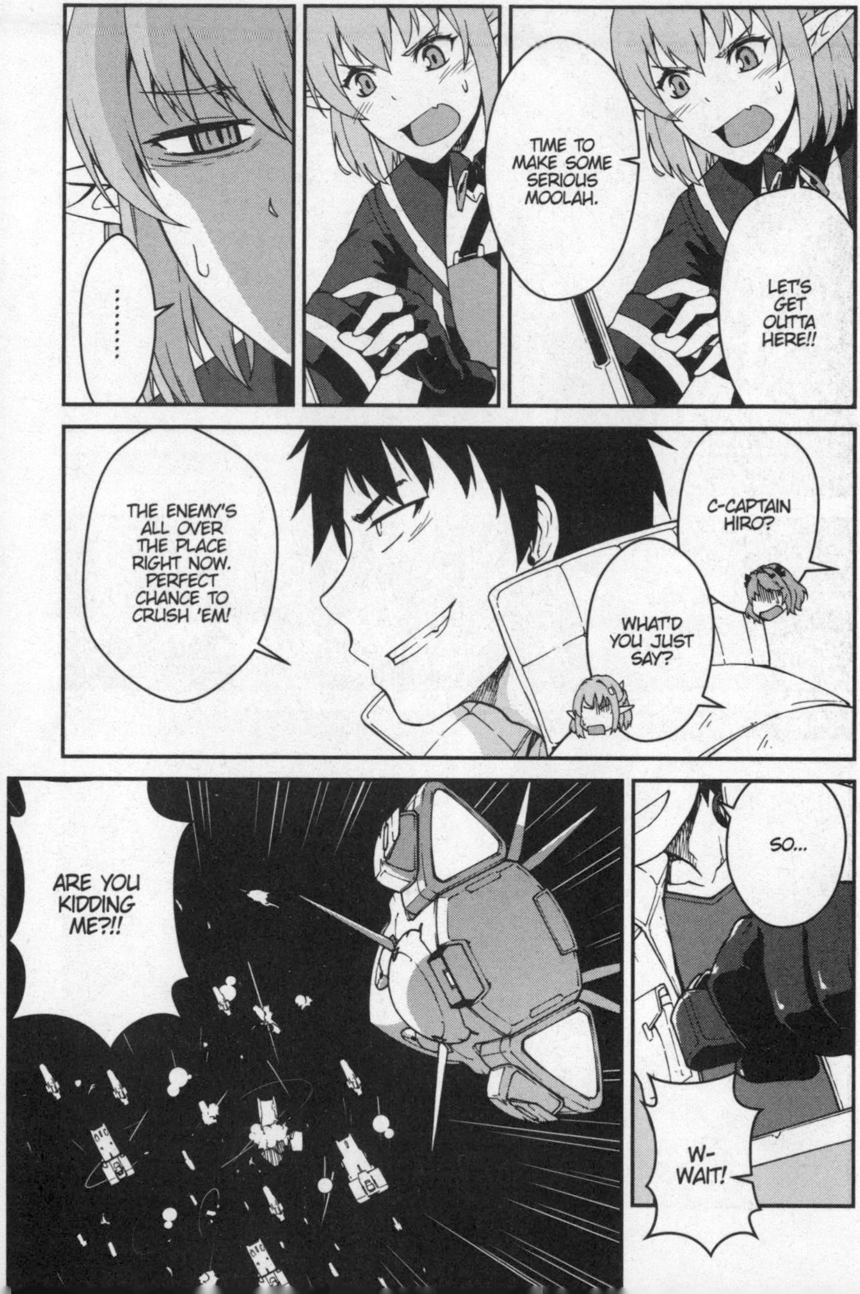
TIME TO MAKE SOME SERIOUS MOOLAH.
LET'S GET OUTTA HERE!!
......
C-CAPTAIN HIRO?
WHAT'D YOU JUST SAY?
THE ENEMY'S ALL OVER THE PLACE RIGHT NOW. PERFECT CHANCE TO CRUSH 'EM!
SO...
W-WAIT!
ARE YOU KIDDING ME?!!

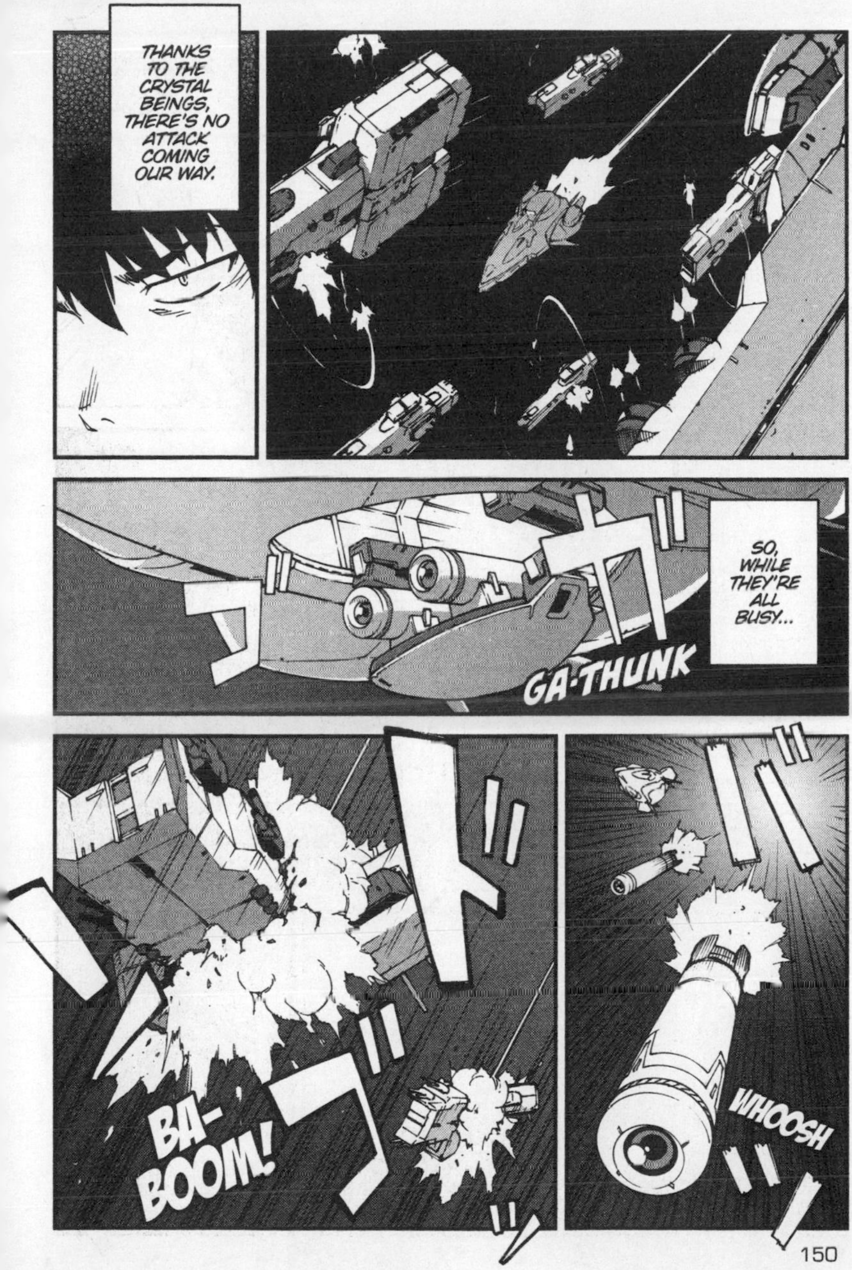
THANKS TO THE CRYSTAL BEINGS, THERE'S NO ATTACK COMING OUR WAY.
SO, WHILE THEY'RE ALL BUSY...
GA-THUNK
WHOOSH
BA-BOOM!

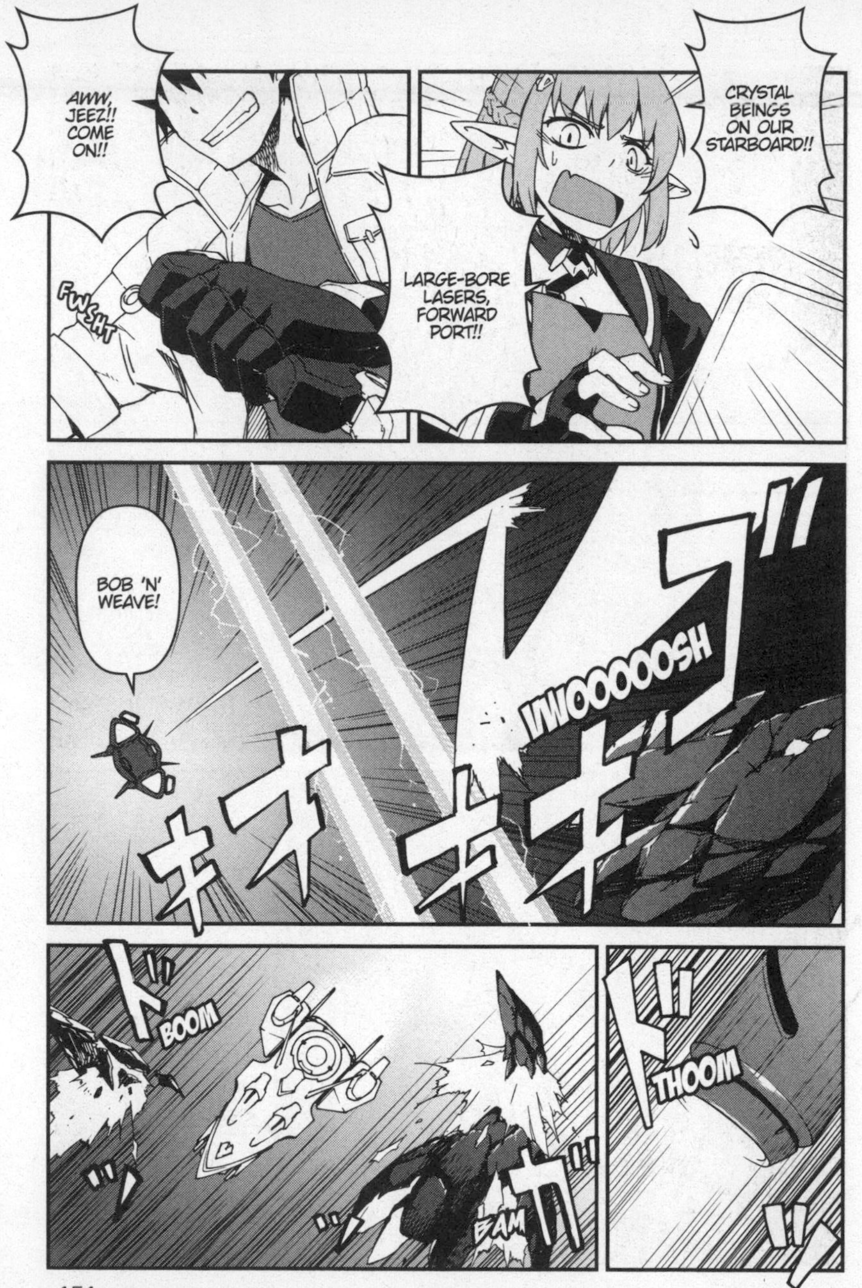
CRYSTAL BEINGS ON OUR STARBOARD!!
AWW, JEEZ!! COME ON!!
LARGE-BORE LASERS, FORWARD PORT!!
FWSHT
BOB 'N' WEAVE!
VWOOOOOSH
THOOM
BOOM
BAM

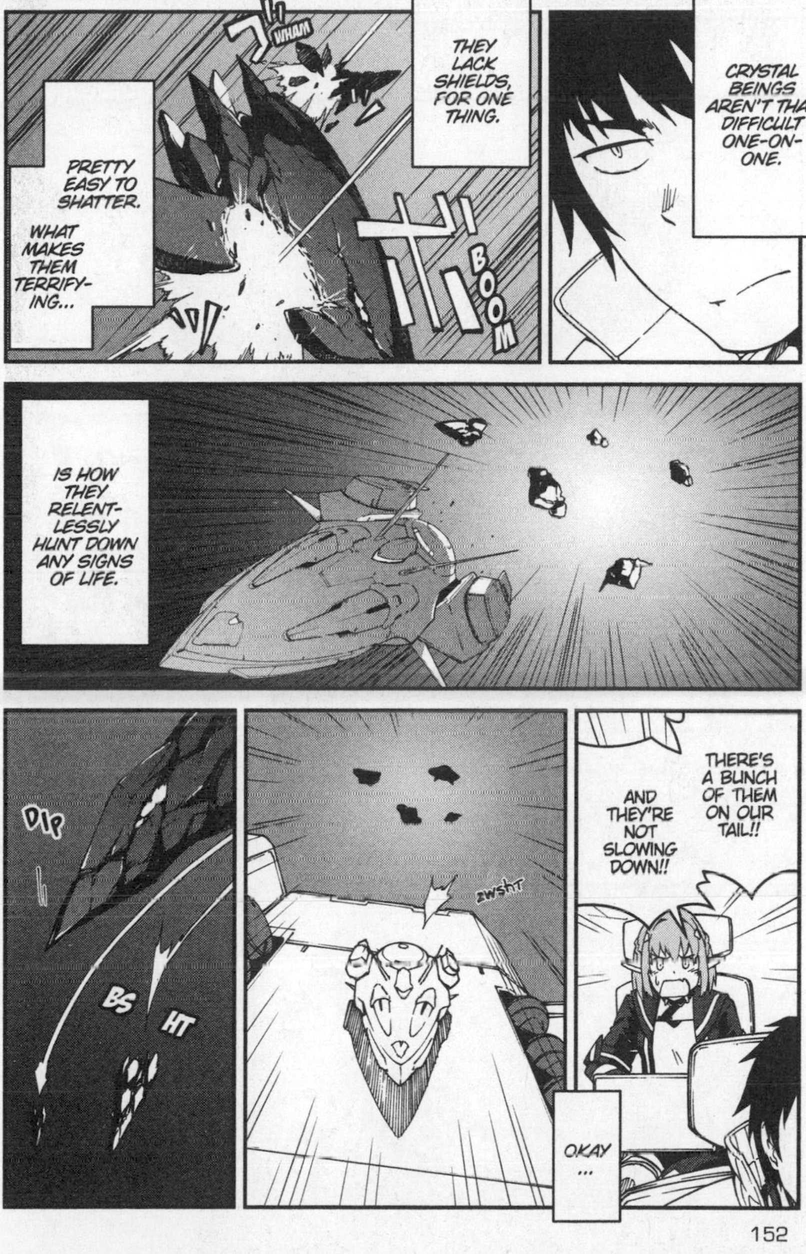
CRYSTAL BEINGS AREN'T THAT DIFFICULT ONE-ON-ONE.
THEY LACK SHIELDS, FOR ONE THING.
WHAM
PRETTY EASY TO SHATTER.
BOOM
WHAT MAKES THEM TERRIFYING...
IS HOW THEY RELENTLESSLY HUNT DOWN ANY SIGNS OF LIFE.
THERE'S A BUNCH OF THEM ON OUR TAIL!!
AND THEY'RE NOT SLOWING DOWN!!
OKAY ...
ZWSHT
DIP
BS HT

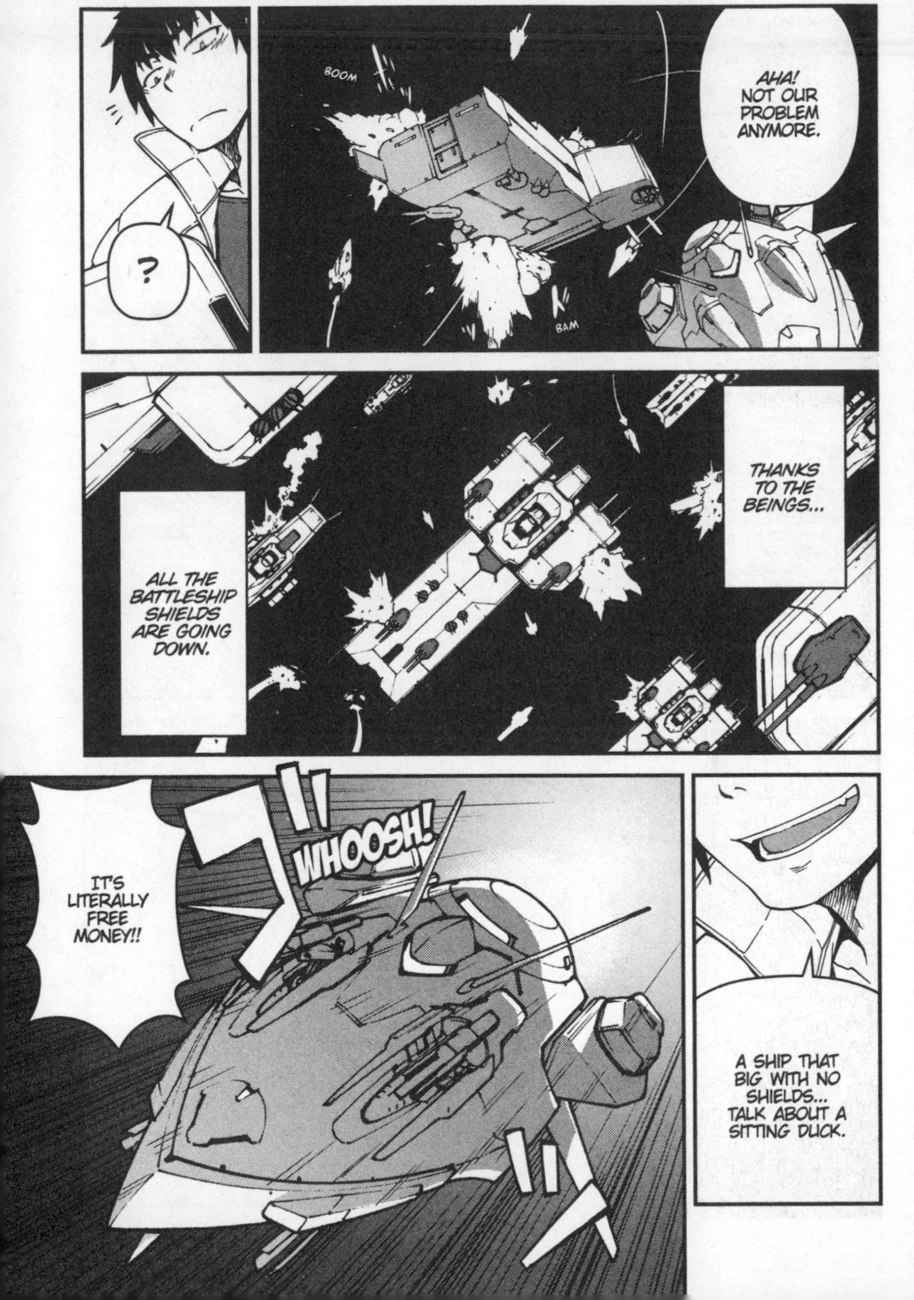
AHA! NOT OUR PROBLEM ANYMORE.
BOOM
BAM
?
THANKS TO THE BEINGS...
ALL THE BATTLESHIP SHIELDS ARE GOING DOWN.
A SHIP THAT BIG WITH NO SHIELDS... TALK ABOUT A SITTING DUCK.
WHOOSH!
IT'S LITERALLY FREE MONEY!!

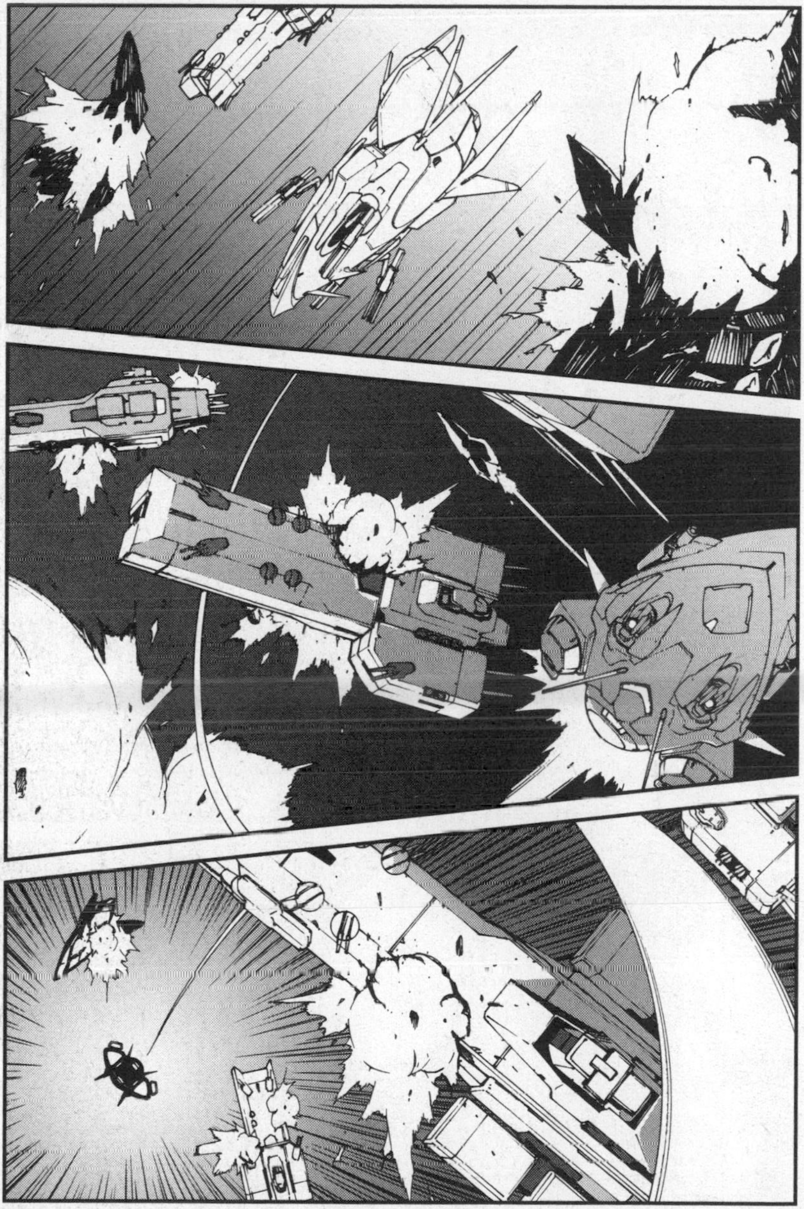

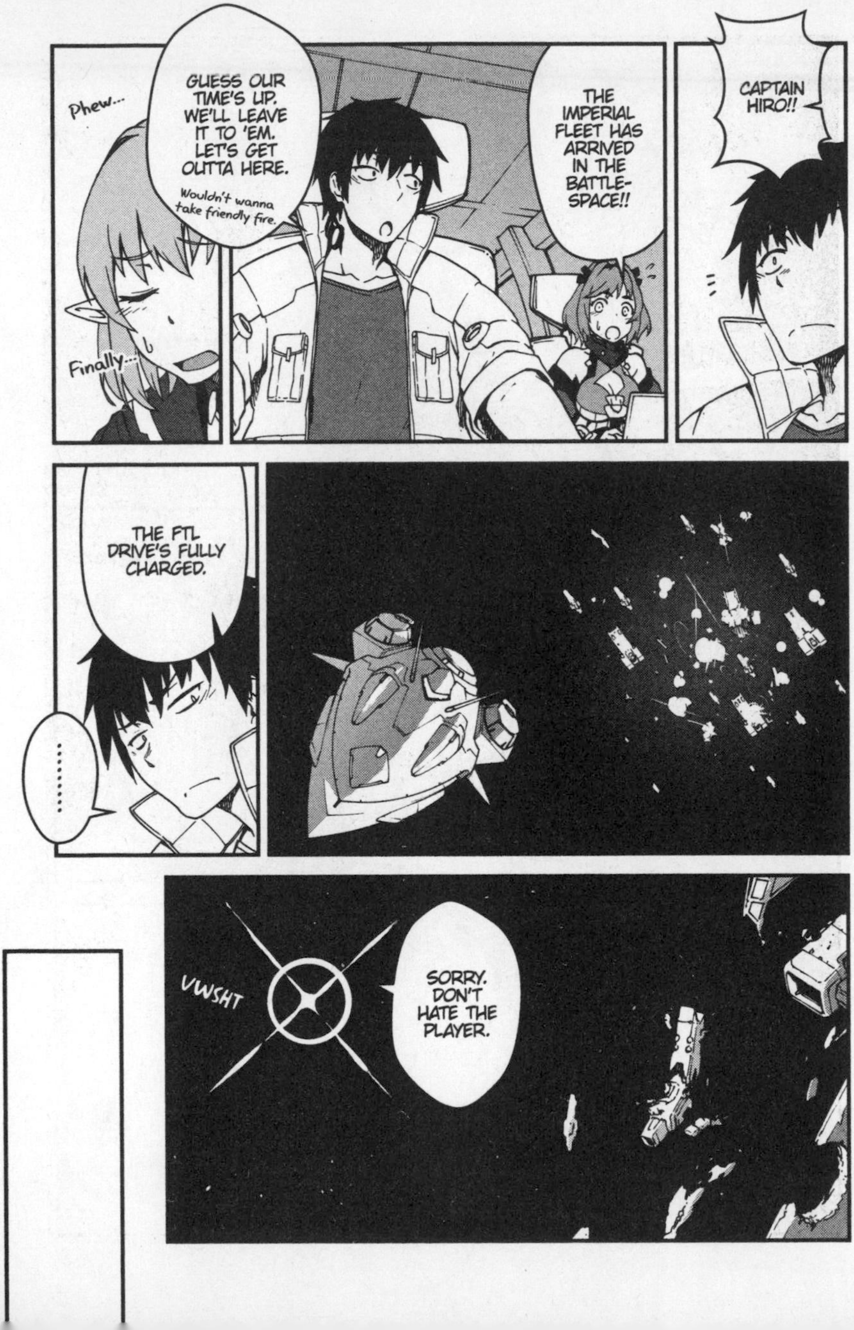
CAPTAIN HIRO!!
THE IMPERIAL FLEET HAS ARRIVED IN THE BATTLE-SPACE!!
GUESS OUR TIME'S UP. WE'LL LEAVE IT TO 'EM. LET'S GET OUTTA HERE.
Wouldn't wanna take friendly fire.
Phew...
Finally...
THE FTL DRIVE'S FULLY CHARGED.
....
SORRY. DON'T HATE THE PLAYER.
UWSHT

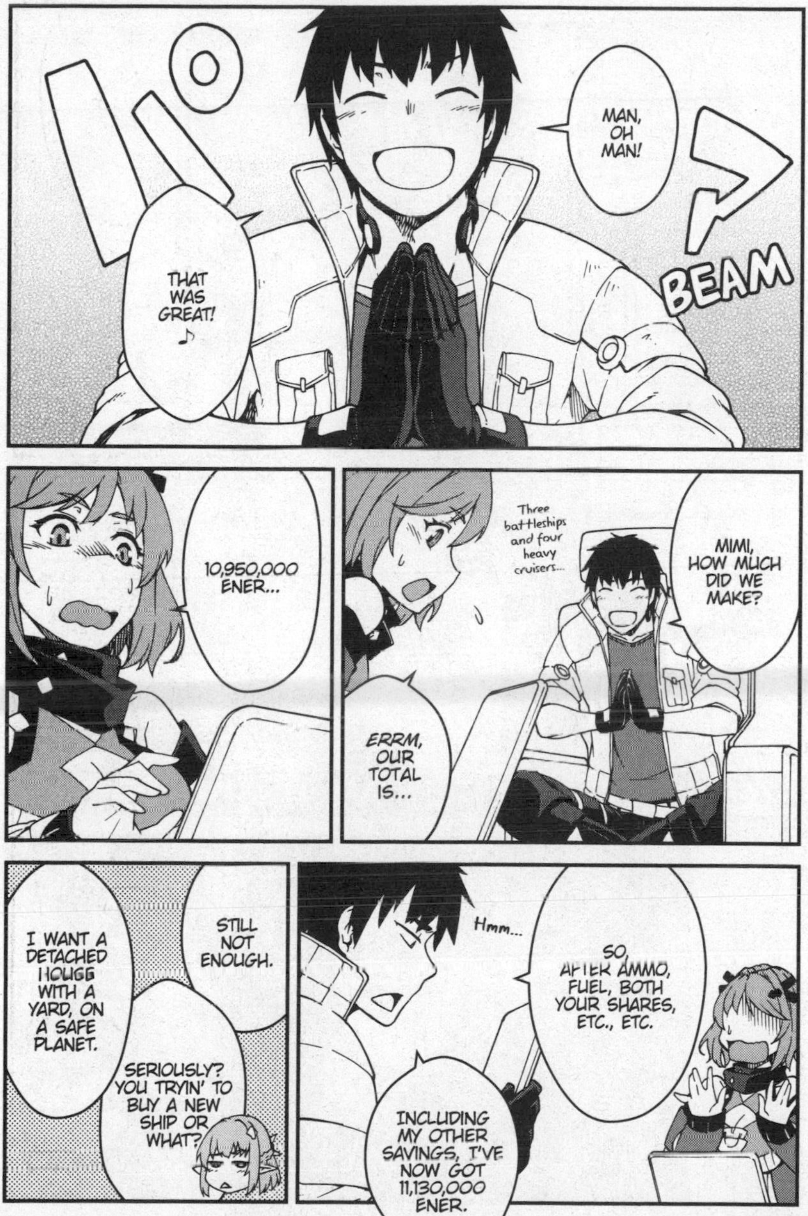
MAN, OH MAN!
BEAM
THAT WAS GREAT! ♪
MIMI, HOW MUCH DID WE MAKE?
Three battleships and four heavy cruisers...
ERRM, OUR TOTAL IS...
10,950,000 ENER...
SO, AFTER AMMO, FUEL, BOTH YOUR SHARES, ETC., ETC.
Hmm...
INCLUDING MY OTHER SAVINGS, I'VE NOW GOT 11,130,000 ENER.
STILL NOT ENOUGH.
I WANT A DETACHED HOUSE WITH A YARD, ON A SAFE PLANET.
SERIOUSLY? YOU TRYIN' TO BUY A NEW SHIP OR WHAT?

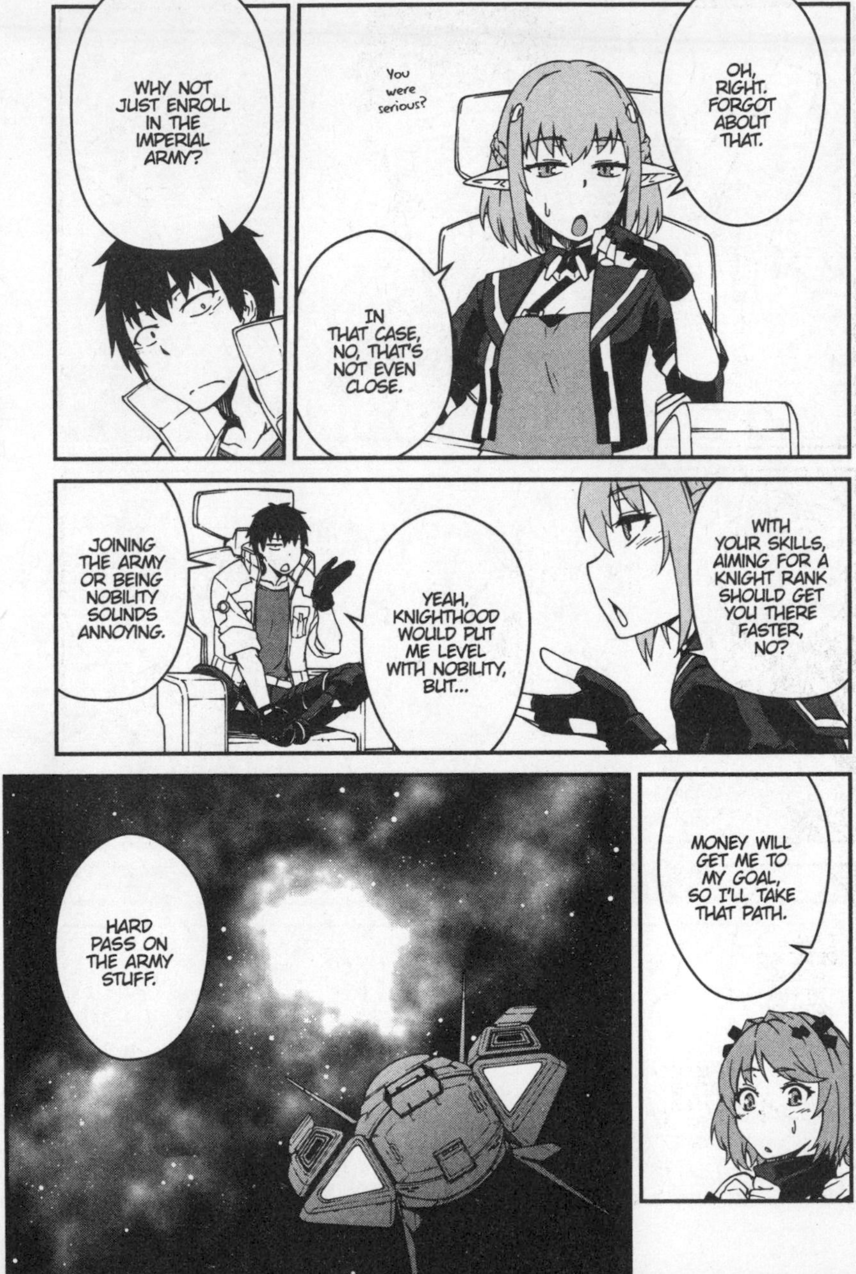
OH, RIGHT. FORGOT ABOUT THAT.
You were serious?
IN THAT CASE, NO, THAT'S NOT EVEN CLOSE.
WHY NOT JUST ENROLL IN THE IMPERIAL ARMY?
WITH YOUR SKILLS, AIMING FOR A KNIGHT RANK SHOULD GET YOU THERE FASTER, NO?
YEAH, KNIGHTHOOD WOULD PUT ME LEVEL WITH NOBILITY, BUT...
JOINING THE ARMY OR BEING NOBILITY SOUNDS ANNOYING.
MONEY WILL GET ME TO MY GOAL, SO I'LL TAKE THAT PATH.
HARD PASS ON THE ARMY STUFF.

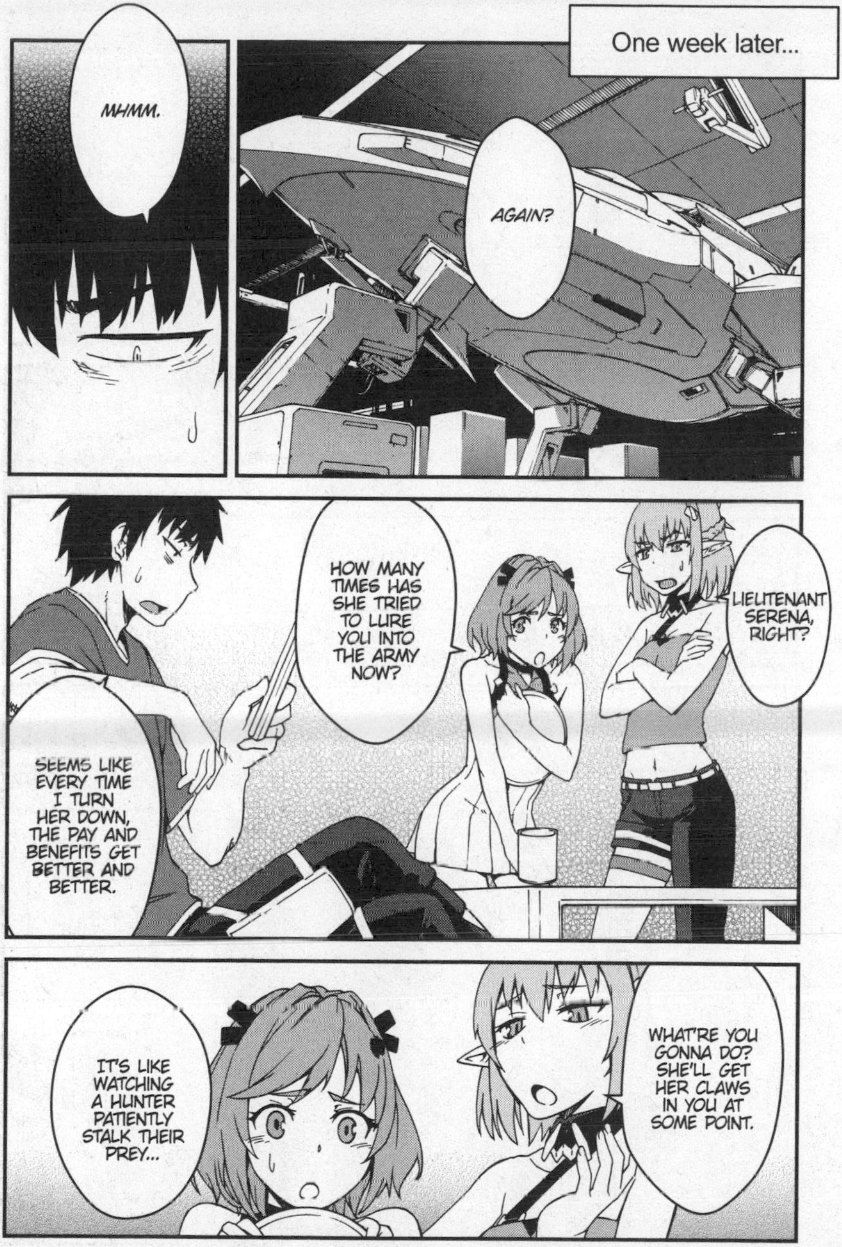
One week later...
AGAIN?
MHMM.
LIEUTENANT SERENA, RIGHT?
HOW MANY TIMES HAS SHE TRIED TO LURE YOU INTO THE ARMY NOW?
SEEMS LIKE EVERY TIME I TURN HER DOWN, THE PAY AND BENEFITS GET BETTER AND BETTER.
WHAT'RE YOU GONNA DO? SHE'LL GET HER CLAWS IN YOU AT SOME POINT.
IT'S LIKE WATCHING A HUNTER PATIENTLY STALK THEIR PREY...

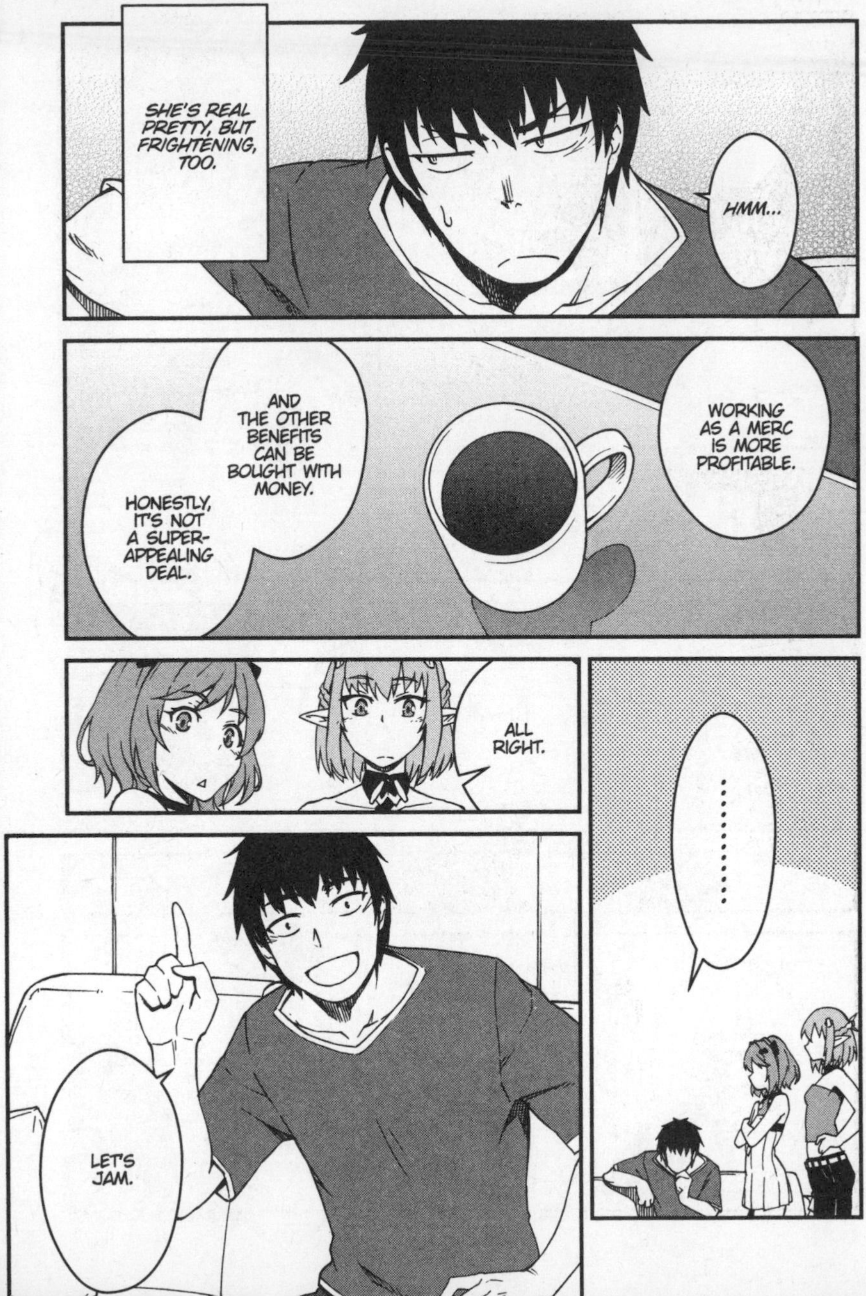
SHE'S REAL PRETTY, BUT FRIGHTENING, TOO.
HMM...
WORKING AS A MERC IS MORE PROFITABLE.
AND THE OTHER BENEFITS CAN BE BOUGHT WITH MONEY.
HONESTLY, IT'S NOT A SUPER-APPEALING DEAL.
....
ALL RIGHT.
LET'S JAM.

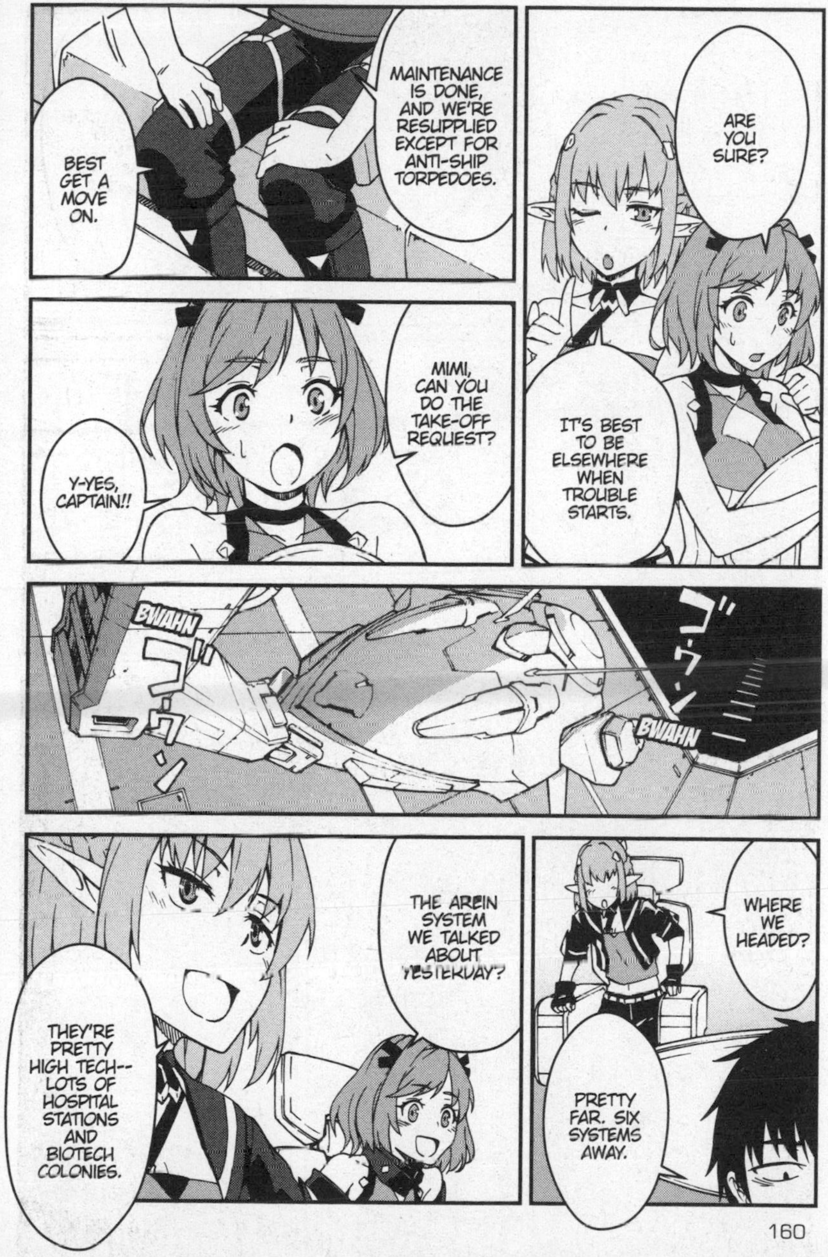
ARE YOU SURE?
IT'S BEST TO BE ELSEWHERE WHEN TROUBLE STARTS.
MAINTENANCE IS DONE, AND WE'RE RESUPPLIED EXCEPT FOR ANTI-SHIP TORPEDOES.
BEST GET A MOVE ON.
MIMI, CAN YOU DO THE TAKE-OFF REQUEST?
Y-YES, CAPTAIN!!
BWAHN
BWAHN
WHERE WE HEADED?
PRETTY FAR. SIX SYSTEMS AWAY.
THE AREIN SYSTEM WE TALKED ABOUT YESTERDAY?
THEY'RE PRETTY HIGH TECH-- LOTS OF HOSPITAL STATIONS AND BIOTECH COLONIES.

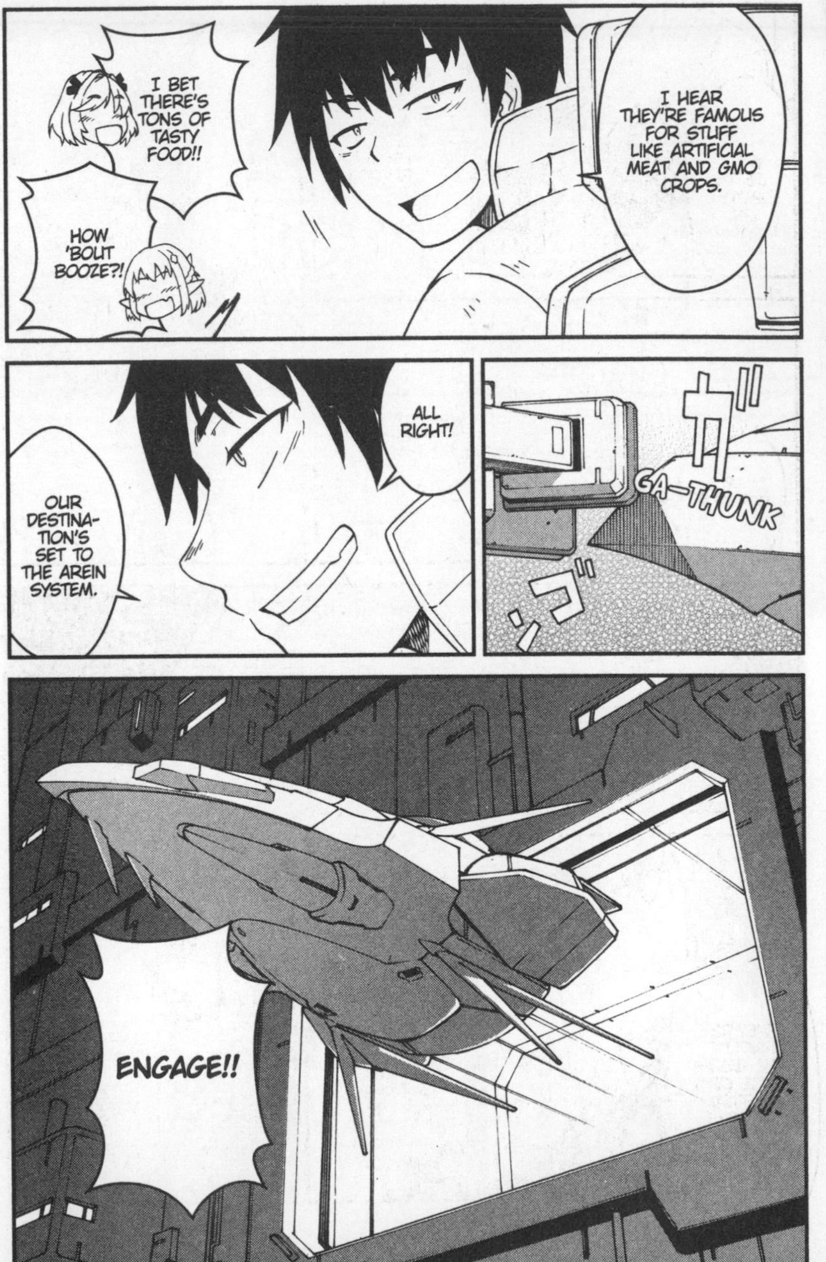
I HEAR THEY'RE FAMOUS FOR STUFF LIKE ARTIFICIAL MEAT AND GMO CROPS.
I BET THERE'S TONS OF TASTY FOOD!!
HOW 'BOUT BOOZE?!
GA-THUNK
ALL RIGHT!
OUR DESTINA-TION'S SET TO THE AREIN SYSTEM.
ENGAGE!!

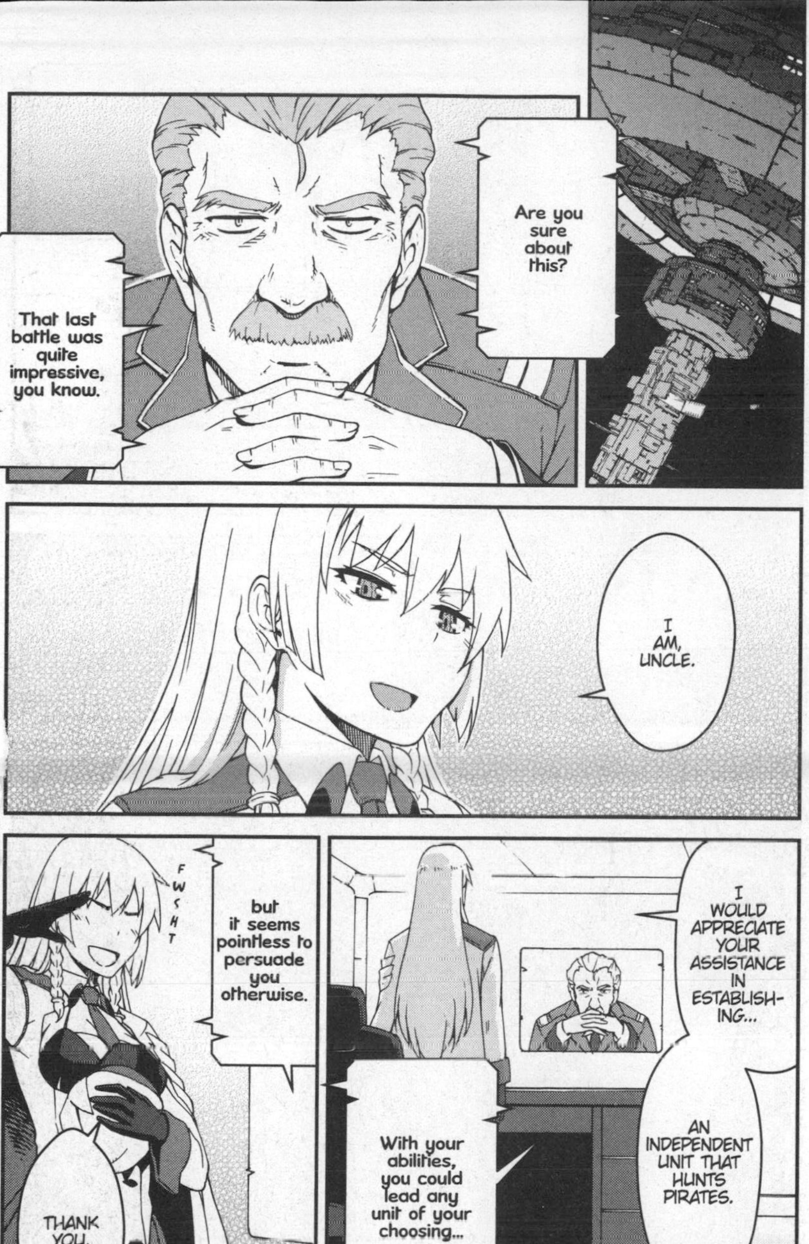
Are you sure about this?
That last battle was quite impressive, you know.
I AM, UNCLE.
I WOULD APPRECIATE YOUR ASSISTANCE IN ESTABLISHING...
AN INDEPENDENT UNIT THAT HUNTS PIRATES.
With your abilities, you could lead any unit of your choosing...
but it seems pointless to persuade you otherwise.
FWSHT
THANK YOU, SIR!

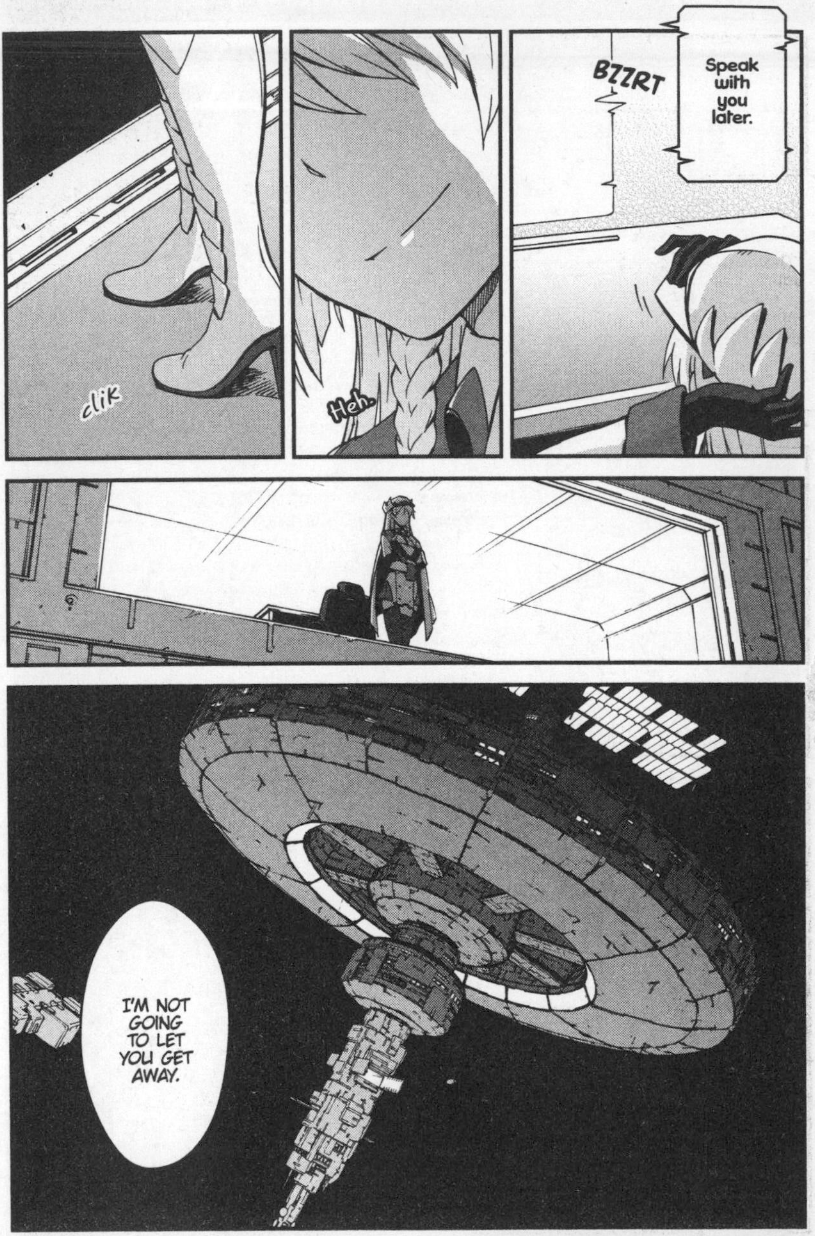
Speak with you later.
BZZRT
Heh.
clik
I'M NOT GOING TO LET YOU GET AWAY.

To Be Continued...

SEVEN SEAS ENTERTA

REBORN AS A SPACE

I WOKE UP PILOTING THE **STRONGEST STARSHIP!** Vol.2

art: **SHUNICHI MATSUI**   story: **RYUTO**   character design: **TETSUHIRO NABESHIMA**

TRANSLATION **Kristjan Rohde**	MEZAMETARA SAIKYO SOBI TO UCHUSEN MOCHI DATTA NODE, IKKODATE MEZASHITE YOHEI TOSHITE JIYU NI IKITAI Vol.2 ©Shunichi Matsui 2020, Ryuto 2020 First published in Japan in 2020 by KADOKAWA CORPORATION, Tokyo. English translation rights arranged with KADOKAWA CORPORATION, Tokyo.
LETTERING **Alexandra Gunawan**	
COVER DESIGN **Nicky Lim**	
LOGO DESIGN **George Panella**	No portion of this book may be reproduced or transmitted in any form without written permission from the copyright holders. This is a work of fiction. Names, characters, places, and incidents are the products of the author's imagination or are used fictitiously. Any resemblance to actual events, locales, or persons, living or dead, is entirely coincidental. Any information or opinions expressed by the creators of this book belong to those individual creators and do not necessarily reflect the views of Seven Seas Entertainment or its employees.
PROOFREADER **Kurestin Armada**	
COPY EDITOR **Dawn Davis**	
EDITOR **Nick Mamatas**	Seven Seas press and purchase enquiries can be sent to Marketing Manager Lianne Sentar at press@gomanga.com. Information regarding the distribution and purchase of digital editions is available from Digital Manager CK Russell at digital@gomanga.com.
PREPRESS TECHNICIAN **Rhiannon Rasmussen-Silverstein**	
PRODUCTION ASSOCIATE **Christa Miesner**	Seven Seas and the Seven Seas logo are trademarks of Seven Seas Entertainment. All rights reserved.
PRODUCTION MANAGER **Lissa Pattillo**	
MANAGING EDITOR **Julie Davis**	ISBN: 978-1-64827-460-2 Printed in Canada First Printing: December 2021 10 9 8 7 6 5 4 3 2 1
ASSOCIATE PUBLISHER **Adam Arnold**	
PUBLISHER **Jason DeAngelis**	

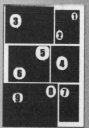
Follow us online: www.SevenSeasEntertainment.com